Visible Thinking

Unlocking Causal Mapping for Practical Business Results

To Jill Buckley
With very
best wishes

John Bryson

Visible Thinking

Unlocking Causal Mapping for Practical Business Results

John M. Bryson
Fran Ackermann
Colin Eden
Charles B. Finn

John Wiley & Sons, Ltd

Other Wiley Editorial Offices

John Wiley & Sons Inc., 111 River Street, Hoboken, NJ 07030, USA

Jossey-Bass, 989 Market Street, San Francisco, CA 94103-1741, USA

Wiley-VCH Verlag GmbH, Boschstr. 12, D-69469 Weinheim, Germany

John Wiley & Sons Australia Ltd, 33 Park Road, Milton, Queensland 4064, Australia

John Wiley & Sons (Asia) Pte Ltd, 2 Clementi Loop #02-01, Jin Xing Distripark, Singapore
129809

John Wiley & Sons Canada Ltd, 22 Worcester Road, Etobicoke, Ontario, Canada M9W 1L1

Wiley also publishes its books in a variety of electronic formats. Some content that appears
in print may not be available in electronic books.

Library of Congress Cataloging-in-Publication Data
Visible thinking : unlocking causal mapping for practical business results
/ John M. Bryson . . . [et al.].
    p. cm.
  ISBN 0-470-86915-1
  1. Decision making.   2. Problem solving.   3. Strategic planning.   4.
Thought and thinking.   5. Cognitive maps (Psychology)   I. Bryson, John M.
  (John Moore), 1947–
    HD30.23.V575 2004
    658.4'03 - - dc22   2004006764

British Library Cataloguing in Publication Data

A catalogue record for this book is available from the British Library

ISBN 0-470-86915-1

Typeset in 11/13pt Plantin by Dobbie Typesetting Ltd, Tavistock, Devon
Printed and bound in Great Britain by TJ International Ltd, Padstow, Cornwall
This book is printed on acid-free paper responsibly manufactured from sustainable forestry
in which at least two trees are planted for each one used for paper production.

To all those who have helped us develop causal mapping as a technique, and to all those who will benefit from using it in the future.

Contents

About the Authors

John M. Bryson is a professor of planning and public affairs at the University of Minnesota in Minneapolis, MN (USA), and has held visiting appointments at the London Business School, University of Strathclyde, University of Oxford and Oxford Brookes University. His research, teaching and consulting interests focus on leadership, strategic management and the design of participation processes. He uses causal mapping in much of this work. Professor Bryson has published ten books and over 80 scholarly articles and book chapters. He consults widely in the US and UK.

Fran Ackermann is a professor of strategy and information systems at the University of Strathclyde in Glasgow (UK). She is interested in working with groups (public or private, multinationals, or small and medium-sized enterprises) on messy, complex, strategic problems and sees causal mapping as a fundamental aspect of this work. She has consulted widely both within the UK and in Europe, Australia and the USA. She is co-developer (with Colin Eden) of causal mapping software – both for individual use and for groups – and continues to explore means of supporting group working through IT. She has written extensively in the area, having published three books and over 70 scholarly articles.

Colin Eden is a professor of strategic management and management science at the University of Strathclyde. His major interests are in: (1) the processes of strategy making in senior management teams, and (2) the success and failure of large projects. He has consulted with the senior management teams of a wide range of public and private organizations in Europe and North America. In all of these activities he uses causal mapping as a part of the process. He is the author of seven books and over 150 scholarly articles in management science and strategic management.

Charles B. Finn is a management professor at the College of Saint Rose, Albany, New York (USA). He has held teaching and management positions at the University of Minnesota and State University of New York. He has worked as a consultant to private, public and non-profit organizations at local, state and federal levels within the USA and has taught and consulted internationally. He has two interests in mapping: (1) how large, diffuse systems can organize for everyday challenges and do the necessary strategic thinking to realize competitive advantages, and (2) how to use mapping to encourage personal and organizational learning and development.

Preface: Creating the Future You Want – Causal Mapping for Individuals and Groups

W E ALL FACE SITUATIONS IN WHICH *THINKING REALLY matters* – either as an individual or as a group – *if we are to create the future we want*. For example, have you had trouble figuring out what was bothering you, making you anxious or keeping you awake at night? If some parts of your life have not turned out well, do you wonder why? Have you puzzled about how to make your job more satisfying, get the raise you want or acquire the resources you need? Have you wondered about how to make the most persuasive case to your boss, staff or customers? Have you pondered how you might create more satisfied clients or customers? Or maybe your organization, church or community group needs to rethink its strategy. Have you wondered about what the content of the strategy should be and how you might go about developing it with the help of others? Would you like more assurance about your decisions, to be more comfortable with your relationships and generally more in control of your life?

These are all examples of situations where – in order to create the future you want – *thinking really matters*. The questions and answers are important and all have to do with our ability or inability to make reasonable sense of the world. They involve *complex, interconnected issues* in which everything seems to be linked to everything else – and that is part of the problem! Indeed, getting clear about what the issues *are* is at least half the battle. Developing effective responses to the issues involves thoughtful exploration of a number of elements, including *goals*, *strategies* and *actions* to address the issues. The answers are *not necessarily obvious* and careful thought might even lead to *surprising outcomes*. In circumstances such as these, typically individuals and groups must *talk things out* in order to know what they should want, why they should want it and how they might achieve it.

The purpose of *Visible Thinking* is to help you understand and use the tool of *causal mapping* to make sense of challenging situations, to get more of what you want out of them and less of what you don't want. Causal mapping is a simple and useful technique for addressing situations where thinking – as an individual or as a group – matters. A causal map is a word-and-arrow diagram in which ideas and actions are causally linked with one another through the use of arrows. The arrows indicate how one idea or action leads to another. Causal mapping makes it possible to articulate a large number of ideas and their interconnections in such a way that people can know *what* to do in an area of concern, *how* to do it and *why*, because the arrows indicate the causes and consequences of an idea or action.

Causal mapping is therefore a technique for linking strategic thinking and acting, helping make sense of complex problems, and communicating to oneself and others what might be done about them. With practice, the use of causal mapping can assist you in moving from "winging it" when thinking matters to a more concrete and rigorous approach that helps you and others achieve success in an easy and far more reliable way.

Visible Thinking is the first book to put the power of causal mapping at the disposal of a general management audience. The book helps people understand the theory and practice of causal mapping. It shows how managers can use and benefit from causal mapping in an almost limitless number of areas – indeed, in almost any area where thinking matters!

When an individual uses causal mapping to help clarify their own thinking, we call this technique *cognitive mapping*, because it is related to personal thinking or cognition. When a group maps their own ideas, we call it *oval mapping*, because we often use oval-shaped cards to record individuals' ideas so that they can be arranged into a group's map. Cognitive maps and oval maps can be used to create a strategic plan, because the maps include goals, strategies and actions, just like strategic plans.

Part I of the book uses several examples to present an overview of the theory and practice of mapping. Part II then focuses on cognitive mapping, while Part III shows how to do oval mapping. Part IV pulls the previous sections together, provides guidance on how to do mapping, and summarizes the benefits and limitations of mapping. All parts of the book are built around cases in which the authors have been involved, so the connection with real-life practice should be immediately apparent. A number of resource sections are also included at the end of the book.

Scope

Visible Thinking therefore introduces the theory and practice of causal mapping and provides practical guidance on how to do it individually and in groups. The book is based on three important premises. The first premise is that *most people do not know for sure what they think about many important matters*. They know that these matters are complex and important, but they do not know what, if anything, to conclude about them. This can be a cause for discomfort, anxiety, opting out or, in the extreme, alienation. Let us be clear that this premise is meant to be a descriptive and not a pejorative statement. We ourselves do not know what we think about many issues: John and Chuck, who are Americans, are not sure what they think about any number of matters ranging from the societal to the personal. For example, they are unsure what to think about the US federal debt, the best way to stop terrorism, or their respective employers' most recent annual budgets. They also are not sure what their local neighborhood groups should do, where their families should go on vacation next year, whether to move from the family home to a condominium (John), how to remodel the family home (Chuck) and so on. Similarly, Fran and Colin, who are Brits living in Scotland, are not sure what they think about the Labour Party, the future of their National Health Service, Scottish independence, European Union decision making, the ideal strategy for their departments, where to go sailing next year, what their career paths should be and so on.

There are good reasons for this. First, the average adult can handle no more than about seven concepts consciously at any given time, and yet most important issues involve many more concepts than that.[1] Because of the busyness of everyday life, we may not know what is important, let alone what to do about it. Even if we do, we are continually distracted by the urgent at the expense of the important. Further, thinking takes time and attention, both of which are often in short supply.

Second, careful thought is not very important for much of what we do. For example, no one has to think very hard about commuting to and from work as long as he or she is familiar with the route, the weather is good, the vehicle is in good repair (legs for Colin, car for Chuck, bus for John, train for Fran), nothing unusual is happening along the route and the journey isn't long enough to be a problem. Indeed, typically we are least conscious of what we do best and do the most often. We simply follow a set of pre-programmed routines that have worked pretty well in the past and are likely to work well in the future. And while executing the routine, we tend to think about what we will do in the near future, not about what we are doing in the present.[2]

Third, we don't need to think much about things we have consciously decided *not* to think about, because it's not worth it. For example, John has decided not to think about his pension investments, other than to monitor quarterly reports, because he is far from an expert in such matters and it might depress him to manage them himself! Instead, he has decided to pay a fee-only financial adviser to think about his investments for him. Fran can't be bothered about car maintenance; she would much rather have her local service station take care of it. Colin doesn't need to think about where the warmest beaches and most sunshine are in the world, because he is not happy being hot. Unlike his co-authors, he does not fantasize about vacationing in the Caribbean. Chuck has decided not to think about changing jobs anytime soon, as he has done so twice in the last few years.

The book is also based on a second premise, namely that *thinking does matter when it comes to deciding what to do about many important issues*. Most of us are unlikely to buy a house, buy a car, buy a new computer, have a second child, change jobs, get a divorce or speak about a serious subject with the president of the company without first spending at least some time thinking about what to do, how to do it and why. If we do any of these things on impulse, the results conceivably might be outstanding, and thinking more carefully would not have made them any better. But a more likely outcome is that the results will not be nearly satisfactory enough – and may in fact be disastrous. We have all found ourselves wondering what would have happened if we had "thought better of it". Beyond our individual experience, however, is the weight of research evidence. Paul Nutt, for example, in a review of 400 strategic decisions, provides clear evidence of the importance of thinking clearly and reasonably *when it does matter*. His research shows that half of all strategic decisions fail![3] Failure to think through the situation, develop a clear direction and find a reasonable, defensible response that addresses key stakeholders' interests and concerns can lead to decision failure, or even a debacle. In contrast, successful thought in strategic decision situations can lead to notable – even exemplary – success. In other words, what people do when thinking matters, *matters*! Said differently, without the thinking you need, you will not create the future you want.

The final premise on which the book is based is our belief that *people need tools and techniques to help them think effectively about what to do in complex issue areas*. We need methods and guidance for clarifying what might be going on in a complex area of concern and for figuring on what to do, how and why. Causal mapping is one of the tools that we believe can help. Indeed, we have found it to be *the* most helpful way of gaining an understanding of important issue areas in such a way that we can figure out effective strategies and actions that will achieve our goals. This is particularly true in situations where we are actually *angry*, *distressed* or *depressed*, either to begin with, or as a result of thinking about the problem but not knowing what to do about it. The anger, distress or depression can get in the way of clear thinking, which simply makes the situation worse. Causal mapping can help us take a more optimistic, objective and action-oriented look at the situation. As a result, we are more likely to take effective action and feel better.[4]

Overview of Contents

The book is designed to introduce the theory and practice of causal mapping to a general management audience. It does so primarily through numerous examples. In each example, thinking clearly mattered. As the book progresses, the guidelines for doing effective causal mapping are gradually introduced and developed.

The book is organized into four parts. Part I provides an introduction to causal mapping, including what it is and why it is important. Part II focuses on answering the question: "What do I think?" In this section we examine cognitive mapping. Part III helps answer the question: "What do we think?" In this section we look at oval mapping. The final section, Part IV, pulls together the main points of the previous chapters, summarizes the benefits and limitations of mapping, and discusses its future.

Part I: What Mapping Is and Why and How It Works

Part I consists of two chapters. Chapter 1 introduces the idea of causal mapping and shows how it can be useful. The general nature, purpose and benefits of mapping are presented. The example in this chapter focuses on how Chuck and his wife Mary used a relatively informal form of causal mapping to find a way out of a recurring argument they were having about who was responsible for doing what around the house. Many people – particularly those in long-term relationships – will nod their heads knowingly as the conflict unfolds, and will appreciate how mapping was used to manage the conflict. While the conflict is a domestic one, the approach to resolving it would apply to almost any interpersonal conflict in a work team.

In Chapter 2, the main example shows how John and Chuck use a more formal type of causal mapping to figure out how to do something they have long dreamt of – sailing from Duluth, Minnesota, to Hilton Head Island, South Carolina, a trip of some four months and 4000 miles. The example is developed as a way of presenting mapping in more detail. The example helps us understand the general structure for maps and suggests a set of simple rules to be followed when constructing them. Again, the example is rather personal, but what it demonstrates is more generally how causal mapping can be used for strategic planning purposes. The example also is not unusual at all in that it provided John and Chuck with a number of surprising revelations that led them to rethink how they were going about pursuing this adventure, and indeed much else in their lives. In other words, when they saw what they said, they were not sure they liked what they saw, and had to figure out what to do to change it.

Part II: What Do I Think? A Guide to Cognitive Mapping

The book's second section helps readers figure out what they think as individuals through showing how to create cognitive maps. Chapter 3 shows how Colin figured out how to negotiate delivery of a new product (a custom-made sailboat) on time and to agreed quality standards. The map helped Colin figure out how he could involve third parties to help him achieve his aim, through inventing ways to tap their self-interest in the service of his own. The example is thus one of creative conflict management and project management.

Chapter 4 shows how Fran figured out where to live, an example that might be thought of more generally as a facility location exercise. Fran used mapping to develop a number of criteria to help her with her search and then used them to find, purchase and move into her new flat. In the process, she discovered some goals she didn't know she had and that discovery helped her more self-consciously pursue a better life.

The final chapter in Part II, Chapter 5, shows how to develop cognitive maps through interviewing another person. In this chapter Chuck interviews John in order to explore options and develop strategies for John to pursue to get a more satisfying job. The example may be thought of more generally as showing how to explore strategic options. It is also interesting because it revealed a dilemma: for John to stay where he was, he had to be willing to leave. The map showed how the dilemma could be managed.

Part III: What Do We Think? A Guide to Oval Mapping

The focus in Part III is on developing *group maps*, or collective representations of the world. These maps are used to show what a group of two or more people think they ought to be doing, how they might do it and why – in short, how to create the future they want.

Chapter 6 shows how a group working for a Scottish public-sector college created a group map – an oval map – to help the college decide whether or not to merge with another organization. Based on the mapping exercise, the college decided not to merge. The example should be useful to anyone interested in collaboration, mergers or acquisitions.

Chapter 7 involves a turnaround situation faced by a non-profit organization – another college – faced with a deteriorating situation and the need to search for a new president. The interim president of the college used a retreat setting to involve a significant number of stakeholders in an oval mapping process. The map was used to guide a subsequent strategic planning effort and a search for a new president. The example shows how mapping can fit into a larger strategic planning and organizational change effort.

Chapter 8 presents a business case in which a group map is created out of individual cognitive maps. The case involves getting a group of people from different departments to work together on creating a new product. The example should therefore be useful to anyone interested in working across organizational boundaries, especially for purposes of developing new products or services.

Chapter 9 involves another business example and shows how mapping was used by a top management team to develop a strategic plan for their company within a very tight time frame. The example is quintessentially about strategic planning – seen as strategic thinking, acting and learning – by a top management team. The example also involves added urgency, since on the one hand the organization was desperately short of cash, while on the other hand the team members were major shareholders in the firm and had much to lose if the planning failed. In the end, the planning exercise worked and the organization is now quite healthy.

Part IV: Summary and Conclusions

The book's final section consists of two chapters. Both are designed to provide a summary of all of the material presented in a form that makes it quick reference material for practical use in the future. Chapter 10 provides a detailed comparison and contrast of the cases along four different dimensions: the nature of the problems and challenges that prompted mapping; the inputs or resources used for mapping; the mapping process itself; and the contributions that mapping made to a successful outcome. The chapter then presents a set of process guidelines designed to help readers create their own maps.

Chapter 11 discusses the benefits, limitations and future of mapping. The chapter concentrates on how mapping enhances learning by individuals and groups. In summary, mapping is what to do when thinking matters.

Resource sections

The book also includes three resource sections that provide supplemental material and information. Resource A is a glossary. Resource B offers guidance on how to analyse maps. Resource C provides a brief history of causal mapping and shows how it is related to other kinds of commonly used word-and-arrow diagrams. Resource D gives information on where to find additional help with mapping. And Resource E presents a complete set of the process guidelines presented in Chapters 2–9.

Audience

This book is meant for any leader or manager who wants help figuring out how to create the future he or she wants in his or her job, organization, life or community, either alone or in partnership with others. Readers simply need to be willing to invest a little time in learning how to do causal mapping.

Mapping, of course, is not the only tool that would help in these situations. Nor is it for everyone. Some people like using pictures to help them think things through, while others prefer to talk things through. Some like to deal only with concrete facts and others enjoy working with ideas and possibilities. Nor is mapping a substitute for technical expertise, useful advice, professional guidance, counselling or therapy. Having said all that, we believe that mapping is a *very* effective way of helping people sort out the many aspects of the situations they face in such a way that they can figure out a strategy for creating the future they want. Mapping can help anyone who is willing to follow the simple rules and think carefully. We wrote this book so that you can understand causal mapping and apply it in situations that matter to you.

Knowledge Base

The knowledge base for the book consists of several sources: personal construct theory in psychology,[5] sense-making theory in psychology and social psychology,[6] social construction theory in sociology,[7] constructivism in education[8] and our own work in strategic management.[9] We also draw on insights from the literature on cognitive therapy,[10] narrative therapy[11] and facilitation.[12]

We build on psychologist George Kelly's notion that we each use a "personal construct system" to make sense of our world, to make predictions about it, to try to control it, and in general to anticipate and reach out to it. Language is central to this process. We make sense of the world through comparison and contrast, in which to know what anything means we need to know at least one thing it is like, and one thing it is not like. In a broader sense, meaning is embedded in context, which consists of a whole set of comparisons and contrasts. People construe the same events differently, which means that shared meaning must be negotiated, and consensual action implies a reasonably shared sense of the consequences of actions. A crucial feature of this view is the idea that you never change anyone's mind (or a group's "mind") *directly*. Instead, all you can do is help them elaborate their view of the world to the point that *they change their own mind(s)*. (Anyone who has had or worked with teenagers knows what we are talking about!) Mapping is a way of helping individuals elaborate, understand and change their individual construct system, and of helping groups develop and negotiate a shared view of the world.

We have written the book in such a way that although the material draws on all of the above theories, the reader does not need to become knowledgeable about them. The book is intended to be highly practical and an expression of the adage that "there is nothing so practical as good theory."[13]

Conclusion

Visible Thinking should provide most of the guidance anyone needs to use causal mapping. We hope that the information and instructions supplied in this book will prompt readers to commit the brief amount of time and energy it takes to learn how to create causal maps and to use them when thinking matters. We hope that our readers' lives will thereby become more satisfying, meaningful and productive, and that their workplaces, homes and communities will also benefit. Nothing would make us happier!

Notes

1 See the classic article on cognitive limitations by G. A. Miller (1956) The Magical Number Seven Plus or Minus Two: Some Limits to Our Capacity for Processing Information, *The Psychological Bulletin*, **63**, 81–97.
2 See A. H. Van de Ven (1986) Central Problems in the Management of Innovation, *Management Science*, **32**(5), 590–607.
3 See Paul Nutt (2002) *Why Decisions Fail*, San Francisco, CA: Berrett-Koehler.
4 Causal mapping can be a tool for learning to be more optimistic, rather than pessimistic; see Martin Seligman (1991) *Learned Optimism*, New York: Alfred Knopf.
5 George Kelly (1963) *A Theory of Personality*, New York: Norton Kelly.

6   Karl Weick (1995) *Sensemaking in Organizations*, Thousand Oaks, CA: Sage.

7   Peter Berger and Thomas Luckmann (1967) *The Social Construction of Reality*, New York: Doubleday Anchor Books.

8   David Hyerle (1996) *Visual Tools for Constructing Knowledge*, Alexandria, VA: Association for Supervision and Curriculum Development.

9   John Bryson (1995) *Strategic Planning for Public and Nonprofit Organizations*, San Francisco, CA: Jossey-Bass; John Bryson and Charles Finn (1995) Development and Use of Strategy Maps to Enhance Organizational Performance, in Arie Halachmi and Geert Bouckaert (eds), *The Challenge of Management in a Changing World*, San Francisco, CA: Jossey-Bass; and Colin Eden and Fran Ackermann (1998) *Making Strategy*, Thousand Oaks, CA: Sage.

10 See, for example, Martin Seligman (1991) *Learned Optimism*, New York: Alfred Knopf.

11 See, for example, Gerald Monk, John Winslade, Kathie Crocket and David Epston (1997) *Narrative Therapy in Practice: The Archaeology of Hope*, San Francisco, CA: Jossey-Bass.

12 See, for example, Roger Schwarz (2002) *The Skilled Facilitator*, San Francisco, CA: Jossey-Bass.

13 Kurt Lewin, quoted in David Johnson and Frank Johnson (2002) *Joining Together*, 8th edn, Upper Saddle River, NJ: Pearson, Allyn and Bacon.

Part I

What Mapping Is and Why and How It Works

1

What to Do When Thinking Matters

DO YOU EVER WONDER WHAT TO DO? ARE YOU EVER CONFUSED about how to proceed? You are not alone. Most of us puzzle about important matters. Often it is hard to know what to do about important issues at work – or even how to think about them. These issues may involve customers, clients or service users; employees, professional groups or unions; suppliers or distributors; bankers or funders; or any of a large number of other stakeholders. Issues at home or in the community may also take serious thought before a satisfactory solution can be found.

The world is often a muddled, complicated, dynamic place in which it seems as if everything is connected to everything else – and that is the problem! The connections can be a problem because while we know things are connected, sometimes we do not know how, or else there are so many connections we cannot comprehend them all. Alternatively, we may not realize how connected things are and our actions may lead to unforeseen and unhappy consequences. Either way, we would benefit from an approach to problem solving that helps us understand just how connected the world is, what the effects of those connections are, and what might be done to change some of the connections and their effects.

Causal mapping is an approach that can help. *The purpose of this book is to help you understand and use causal mapping to make sense of challenging situations – and to get more of what you want out and less of what you don't want out of them.* We will show how mapping can be used to help an *individual* understand a situation better and act effectively on it, and we will also show how *groups* can build understanding and create effective action. The focus is on management challenges and how to manage them.

Causal mapping is a simple and useful technique for addressing situations where thinking – as an individual or as a group – matters. *A causal map is a word-and-arrow diagram in which ideas and actions are causally linked with one another through the use of arrows. The arrows indicate how one idea or action leads to another.* Causal mapping makes it possible to articulate a large number of ideas and their interconnections in such a way that people can know *what* to do in an area of concern, *how* to do it and *why*, because the arrows indicate the causes and consequences of an idea or action. Causal mapping is therefore a technique for linking strategic thinking and acting, helping make sense of complex problems, and communicating to oneself and others what might be done about them.

When can mapping help? There are a number of situations that are tailor-made for mapping. We find mapping to be particularly helpful when:

- effective strategies need to be developed, either at work or at home;

- persuasive arguments are needed;

- effective and logical communication is essential;

- effective understanding and management of conflict are needed;

- it is vital that a situation be understood better as a prelude to any action.

These situations are not meant to be mutually exclusive. Often they will overlap in practice.

Perhaps the most important situations are the ones where *effective strategies need to be developed*, either at work or at home. For example, you might be focused on work-related concerns such as the following:

- How could I make my job more satisfying?

- What might we do to create more satisfied customers?

- How should I prepare for a job interview?

- How do I get more resources for my department?

Another category of situations occurs when *persuasive arguments are needed*. For example, you might be concerned with the following questions:

- How can I make an effective case for funding an important work-related project?

- How can I write a better report?

- How can I communicate my needs in such a way that people really listen, instead of hearing only what they want to hear?

- How do I persuade my boss to give me a raise?

Or you might be in a situation where persuasion is not so much the issue, but certainly *effective and logical communication is needed*. For example, you might wonder:

- How do I give clear directions to my staff?

- How can I better understand what people are saying? How can I improve my listening skills?

Sometimes the challenge is that *effective understanding and management of conflict are needed*. The conflict can be internal, interpersonal or inter-group in nature. Consider the following situations:

- What is bothering me? Making me anxious? Making me fret? Keeping me awake?

- How can I understand and deal with conflict with people who are important to me?

- How can I address a conflict with an employer, supplier or contractor?

Finally, you may simply *need to make sense of some situations*. You need to work out what is going on in order to figure out what you can or should do about it, if anything. For example, you may wonder:

- How do I know if Person X is making sense? They just offered what they say is a "real deal", but how do I know if it is? How do I know what questions to ask to understand more clearly what they are saying?

- All hell just broke loose in this meeting. How do I figure out what happened?

In each of these situations, *clear and logical thinking matters.* The questions are *important.* They involve *complex, interconnected issues* in which everything seems to be linked to everything else. Often they call for *careful exploration* of *values, goals, issues, strategies* and *actions to address the issues.* The answers are *not necessarily obvious,* and careful thought might even lead to *surprising outcomes.*

As we noted above, the purpose of this book is to introduce you to causal mapping and get you to use it to address questions like these. In causal maps ideas and actions are linked to one another in a way that makes sense for purposes of understanding and action. Depending on the circumstances, the connections may be causal, inferential, sequential, temporal or logical in a philosophical sense.

Causal mapping makes it possible to articulate a large number of ideas and their interconnections in such a way that we can better understand an area of concern. Causal mapping also helps us know what to do about the issue, what it would take to do those things, and what we would like to get out of having done so. Causal mapping is therefore a particularly powerful technique for making sense of complex problems, linking strategic thinking and acting, and helping to communicate to others what might or should be done. When an individual uses causal mapping to help clarify his or her thinking, we call this technique *cognitive mapping,* because it relates to his or her own cognition. When a group maps their own ideas, we call it *oval mapping,* because we often use special oval-shaped cards to record individuals' ideas so that they can be arranged into a group's map. Sometimes an oval map is called an *action-oriented strategy map.*[1]

Of course, there are plenty of situations where the problems and issues are not complex and we do not need any special help addressing them. This book is not about such situations, but instead focuses on those issues where help is necessary to get our thinking straight.

An Example

One of the best ways to learn about mapping and its power is through examples. So let us start off with a real example where a small *informal type of mapping* helped improve a situation where clear thinking mattered.[2] The example involves a conflict between one of the book's authors, Chuck Finn, and his wife Mary. While the issue was personal, the conflict they experienced was typical of many that take place at work, home or elsewhere. And the way they used mapping to resolve the conflict shows how it can be employed. Read their story and see how they used mapping to resolve their conflict.

When Chuck arrived home from work – late as usual – he was met by a sullen silence from his wife, Mary. It was clear to him that something was bothering her, but he had no idea what. He recalled that they had parted amicably that morning – or at least he thought they had. As a courtesy, he had called and left a message that he would be late. And he really did not think he was *super*-late. So he was genuinely puzzled why Mary was so angry...

But Chuck had a bad feeling about Mary's anger and decided he'd better take a quick "time out" to gather his wits. So he headed for their bedroom to change into casual clothes – slowly. When he returned, he asked, "What's the matter?"

Her reply was short and to the point: "You never do anything around here!"

Chuck immediately recognized the opening line in a recurrent argument that always left both of them feeling angry and helpless. Even worse, the argument never got resolved, so it happened again and again.

With a sense of foreboding, he replied, as he typically did, "I do help out with things, like fixing the car and other big jobs, but I never seem to be here when you think most of the work needs to be done."

The return salvo was practically scripted. Mary said, "I have to do everything and you don't help even when you are around."

Chuck replied, "I often have to work late, or I'm out of town, and you need to give me credit for the things I do."

Soon the argument was full-blown and each partner retreated to angry silence. Chuck then made efforts to accomplish additional chores, but often had to ask Mary for help, which did not improve her attitude at all.

If the past were any indicator, the result of this argument would be that Mary would continue to do the majority of the work with little or no help from Chuck. And she would resent that. And Chuck would continue to contribute less than he probably should, and he would feel guilty and helpless. And he would nurse his own sullen anger, because he really did think he *was* contributing in other ways. Mary would "let it pass," but of course it really never did...

They both knew they were stuck in a trap. They even remarked about the fact that they could almost predict the exact words each one would use in the argument beforehand! As they both loved each other, the issue clearly was not big enough to pull them apart. On the other hand, not resolving the issue meant it continued to fester and they were routinely unhappy at very predictable times – times when they otherwise might be enjoying each other's company.

Chuck had used mapping for years in his classes and strategic management consulting practice. Later that evening it dawned on him that it just might be of benefit here. He was ready to try anything that would assist Mary and him with getting out of their trap. He started thinking that mapping at least might help him "prove his points". After all, weren't his positions logical and defensible and maybe mapping could help Mary understand how right he was? Therefore, he suggested that they explore their conflict by jointly mapping what was going on and what they might do about it.

Mary was suspicious, as Chuck had quite a reputation for trying new things on the family that most often did not work – or only worked for him! Chuck prevailed this time by assuring her that the technique was very simple and that any subterfuge would be quickly apparent. Mary was still reluctant and said she would only proceed if she were an equal participant. Chuck assured her she would be.

So, with a "cease-fire" of sorts in place, and hoping finally to put this recurrent conflict behind them, they agreed to begin the exercise in the dining room. Chuck assembled some necessary supplies, while Mary cleared the dining-room table. Chuck brought the following materials:

- A flipchart sheet.
- Several colours of $2'' \times 2''$ (5 cm × 5 cm) Post-it® pads.
- A number of felt-tipped pens.

They put the sheet of flipchart paper on the table and began to map the basic argument, which was relatively easy since the parts were so predictable and had been so well rehearsed over the years. They wrote each statement on a separate Post-it using a felt-tipped pen. They then put the Post-it notes on the flipchart sheet and drew in the arrows that indicated the flow of the argument. The basic argument is presented in Map 1.1. The arrows from one concept to another mean that the first's "causes" "may lead to", "might result in" or "may influence" the second. Alternatively, lines rather than arrows were put in where the intention was simply to show a connection. Chuck had used mapping before and inserted a minus sign on the end of the arrow from his "doing some things" to "Mary has to do everything" to indicate that because he did some things Mary couldn't be doing everything!

When Chuck and Mary looked at the map, their first surprise was how little content there actually was to the words they exchanged during the argument. Essentially, they made a few statements and proceeded to repeat them over and over, while becoming ever more angry. Mary would say, as she had this evening, "You never do any work around the house, even when you are home, which means I have to do everything." Chuck would respond, as he had this evening, "I do some things, but I'm often not here to help out, because of work or travel." Chuck would add, "Besides, all of the jobs are done by your rules, which I can't figure out, so that makes it hard for me to help."

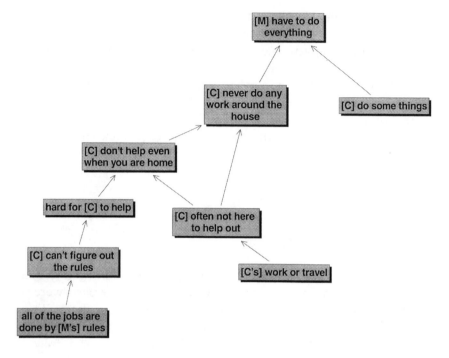

Map 1.1   The heart of the matter.

They considered what this simple map was telling them, argued some more and generally "vented". The emotional discharge helped, as did the almost shocking simplicity of the argument when it was put into map form. The map and venting seemed to "disarm" them.

They continued to map: As the argument typically unfolded (see Map 1.2), they decided to state all of the tasks each of them did. So that these would show up easily, Mary used blue Post-it notes and Chuck used white ones. Mary would list a few of the things she did (such as the laundry, cleaning up, cooking dinner, cleaning the house, doing yard and garden work). She would assert, "You don't help even when you are home." Chuck would respond by listing a few of the things he did (such as fixing the cars, fixing the house, vacuuming the floors, tilling the garden, mowing the lawn). And so on. He then reasserted that it was hard to help when all of the jobs seemed to have to be done following Mary's rules, which he couldn't figure out.

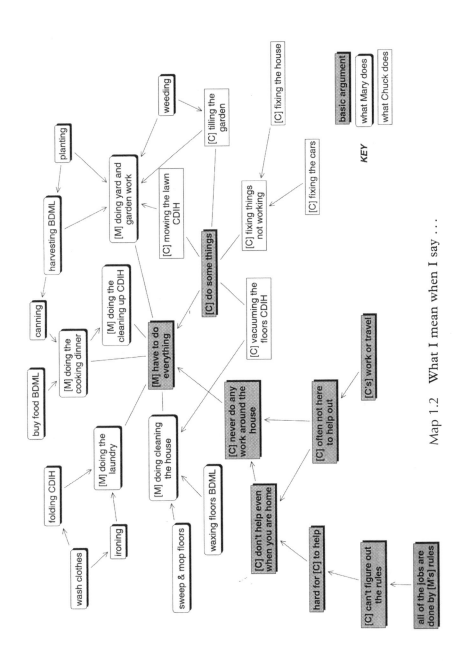

Map 1.2 What I mean when I say . . .

They decided to really focus on what Mary meant when she said she had to do "everything", and what Chuck meant by saying he did "some things". He now knew why he was feeling guilty. Mary clearly did do more of the work around the house. Mary perked up: she was beginning to like mapping!

At the same time, the map helped both Chuck and Mary understand more about each of their arguments. First, they saw that the household chores were clustered into five general areas: laundry, meals, cleaning, fixing things and the garden. Second, they began to understand the circumstances in which each of them did what they did around the house. Specifically, Mary's activities were largely those that had to be accomplished on a regular basis and in a coordinated way, if the household was to function well. Chuck's tasks, on the other hand, were those that Mary did not want, and also were projects that could be done pretty much any time.

As noted, at this point Mary was feeling pretty good about Chuck's new process, as it amply demonstrated that she indeed did do pretty much "everything"! But Chuck was starting to feel pretty good too, since it was becoming clearer why he was not doing as much as he might. He also was beginning to see more clearly what the situation was like from Mary's point of view. Nevertheless, understanding each other's point of view did not solve the problem.

Both Mary and Chuck could see some justification in each other's positions, but neither was happy with the outcome of the conflict. Mary could say, "I can see your point, but that does not deal with my having to do all or most of the work around here!" Chuck could say, "I can see your point, but what can I do about it?"

Exploring the consequences of their situation was an even more sobering activity for both of them. They mapped the consequences using some pink Post-it notes. The consequences are presented in Map 1.3.

The map of the consequences made it abundantly clear that nothing good would happen if they did not agree to do things differently. More importantly, the map allowed each of them to understand more about the pain and frustration they both felt. Mary said that as a result of "doing everything" and "Chuck not doing any work" she

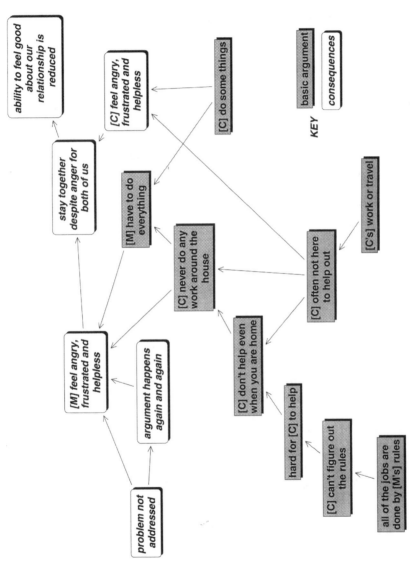

Map 1.3.   The consequences of remaining trapped are not good.

felt "angry, frustrated and helpless". Chuck claimed that because he was "often not here to help out" because of "his work or travel", he was only able to "do some things" and he felt "angry, guilty and helpless". Their inability to get beyond their emotional responses meant that "the problem was not addressed". This meant that "the argument happened again". They "stayed together despite the continuing conflict", but their "ability to feel good about their relationship was reduced".

When they both acknowledged the consequences of their recurrent conflict and saw how much it hurt them, they both felt motivated to find a real and enduring solution. After all, they were smart people and loved each other very much; it was foolish to stay stuck. Besides, now that they had a better understanding of the problem and a tool to help them find a solution, they felt confident they could find a way forward. In addition, whatever they came up with would probably be better than the current situation.

So Chuck and Mary returned to the map and the list of tasks that needed to be done. They decided to look at these tasks and what seemed to go wrong – or right! – with each task. They started with vacuuming. Look again at Map 1.2.

Both claimed to do the vacuuming, but it quickly became evident that Chuck only vacuumed when he was around and was told to do so. This explained why both of them could say they were doing the job, because there were times when each did. They found that the same thing occurred with mowing the lawn, washing clothes, folding clothes and cleaning up.

As they explored this situation further through dialogue, it became clear that Mary often vacuumed, mowed and washed and folded clothes as a way of getting some physical exercise and mental escape after getting home from a mentally demanding but rather sedentary desk job. When Chuck got home – which was almost always after Mary – she was busy doing chores that she would much rather do herself, like cook dinner, and also resenting the fact that Chuck had nothing to do. As they talked further, they agreed that this meant Mary was doing these chores about 75% of the time, and that Chuck only did them on weekends when Mary had not got to them during the week. At the same time, these were jobs Chuck could do whenever he got home, and they both agreed that these were already his responsibility to do when he was available. The result of this pattern of behaviour was that Mary was doing these tasks most of the time and did not need to, and Chuck got blamed and resented for not doing things he was willing to do when he got home.

A light bulb went on for both Mary and Chuck and they agreed to a new rule to govern their behaviour. The new rule was: *When Chuck was not travelling or kept super-late at work, he was expected to do certain jobs (vacuum the floors, mow the lawn, wash and fold clothes, and clean up after dinner). Mary was only to do those jobs when it was obvious that Chuck had very good reasons for not getting to them.* Chuck and Mary wrote "CDIH" – for Chuck Does If Home – on each relevant Post-it on Map 1.2. They decided this was an excellent way to work things out, even though Mary was a little cynical regarding Chuck's good intentions. She also understood that the agreement gave her legitimate grounds to raise hell with Chuck when he did not follow through! A new plan was taking shape.

The map also helped them both understand that there were a set of jobs in which Chuck would have to take Mary's lead, as she was far more of an expert than he was (such as buying food, waxing floors and harvesting the garden). In doing those tasks, Chuck and Mary would have to negotiate a time to work together, or at least to consult regarding what needed doing and how. They wrote "BDML" – Both Do, Mary Leads – on each of these additional Post-it notes.

As a result of the mapping exercise, Chuck discovered how he could do his share of household chores following a set of rules that gave him guidance and some relief from anger, guilt and helplessness. Mary had a set of rules that would result in her doing less work; experiencing less anger, frustration and helplessness; and thinking that she and Chuck had more of an equal partnership when it came to housework. These were desirable consequences and led them to revisit the map to clarify exactly what the consequences of doing things differently were and how they related to one another.

Chuck and Mary decided to revise the map and clearly articulate their new plan. They took off the Post-it notes that described the original argument. They then mapped a new set of consequences

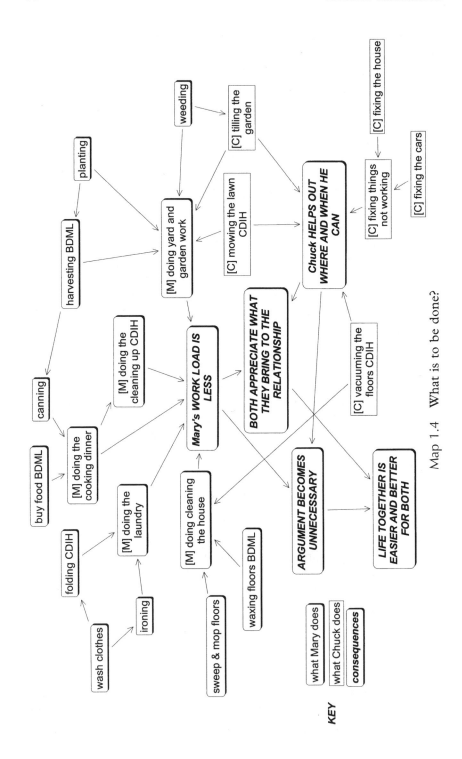

Map 1.4 What is to be done?

onto the "what doing everything means" map (Map 1.2) in order to create a plan for the future. They used CAPITAL LETTERS for the new – and more desirable – consequences. Mary added "Mary's workload is less". Chuck added "Chuck helps out where and when he can". Both agreed that they "both appreciate what they bring to the relationship", their "regular argument is no longer a fruitless topic" and "life together is easier and better for both". Their new plan (Map 1.4) was something they both could support and they certainly liked the new set of results they could anticipate from following the plan.

Mary and Chuck sat back in their chairs, looked at each other and smiled. They had worked together on an issue that had troubled them for quite a while. They had affirmed their relationship through taking one another's issues and concerns seriously. They had discovered some solutions that addressed the issue and satisfied each partner. They had found a tool that helped them with the current issue and they realized could help them in the future. In other words, not only had they dealt with the problem at hand, their future problem-solving capacity had been enhanced. A wink from each indicated it clearly was time to forgive one another, promise to abide by the new rules, and share a well-deserved glass of wine!

In effect, in this case an informal type of mapping played the same role that a wise friend or counsellor might have played, but without having to organize or pay for third-party help. Mapping helped Chuck and Mary sort out the many aspects of the issue that bothered them, and also helped them create a new plan that addressed the issue and produced much better results for both of them.

Conclusion

We have argued that *mapping* is what you should do when clear thinking matters. At their most basic, maps are simply word-and-arrow diagrams. They are textual statements linked by arrows that indicate what causes what, or what actions lead to what outcomes. The basic idea behind mapping is very simple, but also very powerful.

As the example with Chuck and Mary shows, mapping can be used to deal with important questions that involve complex interconnections and emotions. Maps allow exploration of issues and answers through assisting and clarifying the content and logic embedded in discussion and dialogue. Indeed, mapping prompts mappers to articulate what they think and why. And, as in Chuck and Mary's case, mapping can help people articulate preferred goals, strategies and actions for getting out of difficult situations.

Said differently, maps can help make the obvious – as well as the not so obvious – apparent. They can also take the heat out of an emotional situation, while illuminating the nature of the situation and its consequences and possible avenues toward effective solutions. Maps acknowledge that solutions may need many actions rather than a single action.

The family argument example also shows how maps can become tools for building relationships. Chuck and Mary were building – or reinforcing – their relationship while negotiating meaning and creating understanding and action. Their map was a "transitional object", "facilitative device" or "ritual structure" that allowed them to move together to a much better place cognitively, behaviourally and emotionally.[3] Mapping helped them articulate the current "problem story" that was causing difficulty for them, and then to create an "alternative story" that was less problematic, more motivating and generally more satisfying. The new story was created in part out of aspects of the situation that were already present, so the flow from problematic past into more desirable future was facilitated.[4]

When can mapping help? We think it can help whenever thinking matters. In particular, and to recap, we think that mapping can be particularly useful when:

- effective strategies need to be developed;

- persuasive arguments are needed;

- effective and logical communication is essential;

- effective understanding and management of conflict are needed;

- it is vital that a situation be understood better as a prelude to any action.

As we noted, these situations are not mutually exclusive. Indeed, in order to deal with their conflict, Chuck and Mary needed to understand their situation better, develop an effective strategy, persuade each other, communicate effectively, and understand and manage their conflict better. Mapping helped them do all of these.

We hope that the potential management applications of the tool are becoming clear. Chuck and Mary's argument took place at home, but issues like theirs are common in the workplace, and so is the need to develop effective strategies for dealing with issues of many sorts. In the next chapter, we present another example and talk through in more detail how and why mapping works.

Notes

1 C. Eden and C. Huxham (1988) Action-oriented Strategic Management, *Journal of the Operational Research Society*, **39**(10), 889–99.
2 The type of informal mapping introduced at this early stage of the book could be described as a combination of mind mapping (T. Buzan and B. Buzan (1993) *The Mind Map Book: Radiant Thinking, the Major Evolution in Human Thought*, London: BBC Books) and causal mapping. The map's informality makes it less amenable to construction of more complex maps and to formal analysis. Nonetheless, as will be seen in the example, this type of informal mapping provided valuable insights that led to changed behaviour.
3 Chuck and Mary's map acted as what psychiatrist D. W. Winnicott calls a "transitional object"; that is, a device that helps someone make a move from one way of thinking, doing and being to another; see D. W. Winnicott (1953) Transitional Objects and Transitional Phenomena, *International Journal of Psycho-Analysis*, **34**(Part 2), 89–97. Similarly, the map acted as what Arie de Geus calls a "facilitative device", which does for groups what transitional objects do for people; see A. P. de Geus (1988) Planning as Learning, *Harvard Business Review*, March–April, 70–4. The process of mapping provides what John Forester calls a "ritual structure", a patterned and purposeful way for a group to figure out what to do, how and why; see J. Forester (1999) *The Deliberative Practitioner*, Cambridge, MA: MIT Press.

4 See G. Monk, J. Winslade, K. Crocket and D. E. Epston (1997) *Narrative Therapy in Practice: The Archaeology of Hope*, San Francisco, CA: Jossey-Bass, for a discussion of problem stories and how they can be developed into less problematic alternative stories.

2

How and Why
Mapping Works

*The significant problems we face cannot be solved at the same level of
thinking we were at when we created them.*   ALBERT EINSTEIN

QUITE SIMPLY, MAPPING WORKS BECAUSE IT SEEKS TO REPLI-
cate the way psychologists believe human beings make sense of
their world. We make sense of our lives and situations by
constructing, elaborating, revising and re-revising a system of
interconnected concepts (more formally called "constructs"). The
concepts, in turn, embody a set of comparisons and contrasts. In
other words, in order to know what something *is*, we need to know at
least one thing it is *like* – the comparison – and one thing it is *not
like* – the contrast. We then use the relationships among these
concepts (and their comparisons and contrasts) to:

- make sense of our world;

- create distinctions that make a difference;

- anticipate the future;

- take action based on our anticipations;

- make sense of the results of our actions;

- begin again in a context that is in some sense different, at least
  partially as a result of our actions.[1]

An example helps clarify what we mean. Consider John and Chuck's
preferences for exercise: both exercise regularly – a comparison –
but John prefers to run and Chuck prefers to swim – a contrast. The
comparisons and contrasts are developed more fully in Map 2.1.

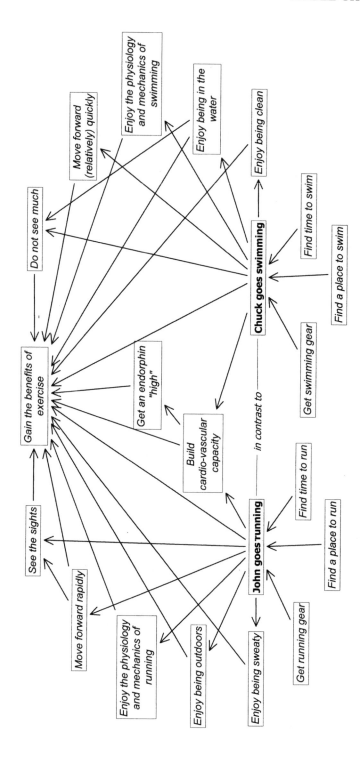

Map 2.1   When they find time to exercise, John and Chuck have the same aim and similar requirements, but they achieve their aims in a completely different manner.

Map 2.1 shows that John runs and Chuck swims. In order to go running, John needs to get running gear, find a place to run and find time to run. Similarly – but a little differently – Chuck needs to get swimming gear, find a place to swim and find time to swim. Each has similar objectives for exercising, which include building cardio-vascular capacity, which can lead to an endorphin "high". Both are part of gaining the benefits from exercise.

There are other similarities and differences as well: John enjoys being sweaty, while Chuck enjoys being clean. John enjoys being outdoors, while Chuck enjoys being in the water. Both enjoy the physiology and mechanics of their chosen form of exercise. John enjoys moving forwards rapidly and seeing the sights. Chuck enjoys moving forwards as quickly as he can while swimming (which is too slow for John), but he does not see much. Both enjoy the benefits of exercising, but Chuck's enjoyment is reduced somewhat – hence, the negative arrow – by not seeing much. So there are many similarities, but also some important contrasts in what exercising *means* to John and to Chuck. Indeed, the dissimilarities are enough for John not to choose swimming as a regular form of exercise and for Chuck not to choose running.

Note that the *meaning* of a concept is not just in its wording, but is actually embedded in the *relationships* it has to the concepts around it.[2] If there are many concepts and relationships, including at least implicit comparisons and contrasts, then the focal concept is *meaning-full*. If there are few concepts and relationships, then the focal concept is relatively *meaning-less*. In Map 2.1, we can see that running and swimming are fairly meaningful concepts for both John and Chuck.

This view of *meaning creation* leads to some important propositions. First, *people construe the same event or situation differently*. Even if they literally see the same thing, they will construe different things in what ostensibly is the same situation, and construct at least partially different concept systems to account for it and to make predictions about the future. In other words, perception is prior to construal; construal is the act of giving meaning to what is seen. Thus in our example, John's view of swimming is not the same as Chuck's and Chuck's view of running is not the same as John's. Second, *success in a problem-solving group depends on the ability of each member to understand how the others interpret the situation.* People need to be able to say, "I see what you are saying." Third, *a group must reach a reasonable consensus about how to construe present and future events if they are to create reasonably coherent and coordinated action.* In other words, everyone must be at least somewhat "on the same page". Mapping is useful precisely because it can help people *literally* see what one another is saying and allow everyone to be on the same page.[3]

Viewing meaning as embedded in personal construct systems also leads to a fourth really fundamental proposition, namely that *you can never change anyone's mind (or a group's "mind") directly; you can only help them elaborate their concept system(s) until they change their own mind(s).* Parents of teenagers understand this – and groan at the knowledge. Mapping works in part simply because it helps people figure out what their concept system is, and how and why they might change it. It helps people *change their own minds,* which is the only kind of persuasion and conversion that really count. For groups to reach consensus, typically each person must change their own mind in some way. Others cannot do it for them, although they can help.

Another Example Involving Personal Planning

Let's look at another example. This shows in more detail how a system of concepts is built up and how the propositions work themselves out in practice. We will also use the example to begin developing guidelines for constructing, using and analysing maps. The situation involves two of the authors doing some personal strategic planning, but the principles apply to organizational strategic planning as well, as subsequent chapters in the book will show.

In presenting this example, we will start providing specific advice on how to do mapping. The advice will be in the form of "process guidelines", that will be highlighted in **bold**. We will also begin indicating new and important understandings for the people doing the mapping that emerged from the mapping process. We call these "learning points" and they will be presented in ***bold italic***.

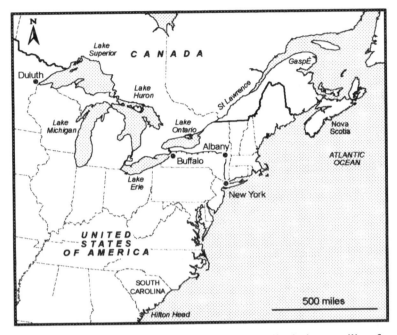

Map 2.2 *The big adventure.* John and Chuck talked about sailing from
Duluth, Minnesota, to Hilton Head Island, South Carolina, across Lakes
Superior and Huron, down the Detroit River, through Lakes St Clare and
Erie, around Niagara Falls, across Lake Ontario and down the St Lawrence
to the Atlantic, around the Gaspé Peninsula and Nova Scotia to Maine and
south to Hilton Head. Or they might lower the mast at Buffalo, New York,
and motor through the Erie Canal to Albany, and down the Hudson River
to New York City. Then they would sail down the East Coast to Hilton
Head. The trip (3000 to 4000 miles) could take all summer and perhaps
into the fall.

The authors all like to sail. Two of them – John and Chuck – have
talked about taking three or four months unpaid leave from their
jobs to sail from Duluth, Minnesota, to Hilton Head Island, South
Carolina. A big reason for the trip is that it will allow John and
Chuck to spend more time together, which has been difficult lately,
since Chuck has moved from Minneapolis, where John still lives, to
take another job in New York. The trip would allow them to do
things they really enjoy – being together, sailing and having a big
adventure.

There are a number of reasons for considering this particular trip.
Chuck grew up in Duluth and learned to sail on Lake Superior.

Much of his family still lives there. Duluth is not too far from Minneapolis. John and Chuck both like sailing on Lake Superior, and it would be good to start from a familiar city in familiar waters. Hilton Head Island makes a good destination because John and his wife know the island well, as they vacation there once a year with their extended families. In addition, mooring or storing the boat should not be a problem.

To make the trip, John and Chuck would sail across Lake Superior, across Lake Huron, down the Detroit River and through Lake St Clare to Lake Erie, across Lake Erie, around Niagara Falls, across Lake Ontario and down the St Lawrence River to the Atlantic Ocean. From there they would sail around Quebec's Gaspé Peninsula and Nova Scotia to Maine and then down the East Coast of the United States to Hilton Head. Alternatively, they might take down their mast at Buffalo, New York, and motor across the Erie Canal to Albany, and then motor and sail down the Hudson River to New York City. From there they would sail down the East Coast to Hilton Head. The distance, depending on the exact route, would be in the order of 3000–4000 miles. To be really enjoyable, the trip would take all summer and perhaps into the fall.

John and Chuck knew that taking this trip would not be easy and that there were many things to consider. So naturally they decided to map the effort. The map would help them develop strategies and actions for pursuing their adventure, and also help them clarify the trip's overall purpose and goals.

It is important to note that at first they thought they would not mention this trip idea to their wives, Barbara and Mary respectively. Before mentioning it, John and Chuck first wanted to figure out whether the adventure was even feasible. It is also true that they were a little apprehensive about how their wives might respond. Chuck was particularly apprehensive. After all, taking the trip would mean that Mary would have three to four months of household chores to do by herself (see Chapter 1)! What follows is John and Chuck's map and how they constructed it.

In order to begin mapping, you need to **have a reason for mapping, assemble the necessary materials and find a place to map** (process guideline). John and Chuck had a purpose; now

Map 2.3   What do John and Chuck want to do? Sail halfway across America.

they needed the following materials (essentially the same materials Chuck and Mary needed to address their argument):

- One sheet of flipchart paper.

- Two $2'' \times 2''$ Post-it pads.

- Two felt-tipped pens.

- Two soft-lead pencils.

- A large flat surface, such as a tabletop or wall.

John and Chuck chose to sit at a table. They placed the flipchart sheet lengthwise on the tabletop in front of them. They each took one of the felt-tipped pens and a Post-it pad. One of them wrote "Sail from Duluth, MN to Hilton Head, SC" on a Post-it and placed it in the middle of the flipchart sheet, about one-third of the way down from the top. They were beginning to create an action-oriented map by first asking themselves the question: *"What do you want to do?"* (see Map 2.3).

John and Chuck knew that **the answers to the question "What do you want to do?" (or "What might you do?") would most likely turn out to be possible strategies**. Our experience indicates that this is the best place to start constructing an action-oriented map, rather than with goals. In other words, **start mapping with what people can imagine doing, or with issues they think they face (that is, with some source of "pain")**, rather than with goals. Starting with "doing" or with some pain is a way of making the exercise more realistic, both immediately and in the longer term as well.

Typically, the next appropriate step in creating an action-oriented map is to ask, *"How would we do that – that is, sail from Duluth to Hilton Head? What would it take to do that?"* John and Chuck knew that **the answers to this question would**

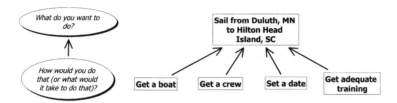

Map 2.4   Before the "big adventure" – sailing halfway across America –
John and Chuck need to do a number of big things first.

produce strategic options and possible actions. Each wrote a
couple of ideas on separate Post-it notes, one idea per note. They
decided they needed to:

- get a boat;

- get a crew;

- set a date;

- get adequate training.

Note that all of these **statements, as options or actions, have an
active verb in them**.

These Post-it notes were placed underneath the first note and
arrows were drawn from each to the first using a soft-lead pencil (see
Map 2.4). As we noted in the previous chapter, the arrows mean
"would be needed to" (or "may lead to", or "might result in", or
"may influence"). In other words, getting a boat and crew, setting a
date and getting adequate training probably would be needed to sail
from Duluth to Hilton Head. It is hard to imagine making the trip
without doing them!

John and Chuck then decided to ask themselves, *"OK, now what
would it take to do those things?"* The results of answering this
question will be found in Map 2.5. One of the first challenges is
figuring out how to "get a boat", since neither John nor Chuck
owned a large enough sailboat when they did the map. They could
either "buy a boat" or "charter a boat". Either way, they need to
"get money", probably a lot of it. One option they might pursue to
"get money" would be to "build up savings". To do this, they could
either "do extra consulting" or "reduce consumption". But in order

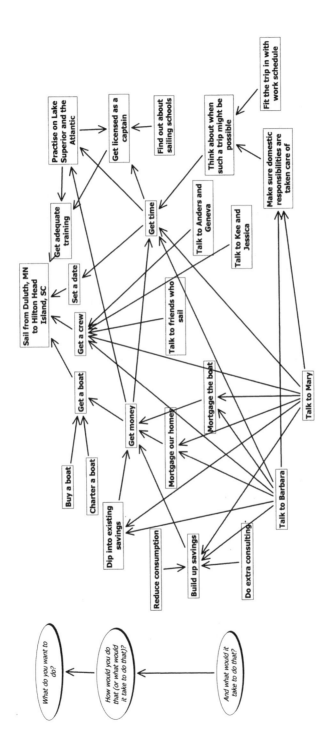

Map 2.5   Careful examination of the "big" actions shows that there are many smaller, but very important, actions that need to be done in order to accomplish the "big" actions.

to pursue either option, John will need to "talk to Barbara", while Chuck will need to "talk to Mary", since the understandings they have with their spouses will need to be renegotiated.

Another way to "get money" would be to "mortgage our homes" or, preferably, "mortgage the boat". Either way, John needs to "talk to Barbara", while Chuck needs to "talk to Mary".

The next challenge is to "get a crew". One option would be to "talk to friends who sail". The likely prospects would be Colin and Fran, but neither of them is particularly interested. Colin would rather sail around the Hebrides off the west coast of Scotland, an area he thinks provides some of the best sailing in the world. Fran grew up in Australia and would prefer somewhere like Scotland, but warmer. Another option would be to "talk to Barbara" and "talk to Mary". Children might also be interested in crewing, so John could "talk to Kee and Jessica" and Chuck could "talk to Anders and Geneva".

Once the boat and crew are in hand, the next task is to "set a date". But in order to set a date, both John and Chuck will need to "get time" – specifically, four months off. To do that they will first have to "think about when such a trip might be possible". With kids in college, taking time off will be a challenge. If John and Chuck are to take this trip before their kids are out of college (or after, for that matter!), they will need to "get money", which takes them back to that part of the map. Assuming they have the money, somehow they will need to "fit the trip into their work schedule". They also will need to "make sure their domestic responsibilities are taken care of". To do that, John will need to "talk to Barbara", while Chuck will most certainly need to "talk to Mary".

Finally, both John and Chuck need to "get adequate training". Chuck is a more experienced big-water sailor than John, but he still needs to get some training. They both would like to "get licensed as a captain" and in order to do that, they will need to "find out about sailing school" and will need to "get money" and "get time". They also need to "practise on Lake Superior and the Atlantic", which will also mean they have to "get money" and "get time". Note that what John and Chuck have been doing to develop the part of the map shown in Map 2.5 is to keep working down a chain of arrows by asking the question "How would you do that?" or "What would it take to do that?"

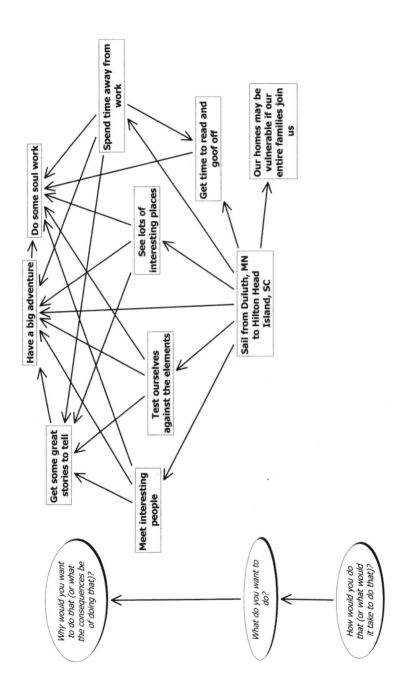

Map 2.6 Asking themselves why they would want to sail halfway across America brought out the real reasons for John and Chuck's big adventure.

So what do John and Chuck conclude so far? They have to **examine the map frequently to understand what it is saying**. They **look especially for "busy" concepts – those that have lots of arrows coming in and going out – and "potent" concepts – those that lead to many concepts further up the map**. The "busy" concepts are likely to occupy a central role in their thinking, while the "potent" concepts are likely to be key leverage points for achieving their goals. It appears that the big challenges (indicated in part by their busyness) are the need to "get money" and "get time". Those are really important means to the end. ("Get crew" is also busy, but all John and Chuck really need is themselves for crew, and all they need for that is to "get time". Additional crew would be helpful and pleasant, but not actually "needed".) And it turns out that the two most potent options are talking with their spouses. That is where it all starts, and they cannot achieve their goals without doing so. *So putting off talking to Barbara and Mary is out of the question* (learning point).

Now John and Chuck needed to start identifying and clarifying what their goals, or ends, really are. "Sail from Duluth, MN to Hilton Head, SC" is not the ultimate end, but is merely a strategy for pursuing more important ends. **To find out what their real goals are** John and Chuck have to **ask "Why would we want to do that?" or "What would be the consequences, or results, of doing that?" Those consequences that are *good in their own right* are likely goals.** The results of their inquiry are presented in Map 2.6.

The first set of consequences of the trip that came to mind are that John and Chuck would "meet interesting people", "test themselves against the elements", "see lots of interesting places", "spend time away from work", and "get time to read and goof off". As far as Chuck and John are concerned, this would not be a bad set of outcomes. In fact, each would be a *goal* for them – good in its own right. Unfortunately, there is another possibility. John and Chuck thought they may "make their homes vulnerable to theft, vandalism and fire" if they make the trip and their wives and children come along as crew. Something will have to be done to guard against those negative outcomes if their families come along. The possibility that the houses will be vulnerable to damage is what we would call a *negative goal*. A negative goal is a natural and logical consequence of doing what you want to do, and is at the same level of abstraction as a goal, but involves a negative outcome, not a positive one. "Making their houses vulnerable" is an undesirable situation that must be managed. (Note that not all outcomes are goals or negative goals; some outcomes may simply be consequences and not labelled either as goals or negative goals.)

Are there additional consequences resulting from the initial set? Yes. John and Chuck would "get some great stories to tell" (they are both inveterate story tellers!) and they would "have a big adventure" (they both love big adventures). But there is an even more important consequence to be gained from the trip, and that is that both would "do some soul work". On a trip like this – poised between the heavens and the deep, and in tune with nature – they would have plenty of time to explore the meaning of friendship, work, spirit and life itself. *And – to their surprise – doing soul work is apparently the ultimate purpose of the trip.* **By pushing on the consequences of what they might do, they have found what the real purpose is of doing that thing.** At this point, they stopped, looked at each other and let that realization sink in.

After talking about what the apparent purpose of their trip is – soul work – *John and Chuck came to another major realization: they do not have to sail from Duluth to Hilton Head to do soul work!* There are actually plenty of ways to do soul work that do not involve nearly as much risk and money. They will have to think about that. In other words, they will need to keep in mind the larger lesson that **once you have clarified your real purpose, it is important to reexamine the possible strategies for achieving it to see if there are additional ways to pursue the purpose and its attendant goals.**

John and Chuck now looked at the whole map. A map initially consists of a set of *possible* purposes, goals, strategies, options and actions. Through dialogue it should be possible to agree on *actual* purposes, goals, strategies and actions. They therefore discussed the map in order to **decide which concepts among the various possibilities represented the actual purpose, goals, strategies (or strategic issues) and actions to implement the strategies** (see the Glossary on p. 309). In the case of any

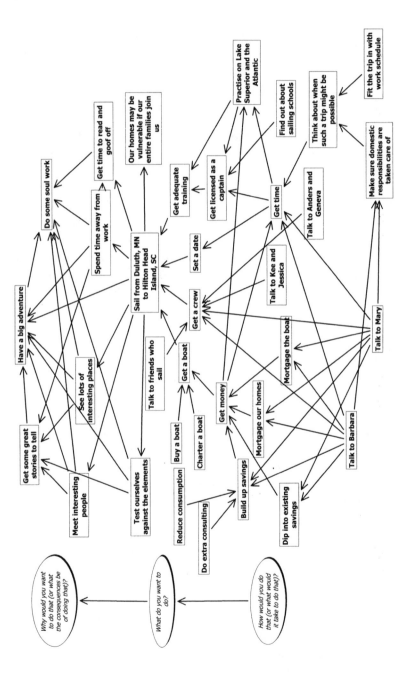

Map 2.7   The "big picture" of the "big adventure". Everything that John and Chuck need to do to sail halfway across America, and everything they want to gain from the big adventure.

disagreements or new insights, they could always add, delete or change the concepts on their map. Their final map is presented in Map 2.7.

To summarize, John and Chuck *used mapping and the map to bring their differing views of the world together*. They used the mapping process to develop a shared understanding of what might be involved in their big adventure and why they might wish to pursue it. In other words, they built a shared concept system that embodied a variety of mostly implicit comparisons and contrasts, as well as explicit predictions about the future. They agreed on the current situation, the purpose of the trip, and steps each would need to take to make the trip happen.

The mapping effort has resulted in three major insights that John and Chuck did not possess before they started. First, they need to start talking with Barbara and Mary early on if they want to make this trip. Second, what they really want to do is some individual soul work. And third, there are many other strategies for doing soul work. They have to explore some of them further before deciding whether to sail from Duluth to Hilton Head.

Note again that this mapping exercise started with what turned out to be a *strategy*, not with goals. Actually, *John and Chuck did not know – and probably could not have known – what their ultimate purpose and goals were until they had constructed much of the map*. In our experience this is quite common, and for that reason we generally advise mappers *not* to start with goals or objectives, but instead to begin what they can imagine themselves doing – that is, to start with strategies – before exploring what the goals might be that those strategies help achieve. This approach will no doubt seem very odd to many people, but based on our experience it usually works best. Said differently, people usually need to talk their way into their goals and purposes; they need to see what they believe they want to do before they can articulate why they want to do it. Belief about doing leads to seeing the reasons for believing in the first place – and perhaps to changing one's mind about what one believes and says.[4]

The Structure and Logic of an Action-Oriented Map

Action-oriented maps like the maps presented in this chapter have a characteristic structure and logic, which is presented in Figure 2.1. The logic is that of argumentation. The structure is that of a strategic plan.[5]

John and Chuck began by asking themselves "What do we want to do?" This is the middle question in the left-hand column. Once they answered that, they had identified a *possible strategy*: "Sail from Duluth, MN to Hilton Head Island, SC" (see the middle column of Figure 2.1). Said somewhat differently, they had identified a *strategic issue* that consisted of an as yet unarticulated set of possible *action options* they might pursue to address it. They then explored those options by asking themselves "How would we do that?" or "What

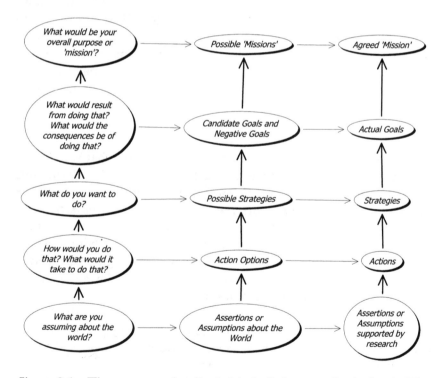

Figure 2.1   The structure that lies behind all the maps in the book. The refinement of the statements and the analysis moves from left to right and from top to bottom – or from bottom to top.

would it take to do that?" The answers to these questions resulted in the set of options. For example, it was by asking these questions that they realized (the obvious!) that John needed to talk to Barbara and Chuck needed to talk to Mary. (Again, refer to the Glossary on p. 309.)

They could then have asked yet another question – though they did not – and that is "What are you assuming about the world?" In other words, what do you believe or assert about the world that provides the deep foundation or platform on which the scaffolding of the rest of your argument is built? Had they asked that question, it would have become explicit that both wanted to stay married to their wife and remain friends with the other's wife. They did not ask the question because staying married to their soul mates and friends with the other's wife is so much a part of their "assumptive worlds" or "world-taken-for-granted" that they did not need to ask it.[6]

After exploring action options for pursuing their strategy, they then asked "What would result from that?" (sailing from Duluth to Hilton Head) or "What would the consequences be of doing that?" The answers to these questions produced *candidate goals* and *negative goals*. Finally, they asked themselves "What is our overall purpose?" It was only by pursuing the consequences of the sailing trip far enough that they discovered that doing soul work was the *real* purpose.

Once a map has been developed, the logic connecting purpose, goals, strategies, actions and assertions should be clear, and commitments can be made (although whether they will be or not is another question). The logic should make sense whether it is *deduced* from top to bottom (purposes and goals to assertions) or *induced* from bottom to top (assertions to goals and purposes).

No matter what, as we noted above, the logic structure is the same as the structure of a strategic plan. In other words, starting from the top (see the right-hand column in Figure 2.1), it should be clear how the purpose and each of the goals might be achieved by a set of "strategies". It should be clear how each of the strategies may be pursued by a set of actions. And it should be clear how key assumptions or assertions about the world underpin important actions. Alternatively, it should be clear how actions are based on assumptions or assertions; how the actions bundle together as strategies; how the strategies accomplish the goals; and ultimately how pursuit of the goals will achieve the overall purpose. We should be able to move up and down these chains of argument and understand each link in the chain.

As noted above, Chuck and John began the map of their sailing trip "in the middle"; that is, they started with what was actually a possible strategy. That is a fairly typical place to start, and in our experience is usually one of the best places to begin. As we shall see later, it can also be good to start by outlining the issues that are being faced, and then exploring the consequences of *not* acting on them. For Chuck and John it was certainly more appropriate to start with a possible strategy. For both starting positions, it is presumed that goals are not fully understood, or may be idealized rather than realistic. For John and Chuck, only after figuring out what options they had for pursuing their strategy did they explore what their candidate goals might be, and only through that exploration did they find their real purpose.

The example actually demonstrates one of the beauties of mapping: there is no presumption that you know everything in advance when you start, although most people know what many of their issues are or what possible strategies (sometimes ill thought out) they might pursue. Indeed, the presumption is quite the opposite: mapping is primarily a tool for *creating* or *discovering* what you really think. Alternatively, as the ancient Roman philosopher Seneca said, "If one does not know to which port one is sailing, no wind is favourable." Mapping helped John and Chuck figure out what their real port was and which winds might help them get there.

Summary and Conclusions

Mapping works because it builds on the way human beings make sense of their world. It also helps us become self-conscious about our thinking process and logic. The educational psychologist R. Samson argues that there are eight fundamental thinking processes.

These are representing in context, describing attitudes, comparing, categorizing, part–whole relationships, sequencing, cause-and-effect reasoning and relational reasoning (or reasoning by analogy).[7] Mapping helps with all of these processes – and helps us be self-conscious about using them. And by doing so, it helps us effectively construct, elaborate and change our system of interconnected concepts so that we can figure out what we want, how to get it and why. Once again, we think that *mapping should be the tool of choice when thinking matters.*

Process guidelines emerging from this case

- Have a reason for mapping, assemble the necessary materials and find a place to map.

- Answers to the question "What do you want to do?" (or "What might you do?") will most likely turn out to be possible strategies.

- Start mapping with what people can imagine themselves doing, or with issues they think they face (some "pain"), rather than with a statement of goals.

- A useful step in creating an action-oriented map is to ask *"How would we do that? What would it take to do that?"*

- Statements, as options or actions, have an active verb in them.

- Examine the map frequently to understand what it is saying.

- Look especially for "busy" concepts – those that have lots of arrows coming in and going out – and "potent" concepts – those that lead to many concepts further up the map.

- To find out what the real goals are, ask "Why would we want to do that?" or "What would be the consequences, or results, of doing that?" Those consequences that are *good in their own right* are likely goals.

- By pushing on the consequences of what might be done, you can find out what the real purpose is of doing that thing.

- Once goals are clarified, it is important to reexamine the possible strategies for achieving them to see if there are additional ways to pursue the goals.

- Decide which concepts among the various possibilities represented the actual goals, strategies (or strategic issues) and actions to implement the strategies.

Learning points for John and Chuck

- They had used the map to bring their differing views of the world together.

- There are three major insights that John and Chuck did not have before they started. First, they needed to start talking with Barbara and Mary early on if they wanted to make this trip. Second, what they really wanted to do is some individual soul work. And third, there are many other strategies for doing soul work. They would have to explore some of them further before deciding whether to sail from Duluth to Hilton Head.

- John and Chuck did not know – and probably could not have known – what their ultimate purpose and goals were until they had constructed much of the map.

- Looking at their map – which showed them that doing soul work was their real purpose – John and Chuck came to another major realization: they do not have to sail from Duluth to Hilton Head to do soul work!

Postscript

At the time of writing, John and Chuck have not absolutely decided to make the trip, but they have taken some important steps in that direction. For example, Chuck and Mary have sold their vacation home in Minnesota's North Woods (after Chuck made sure to "talk to Mary"!) and Chuck has bought a used 36-foot sloop, which he is making totally seaworthy. He is also taking the classes necessary to become a charter boat captain. John has "talked to Barbara" and they have purchased a vacation home on Hilton Head Island, which pleases Barbara immensely. John also has plans to take courses in seamanship, navigation, meteorology and diesel engine maintenance and repair. He also will go to charter boat captain school. And both will find time to practise sailing together on the Great Lakes, the Atlantic and elsewhere. Even if the big adventure ultimately does *not* take place, they will still have the pleasure of each other's company for extended periods of time, John will get to study subjects he has always wanted to know more about, and both will have found ways to attend to their soul.

Notes

1 Readers who would like to pursue further the theories on which this paragraph is based should start with Karl Weick's fascinating and very readable book on how humans "make sense" of their world (K. E. Weick (1995) *Sensemaking in Organizations*, Thousand Oaks, CA: Sage) and George Kelly's guide to what is called "personal construct theory" (G. Kelly (1963) *A Theory of Personality*, New York, NY: Norton). Our approach to causal mapping has been strongly influenced by both authors, and by links to action research theory (C. Eden and C. Huxham (1996) Action Research for Management Research, *British Journal of Management*, 7, 75–86.

2 C. Eden, S. Jones and D. Sims (1983) *Messing about in Problems*, Oxford: Pergamon Press, p. 46, make this argument and show this graphically.

3 The three propositions come directly from Kelly, *op. cit.* Interesting applications of the propositions to planning and management situations (though without reference to Kelly) will be found in J. E. Innes (1996) Planning through Consensus Building: A New View of the Comprehensive Planning Ideal, *Journal of the American Planning Association*, 460–72; J. Forester (1999) *The Deliberative Practitioner*, Cambridge, MA: MIT Press; and L. Susskind, S. McKearnon and J. Thomas-Larmer (1999) *The Consensus Building Handbook: A Comprehensive Guide to Reaching Agreement*, Thousand Oaks, CA: Sage.

4 The discussion about the links between believing and doing is based on Weick, *op. cit.*

5 For more on the nature and logic of argumentation, see H. W. Simons (2001) *Persuasion in Society*, Thousand Oaks, CA: Sage. For more on the logical structure of a strategic plan, see C. Eden and F. Ackermann

(1998) *Making Strategy: The Journey of Strategic Management*, London: Sage.

6 The terms "assumptive worlds" and "world-taken-for-granted" come from C. Eden (1992) On the Nature of Cognitive Maps, *Journal of Management Studies*, **29**, 261–5.

7 Samson's work is cited in D. Hyerle (1996) *Visual Tools for Constructing Knowledge*, Alexandria, VA: Association for Supervision and Curriculum Development, 105–6.

Part II

What Do I Think? A Guide to Cognitive Mapping

3

How not to Miss the Boat

The obvious is not always apparent.
(Paco Underhill, *Why We Buy*)

IN THIS CHAPTER WE PRESENT A STORY INVOLVING BARGAIN-
ing and negotiation between a customer and a supplier. The case
is unusual, in that it involves conflict over when and in what
condition a custom-built yacht will be delivered. However, all of us
get involved in bargaining and negotiation both at home and at
work. Indeed, it is sometimes one of the most important aspects of a
manager's job. Look at this case as an example of a commonly
encountered set of circumstances and see the guidelines as
applicable to other, more frequently encountered situations involving conflicts between customers and suppliers, superiors and
subordinates, citizens and governments, boards and staff and so on.

The four authors of this book all like to sail, but none is more avid
than Colin. He has been sailing for over 30 years, goes on at least
one major sailing vacation each year and sails on as many weekends
as he can. Part of the reason for his move 15 years ago from the
University of Bath in southern England to the University of
Strathclyde in Glasgow, Scotland, was to be close to what he thinks
is the best sailing in the world. Specifically, he wanted to be close to
the islands of the Inner and Outer Hebrides off the west coast of
Scotland.

Colin has owned a succession of boats. He started sharing boats and
then built a 26-foot boat from scratch in his back garden. More
recently these have been expensive boats, to say the least, and Colin
has upgraded in quality over time as his finances have improved.
His latest boat is a 31-foot beauty named *Maalesh*. The boat
was custom-made by a shipwright based in southern England,

approximately 600 miles by sea, or 400 miles by land, from Glasgow. Colin is quite happy with the boat. However, there was a time when he was very worried that it would not be delivered on time and to the quality standard he wanted. In this chapter we tell the story of how he used mapping to make sure the boat got delivered on time and in good shape.

In order to understand the story, some background information is necessary on Colin's life and on how the sailing world is organized. Colin is a very busy professor. At best, in any given year he can work in one two-week sailing trip in the late spring, in addition to his sporadic weekend sailing. If he misses his two-week window, it is gone forever. So when he signed the contract for his new boat early in the year, he had in mind that he would have his long sail in September, before the summer ended. If the boat was delivered too late, Colin would have to wait until the following May for some decent sailing.

Also important to know is that in order to pay for the new boat, Colin had to sell his old boat to come up with the down payment. He sold the boat through the boat builder's local agent in Glasgow. Then Colin was without a boat of any kind.

Custom boat builders are not as fussed about deadlines as their customers are, nor are they bothered by the fact that their customers are temporarily without a boat. What the builders typically do is sign a contract for a boat, start building it and then get going on the next boat. That way they can smooth out their workflow and also keep their next customer happy. This problem of dragged-out deadlines for custom-built boats is a common one, known throughout the industry. Colin knew about it and tried to factor into the contract a reasonable delay in the delivery deadline. In other words, he reckoned that the boat would be delivered late and tried to take that into account in such a way that he would still get some sailing in late in the season.

However, it turned out that delay was not his only problem. Increasingly, he became bothered about many small happenings with the ship builder as time went on, but wasn't sure exactly why he was bothered. Colin decided it was time to get his thinking straight, and so he opted to produce a map. What follows is Colin's story. We will use the way he constructed his map to draw out more guidelines for producing maps.

I was worried that the boat would not be completed on time, and I was bothered by not knowing what to do about it. I love sailing and was really looking forward to this new boat. But time was marching on. I did not have a boat, had spent a lot of money and still had to make a final payment. And yet I might lose the whole sailing season if the new boat was not completed on time. At that moment I seemed to be in a tough situation: out of a lot of money, but with no boat. I had a contract that ultimately was enforceable, but maybe only after I had lost the sailing season.

I really had to get my thinking clear about this problem. So I decided I had to map the situation to make sure I knew exactly what was really bothering me, and to see if I could do anything about it. I guessed it would take a couple of hours or so, which is nothing compared to the loss of an entire sailing season. So I chose to devote a long lunch hour to making the map. An hour seemed reasonable, since I had already thought a lot about this problem and had discussed my situation with friends (including Fran, John and Chuck) on several occasions.

The first thing I did was **assemble the materials I would need to create the map**. These included:

- one small Post-it pad;

- two sheets of flipchart paper (one as a spare);

- two soft-lead (2B) pencils with erasers;

- five felt-tipped pens, each one a different colour (red, purple, blue, orange and black, in order to indicate different categories of statements on the map);

- masking tape or "sticky putty" (in case I wanted to tape the map to the wall to look at it).

Once I had the materials, I closed my office door and spread the flipchart sheet out lengthwise on the table. I then began to write any thoughts I had as quickly as possible onto the small Post-its, one thought per note. I was simply trying to **"dump" as many ideas**

as I could, so I made a point of not censoring myself, or setting out the material in any specific order.

I tried to **keep each statement to no more than eight words,** as a way of making sure I did not have more than one thought on each slip of paper. I placed my initial Post-its – 25 of them – on the flipchart sheet as I thought of them, and drew in causal links (arrows "in" or "out") as I worked. I knew that the location of the slips was likely to change, as were the arrows, while I worked, but I wanted to move as quickly as I could.

As they were dumped, it became clear that some of the **statements represented different aspects of the problem, and so these differences were identified using the coloured pens.** The first idea on the map (numbered 1) I marked in red and was as close as I could come to putting a label on my distress: "Boat delivery has become unpredictable [rather than] just late as expected [1]". Note that **the shorthand convention for "rather than" is an ellipsis (...), which saves time and space.** I placed this idea in the very middle of the flipchart sheet so that I had room to "ladder up" to explore consequences, as well as room to "ladder down" to explore the causes of my distress.

Figure 3.1 shows a photograph of the map after about 15 minutes of work. The initial dump of ideas had taken place and I had done some "structuring" of the issue with links. I **numbered every statement based on the order in which I thought of them.** These numbers can be helpful if it ever makes sense to reflect on what materials seemed to be foremost in your mind, and also how writing one statement acted as a prompt for another.

As noted above, the first statement was my best shot at giving a label, or headline, to the problem I faced. I also **thought carefully about the contrast – the circumstance that would have meant it was not a problem for me.** Thus I was fussed that the "boat delivery has become unpredictable *rather than* just late as expected [1]". I then asked myself why this situation was making me angry and reckoned that "my work planning is becoming increasingly difficult... *rather than* diary becomes fixed [2]". In other words, because I did not know exactly when the boat might be done, I was having trouble arranging the rest of my life.

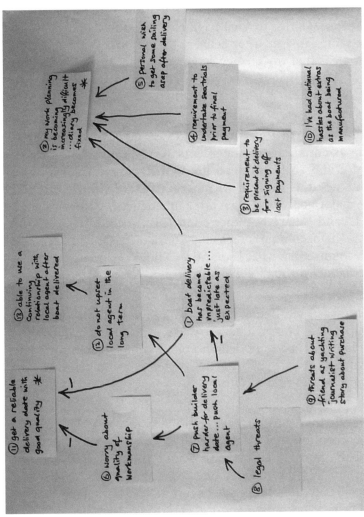

Figure 3.1   A photograph of Colin's first thoughts on the problem – not merely late delivery, but unpredictable delivery as well as worries about the quality of the finished boat – and the effects of this uncertainty on his ability to organize his life.

Colin used red to indicate his distress [1]; black with an * for goals [11]; black for negative goals (significant negative outcomes) [2, 13]; grey for constraints [3, 4, 5]; purple for options [8, 9]; and blue for others [6, 7, 10, 12] – all shown in black in the photograph. Note also the use of "…" as a shorthand for "rather than".

But why was that a problem? And so I offered an explanation (in arrow) to be clear that I was not merely worried for its own sake! The first reason that came to mind was the "requirement to be present at delivery for signing off last payments [3]". The way things were going I might have to fly to the South of England on short notice. Then I quickly noted two other reasons: "requirement to undertake sea trials prior to final payment [4]" and "personal wish to get some sailing in asap after delivery [5]". It was at this point – when it was clear that my chance to go sailing in the Hebrides this year was at risk – that *I clearly understood why the red statement [1] was such a distraction*!

As I looked at the map I was **writing down circumstances that were acting as constraints** (statements 3 and 4) as well as one goal (statement 5), and so I **coloured goals differently (in big bold black) from what I thought of as constraints (black but not bold)**. The major goals were "get a reliable delivery date with good quality [11]" and "diary becomes fixed [2]", the contrast of "my work planning is becoming increasingly difficult". Of course, I also needed to recognize that what I was now calling constraints might be removed somehow through actions I had not yet considered.

But what else was I worried about? I had a "worry about quality of workmanship [6]". This statement was a little like the initial red statement, but I left it in my default colour (blue). Then for some reason I switched back to the starting statement and asked myself "What can be done about it?"

I thought, surely this must be an easy problem to crack. There must be some clear options for dealing with an unpredictable delivery date. I used the purple pen to mark what I thought were options. The first option was the obvious one – one that I had been trying already. Specifically, I had recently begun to "push the boat builder harder for a firm delivery date *rather than* push the local agent [7]". I had mainly tried pushing on the boat builder by making "legal threats [8]". After all, I had a signed contract. But I also considered having a "yachting journalist friend write a story about the purchase [9]". I actually thought this was a rather creative option, but the problem was in making sure it was not an idle threat. In other words, if I made the threat and then the friend did not write the story, I might look pretty foolish and end up with less bargaining power than I started with.

As I was noting statements about the situation, I wrote "I've had continual hassles about extras as the boat being built [10]" but wasn't sure how it connected with any of the other statements. Never mind – it was **more important to get down my stream of consciousness about the situation than build a tidy map**! Most importantly, I made a note of an outcome I wanted very much, "get a reliable delivery date with good quality [11]", and this was unlikely given the situation of the boat delivery being unpredictable [1] and my worry about the quality of workmanship [6].

The map clarified why I wanted to push on the boat builder and not the local agent. I wanted to make sure I "do not upset the local agent in the long term [12]" because it was important that I be "able to use a continuing relationship with local agent after boat delivered [13]". I would have to depend on this agent for follow-up work and did not want him mad at me. Indeed, I wanted him to think of me as a valued customer and even a friend.

Looking at the map, I now *saw clearly what the obvious dilemma was with pushing on the boat builder*. If I pushed too hard, there was a clear likelihood of a *positive impact* on the delivery time *and a simultaneous negative impact* on quality. I guess I knew this already, but it had not been so glaringly apparent to me. It is always disconcerting when you find you have not seen the obvious yourself! *The map also made it clear why I did not know what was the best action to take.* Pushing in the obvious place might get me only half of what I wanted, when I actually needed all of what I wanted.

And so the initial picture of the problem began to take shape. After 13 statements I found that I needed to understand more about the context, or background, of the problem. **Context sometimes gives helpful additional meaning to the problem, so elaborating the context will make for a more "meaning-full" exploration of the problem and very often turns up new solutions.** Maybe then I could figure out better options for addressing the situation [1].

I started to add some Post-its, but I knew I still had many to add and thought it was eventually going to become difficult to keep moving the slips of paper around. So I recreated the map on a computer screen using a special, easy-to-learn mapping software called *Decision Explorer.*[1] The software allowed me to custom-design styles for different types of statement. I did this, using different colours for each type of statement I had already worked with.

In order to **understand things from other points of view, particularly those with whom I was in conflict**, I elaborated the context to gain more insight into the builder's frame of reference. No doubt now – unlike when I negotiated my contract – his "factory is overloaded with work [14]". This led me to reflect on the fact that my "contract was good for me, but lousy for them [the builder] *rather than* providing a good profit in delivering the boat soon [15]". They really needed my business when we negotiated the deal. It was a buyer's market and they "signed the contract when they were short of work [25]". Part of the lousy deal for them, in addition to being a source of little profit, is the fact that "I've been a difficult customer [16]". I made "lots of visits to the factory [17]" and "no room for negotiation of costs and extras for them [19]", because "everything was confirmed in writing by me [18]". In contrast to when I signed the contract, now "other customers must be pushing against late deliveries [20]" since they, too, know that the " 'squeaky wheel' is the standard for getting attention over others [23]". Unfortunately, *I now had the distinctly uncomfortable feeling that by hard bargaining and real diligence I may well have outsmarted myself!*

Two other contextual features completed the picture. My visits to the factory had convinced me that the "factory is ineffectively run [24]". As a consequence of this ineffectiveness, "I've had continual hassles about extras as the boat is being built [10]". In other words, the factory probably could handle more squeaky wheels, if it were well managed. But it was not, and so disruption and delay[2] were natural consequences of more customers complaining about their boats.

I now had a first draft of the problem (see Map 3.1) and decided to **sit back and look at the properties of the map**. I had 25 statements. Six of them were "endpoints" or "heads". Typically, a

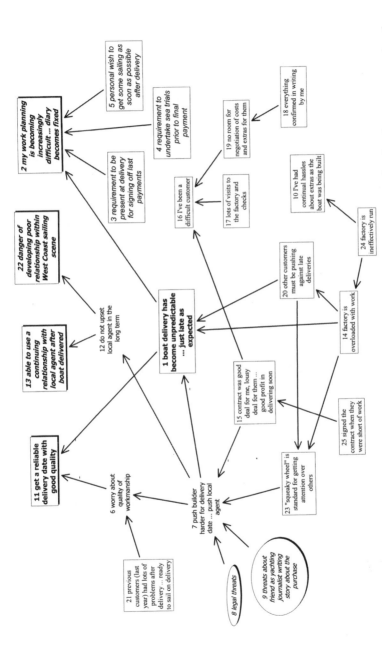

Map 3.1 *Adding context.* Colin drove a hard bargain and is a difficult customer, a reputation he does not want, but how does he get his boat when and how he wants it without becoming notorious among his fellow sailors? (The *Decision Explorer* colours used for different types of statement have been converted into different monochrome styles; see Figure 3.2 for a key.)

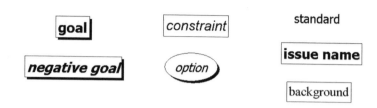

Figure 3.2   Key to *Decision Explorer* statement styles.

genuine endpoint is a goal or negative goal. Two of the six endpoints clearly expressed my goals as I understood them. The first was to "get a reliable delivery date with good quality [11]". The second was to avoid the negative goal of "my work planning is becoming increasingly difficult [2]" or, said positively, "to allow my diary to become fixed". But the four other endpoints needed further exploration to see if they really were endpoints. At present, two of the remaining endpoints were background statements ("I've had continual hassles about extras as the boat being built [10]" and "I've been a difficult customer [16]"), and two were constraints ("able to use a continuing relationship with local agent after boat delivered [13]" and "danger of developing poor relationship within West Coast sailing scene [22]"). It was unlikely that they really were goals or negative goals.

In addition, I only had two options: legal threats and the threat of getting a friend to write a damaging article about the purchase. *Neither option was very potent – in the sense of ultimately hitting several goals – and both might backfire on me*. I needed to continue mapping, or else simply give up and plan on losing the entire sailing season. Not surprisingly, I decided to keep mapping!

So, version two of the map was constructed (see Map 3.2). As I considered the map, I thought it might help me to be more explicit about why I was worried that I might "develop poor relationships on the West Coast sailing scene [22]". Maybe it did not really matter. It did, nevertheless. I might "get to be known as a difficult customer [26]", which might mean I "can't get decent service on the West Coast [27]". But on the other hand, "all payments have been made by me exactly on time [28]" and I had "provided good help with

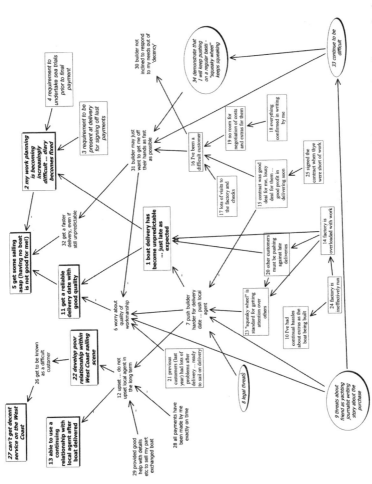

Map 3.2 *The real problem comes to light: no boat – no sailing.* Colin decides that his reputation is worth the risk; the squeaky wheel needs oil. Getting the boat delivered in time for two weeks' sailing is what matters. (See Figure 3.2 for a key to statement styles.)

details etc. to sell my boat [29]". Each of these would reduce any "upset" on the part of the local agent. (Note that the negative arrows from statements 28 and 29 go to the first part of statement 12. If the second part of statement 12 had come first, the arrows would not be negative.)

Significantly, it was during this stage of thinking about and mapping the problem that *at last* **I noted the key goal of "get some sailing asap (having no boat is not good for me!) [5]"!** That is what I wanted most of all. Again, the obvious was not apparent and only mapping had made it so.

This second stage was mostly about tidying up the map, including checking the endpoints or heads and making sure I had all the right links. This is actually easier to do on the computer. Moving the mouse around and using left and right clicks was all that was required – in addition, of course, to *thinking* about the content and relationships I was mapping!

I decided to explore more about me being a difficult customer (statement 16). It could be simply that the "builder is not inclined to respond to my needs out of 'decency' [30]". In that case, I am just plain out of luck. But I also thought that if I am a difficult enough customer, maybe the "builder may just want to get me off his hands as fast as possible [31]" If that happened, then I would "get a faster delivery, even if it were still unpredictable [32]" And *that* would lead to "getting some sailing asap [5]"!

So what options did I have to "hit" statement 31 with? I guessed it simply meant I had to "continue to be difficult [33]", which also meant I had to "demonstrate that I will keep pushing on a regular basis – the squeaky wheel will keep squeaking [34]".

On I went to the third stage. This was the really important stage. I had explored the problem in some detail and now was starting to develop a way forward. Unlike some of the other examples in the book, this problem was not life-shatteringly significant. It did not involve the strategy for a whole organization, or a long-standing conflict in my marriage, or where I lived or my career, and it would go away in the relatively near future. Nevertheless, I had to take some action soon if I was to salvage the sailing season.

In the third stage I started developing and checking the options (see Map 3.3). Whatever else I did, I needed to find ways of addressing statement 1 – the basic problem – and statement 6 – my worry about the quality of workmanship. I also had to find a way to figure out actions that took account of the endpoints. In other words, I had to figure out ways to achieve my goals, as well as to take into account those things I had decided were acting as constraints. (The constraints were nevertheless quasi-goals, in the sense that they were outcomes to avoid, or negative goals.) I had already noted four options (8, 9, 33 and 34) and so I worked at making these practical.

I decided that yes, I would continue to be difficult and be a squeaky wheel. And I would continue to make legal threats. And I would pursue my threat about prompting a story to be done about the purchase in a widely read yachting magazine. But I knew that each "threat must be seen as real *rather than* a threat that everyone else will or can use [35]". In other words, if everyone made the same threat, my situation would not change; I would be stuck in the same spot.

So I put together a package of actions that I actually thought might work. I decided to call up my friend, who writes for a yachting magazine, to discuss my situation and suggest I could "provide him with a promising story [37]". He owed me a favour, so I was going to "call in the favour [38]" and have him "call the builder and show an interest [36]" in doing the story. The builder clearly would not want to be the subject of an unflattering story.

What would my friend ask the builder about? I would tell my friend the "story about a plate rack, which the local agent described as bizarre [39]". The builder proposed a plate rack made of a plastic moulding, which was fine, except that I could find no plates that would fit the apertures. I pointed this out to the builder, arguing that they should be larger, unless they could locate plates that would fit. They refused to look for plates to fit and yet insisted on the proposed plate rack because that was the moulding they had available. I insisted that this was wholly impractical and that having

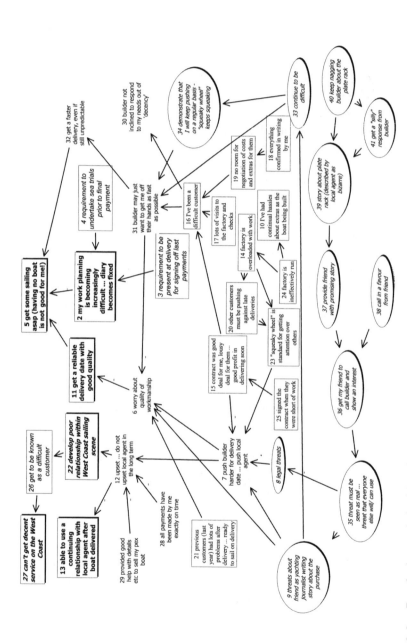

Map 3.3 *Developing and checking options.* Whose reputation? Colin decides to "threaten" the boat builder with a loss of reputation through a story in a sailing magazine about poor-quality work. (See Figure 3.2 for a key to statement styles.)

a plate rack that could not take plates was silly. To add some juice to the story, before my friend called the builder, I would "keep nagging the builder about the plate rack [40]" and expect to continue to "get a 'silly' response from the builder [41]". My friend could recount the story to the builder, as if checking it out, and by doing so the threat might be seen as real to the builder. The "reality" of the threat would be increased because late deliveries were a standard problem in the custom-built yachting industry, and my friend could say he was doing a story on that, and merely wanted to confirm some details on a particularly "bizarre" instance of misbehaviour by the builder.

The set of actions made sense. I just might get the builder to finish the boat on time and to my quality standards in order to avoid being the subject of negative publicity in a journal that most of his potential customers read. I was pleased with the approach, because the threat provided an incentive for the builder *not only* to deliver the boat on time, but also to the contractually agreed quality standard. Only by delivering the boat on time and in good shape could he get out of being featured in the story. The package of actions thus tapped into the *builder's self-interest*, which was crucial.[3] ***Only by helping me achieve my goals could the builder achieve one of his important goals – maintaining a good reputation with potential customers***. I became sure that I had made a break-through! I had a mixed package of actions that seemed to satisfy all of the aspects of the map. I knew it was unusual for any single action to suffice in this type of situation, and so was pleased to have a portfolio of actions to implement.

Postscript

What happened? I took all of these actions and they had the desired effect. The boat was delivered within two days of a newly negotiated date, and so far (touch wood!) I have had only one minor problem with its quality. Follow-up comments by the local agent suggest that the actions worked exactly as expected. So mapping helped me succeed where most others fail, and it only took about an hour to do the map – after having thought about the problem for a while and discussed it with friends. As noted earlier, very few custom-built boats are delivered on time, and even fewer are delivered without some non-trivial problems. Without mapping I never would have figured out a set of actions that created incentives for the boat to be delivered on time to a high quality standard. And yes, I did get to go for a long sail before the season ended!

Conclusion

As we have seen, mapping is a way of helping an individual figure out what they want, how to get it and why. In this case, Colin wanted his boat delivered relatively on time and to a high standard. The challenge was to keep exploring the context and options until he could find the right set of actions that would also motivate the builder to deliver on both goals. Clarifying exactly what the problem was, including an exploration of both constraints and background factors, was a necessary prelude to figuring out actions that would work. It was particularly crucial to figure out actions that would tap into the "target's" frame of reference and incentives and so manage a negotiation with the builder. Without helping the builder "elaborate his construct system" to the point where he saw things differently – and, in particular, saw that his own self-interest would be served by helping Colin – there was little hope that Colin would achieve his own goals.

> You can never change anyone's mind. You can only help them elaborate their construct system until they change their own mind... Or until both of you change your mind...

The story is unusual in that it involves bargaining and negotiating delivery dates and quality for an expensive yacht. However, the general problem of bargaining and negotiating in difficult circumstances is not unusual at all. Nor is the problem of getting clear about your own situation and goals, while simultaneously trying to figure out an adversary's situation and goals. Following the guidelines developed in this chapter should help in any situation where what is known as "interest-based" bargaining and negotiation is desirable.

Process guidelines

- Assemble the materials needed to create the map.

- "Dump" as many ideas as you can, and make a point of not censoring yourself.

- Keep each statement to no more than eight words.

- Some statements represent different aspects of the problem and these differences can be identified using coloured pens.

- The shorthand convention for "rather than" is an ellipsis (...), which saves time and space.

- Number every concept based on the order in which you think of them.

- Think carefully about the contrast – the circumstance that would have meant it was not a problem for you.

- Write down circumstances that are acting as constraints.

- Colour major goals differently (in big bold black) from what are thought of as constraints (black but not bold, in this case).

- It is more important to get down your stream of consciousness about the situation than to build a tidy map.

- Context sometimes gives helpful additional meaning to the problem, so elaborating the context will make for a more "meaning-full" exploration of the problem and very often turns up new solutions.

- Understand things from other points of view, particularly those with whom you are in conflict.

- Sit back and look at the properties of the map.

Learning points

- I clearly understood why the red statement [the starting description of the issue] was such a distraction.

- I saw clearly what the obvious dilemma was with pushing on the boat builder.

- The map made it clear why it I did not know what was the best action to take.

- I now had the distinctly uncomfortable feeling that by hard bargaining and real diligence I may well have outsmarted myself!

- Neither option (legal action or the threat of a damaging article in the press) was very potent – in the sense of ultimately hitting several goals – and both might backfire on me.

- At last I noted the key goal of "get some sailing asap (having no boat is not good for me!)".

- Only by helping me achieve my goals could the builder achieve one of his important goals – maintaining a good reputation with potential customers.

Notes

1 See http://www.banxia.com for more information on *Decision Explorer*.
2 "Disruption and delay" is a term used in project management to describe conditions where apparently small disruptions can finish up causing massive delays. For a description of how these circumstances arise, see C. Eden, T. M. Williams, F. Ackermann and S. Howick (2000) On the nature of disruption and delay, *Journal of the Operational Research Society*, **51**, 291–300.
3 The art of negotiating in a manner that seeks out new options rather than fighting over old options is discussed by R. Fisher and W. Ury (1982) *Getting to Yes*, London: Hutchinson.

4

House of the Rising Fun

IN THIS CHAPTER WE PRESENT A CIRCUMSTANCE WHERE A person feels they should be doing something about a particular situation but is not quite sure what. In this case, Fran felt she should be moving but wasn't quite sure why or what exactly this involved. The different possibilities open to her required considering *what* was driving this particular sensation (that is, why did she want to move?) and what the options were. Specifically, Fran had reached a transition point in her life. Her career was going well, she had accumulated savings and she was pretty sure she wanted a new condominium, or "flat" as they say in Britain. But she was not sure what kind of condo she wanted, where she wanted to live or even why she wanted to move. She just *knew* she wanted to move. As the story opens, Fran lives in Glasgow, Scotland, and wants to move to somewhere else within the city, but that is all she knows for sure.

This circumstance is not unusual either in personal life, or in business. We are frequently presented with opportunities whereby we feel we should act but are not clear why and how. Fran's story therefore is a classic example of "planning from thrust" rather than "planning with goals".[1] Situations of this sort are very common, particularly in people's personal life. Often someone feels strongly that they *want* to do something – or may even think they *have* to do it – but without knowing *how* to do it, *where* to do it, *with whom* to do it or *why*. These situations, of course, are also quite common in organizational life, where strategies are often "emergent" rather than "deliberate". Mapping can help a person (or group) clarify and sharpen their thinking about what the real issues are, what can be done about them and what they might be trying to achieve. Quite often mapping leads to new insights, a host of previously unconsidered actions and thoughtful consideration of the purpose behind the desire to change. This story tells of how mapping helped Fran think through the issue.

Getting Started

I wanted to move. I was fed up with my old flat and was pondering moving somewhere else. Unfortunately, beyond that I was not sure exactly what I wanted. And I am not actually certain why I decided to map my thinking. But I teach mapping and so I suppose it just came naturally. With a fresh-brewed cup of tea in hand, I sat down at the computer and started to map.

I used the computer, rather than pencil and paper or a flipchart sheet, for several reasons. First, I thought the map might get quite large – which it did – and the computer allows you to manage larger maps easily. Second, I wanted to use the analysis capabilities of the mapping software. Third, I wanted to be able to make copies of my file easily so that I did not run the risk of losing my only copy. Fourth, I wanted the portability afforded by floppy disks, so that I could work on my map in odd moments and various places. And finally, I wanted to be able to transmit my map electronically between home and the office, and to friends.

I began with the issue that concerned me, which was that I wanted to "buy a new flat *rather than* stay in the existing one[2] [1]" (see Map 4.1). I was pretty sure I did not want to stay in my current place, but I figured that I would get a better understanding of what I wanted to do by considering that possibility. At the very least, I knew I could afford to stay where I was, and that staying would save me a lot of work. Therefore **capturing the alternative aspect – *the rather than* – of a statement was important**.

I then began to **enter thoughts into the computer as they occurred**. Here I put down anything that came to mind. I wanted to include everything related to the subject, and so made a point of avoiding self-censorship. I simply "dumped" ideas, assertions, facts, options and assumptions onto the page, **avoiding too much consideration of their position or wording**. It was important just to let the ideas flow onto the page.

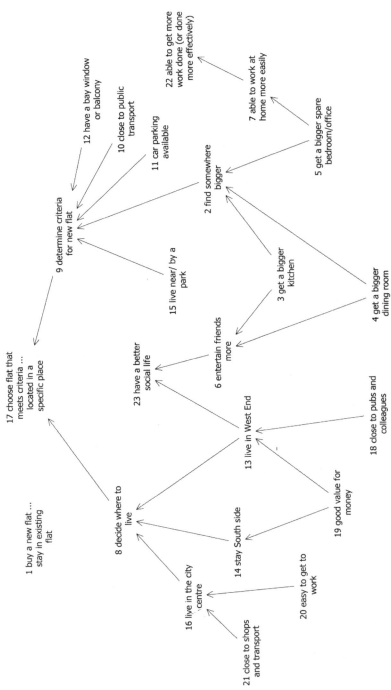

Map 4.1 *Just do it.* In the first map I wrote down everything I could think of related to the issue that concerned me. I avoided self-censorship – I just let the ideas flow.

Where an idea appeared to link to another, for example "get a bigger dining room [4]" would mean that I could "entertain friends more [6]", I would **draw in the causal link**.

I ended up with an initial collection of 23 fairly unconnected ideas, which looked like Map 4.1.

When a particular thought occurred to me I often tried to explore it further by "laddering up" to consequences or "laddering down" to causes or explanations, but I did not necessarily put in all the appropriate links. For example, you will note that while I started with statement 1, I did not link anything to it. On this first attempt at mapping the issue, statement 1 sits by itself – a sort of title. On the other hand, when I was thinking about "find somewhere bigger [2]", that caused me to think about "get a bigger kitchen [3]," "get a bigger dining room [4]", and "get a bigger spare bedroom/office [5]." All of these were more specific reasons for why getting somewhere bigger was important. This **capture of detailed options and linking them to the generic option helped flesh out the idea**. From here I jumped to wondering why I wanted to "get a bigger kitchen [3]". It occurred to me that it was to "entertain friends more [6]". And it then occurred to me that if I were to "get a bigger office [5]", I might be "able to work at home more easily [7]". This process of jumping around pursuing different lines of thought meant I could **avoid getting worried about finalizing endpoints** – these could be explored later on as I began to tidy and refine the map.

I then began to be more disciplined about putting in links. Sometimes this focus occurs early on in a mapping exercise, as in my case, because I was thinking about links anyway. But sometimes it can occur quite late in the process. The choice of a "link-as-you-go" strategy, or a "dump-first, link-later" strategy, depends on whether you fear you might forget ideas that are not recorded right away, or whether there are a number of clear links in your mind that are easy to capture. If you think you will forget important ideas, get them down immediately and worry about links later. You can always cycle around dumping material, linking up the statements and then dumping some more material.

I now began to note further aspects of the issue as they occurred to me. For example, I recalled that in trying to think about why I wanted to move, I started with what was bugging me – namely, space or the lack of it! Having got some material down about that, I then began to think more proactively, which resulted in "decide where to live [8]". And that made me realize that I probably ought to "determine criteria for the new flat [9]." In effect, I had been naming criteria when I focused on wanting a bigger kitchen, dining room and spare bedroom or office. This led me to identify some additional criteria. I wanted to be "close to public transportation [10]", have "car parking available [11]", and I really wanted to "have a bay window or balcony [12]".

I next decided to focus on statement 8, deciding where to live. I thought I was pretty sure I wanted to "live in the West End [13]". But it occurred to me that I just might decide to "stay on the South Side [14]". As I was mulling over that option, I realized that wherever I lived, I wanted to "live near or by a park [15]", which I linked to my criteria list. When I went back to deciding where to live, I realized I also could "live in the city centre [16]". So I was willing to consider three different locations, the West End, South Side and city centre, and I would "choose a flat that met my criteria *rather than* pick one located in a specific place [17]". I linked "determine criteria for new flat [9]" to statement 17 [9→17] to complete that part of the argument.

This process of reflecting and idea creation helped increase my understanding – I felt that I was **beginning to get to grips with what it was I was looking for**, which made me feel more in control. To get more understanding I next began to explore up and down the chains of argument and add or change links as needed.

By asking myself questions like "Why is this important?" or "What would result from doing that?" I could ladder up the chain. So I asked myself, what would happen if I were to "live in the West End [13]"? I realized that I would "have a better social life [23]". Seeing this, I immediately cheered up. **And then it hit me emotionally – as opposed to intellectually – that I did not have much of a social life!** I had been working so hard that I had forgotten that having a good social life was important to me. I quickly linked statement 23 to "entertain friends more [6]", because entertaining friends would lead to a better social life. In fact, spending time with friends is a significant part of what having a social life means to me.

I then decided to ladder down the chain of argumentation, by asking myself "What would lead me to do that?" So I asked myself, what would lead me to live in the West End? An answer was being "close to pubs and colleagues [18]". I then realized that finding "good value for money [19]" would lead me *not* to live in the West End, since it is very expensive. Through **capturing the negative links as well as the positive links** I could begin to **identify some of the dilemmas or trade-offs**: if I moved to the West End there were the pubs, *but* it would be expensive. However, finding "good value for money [19]" supported the idea to "stay on the South Side [14]". Similarly, if I wanted my flat to make it "easy to get to work [20]" and to be "close to shops and transportation [21]", I should "live in the city centre [16]".

Finally, thinking about work took me back to statement 7, about being "able to work at home more easily", and I decided if I could do that I would be "able to get more work done (or done more effectively) [22]". So by the end of this initial stage I had 23 ideas linked together, except for my initial problem statement, which still stood alone. I had begun to get some new insights and also had plenty of material with which to work. I did not have an answer about where to live, but I had made some headway on figuring out criteria with which to make the decision. I also realized that it was pretty important for me to have a better social life no matter where I lived.

Building up and Beginning to Reflect on the Map

I sat back and started looking at where I was in some more detail. I began to think about criteria for deciding where to live and listed some additional considerations (see Map 4.2). I wanted the flat to involve "low maintenance [24]" and I wanted it to "fit my budget [25]".

I also tried to figure out how to link my starting point, "buy a new flat . . . stay in existing flat [1]" into the map. Statement 17, "choose

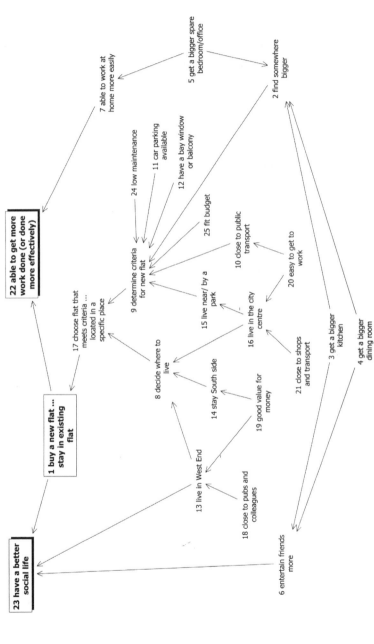

Map 4.2 *Means and ends.* There are no new statements in this map but the structure is developing. Buy a new flat . . . stay in existing flat, is not a goal, but an issue. My goals are now to have a better social life and be able to get more work done or done more effectively.

flat that meets criteria . . . located in a specific place" was an "arrow in", as it indicated what I should consider when making the choice.

I then decided that statement 1 actually was a *key issue*, and therefore I **gave this new category a different style (different colour and font)**. This act suddenly made me realize that *buying a new flat actually was an issue and not a goal*, which was something of a breakthrough for me, because previously I had thought that buying a new flat was my goal. Seeing a new house as more of a *means* to some *end* really opened up my thinking.

So I asked myself to **question what the goals are** in moving? This helped me realize that I wanted to be "able to get more work done (or done more effectively) [22]" and to "have a better social life [23]". To highlight the fact that they were goals, I created a new style for them.

Recognizing what some of my real goals were – at least those that I had been able to identify so far – led me to think about the fact that there were probably other strategies for achieving them than buying a new house. I did not go anywhere further with that thought for the moment, but thinking about it did make me realize that I had been considering only the positive aspects of buying a new flat. *I had got caught up with the emotional rush of moving without considering some of the downsides*. So what were some of the hassles? A flood of things suddenly occurred to me, which maybe reflected a more realistic approach to the issue (see Map 4.3).

Clearly, I would have to "cope with the hassles of moving", which would diminish (a negative link) my desire to "buy a new flat *rather than* stay in the existing flat [1]". Coping would mean I would have to "find a new place [27]", "pack up my belongings [28]", which were not only hassles in and of themselves but would also mean that I would have to "clean up the flat (for would-be buyers) [31]". These were just part of "sell existing flat [29]". This line of thinking led to more hassles being identified: "cope with legal requirements [32]", "negotiate a new mortgage [33]", "work on new flat to get it right *rather than* be able to live in it right away [34]", "review my financial situation [36]", "deal with real estate agent for selling my house and buying a new one [37]" and "open my house to buyers (put up with intrusions and keeping tidy) [40]". So before long I had

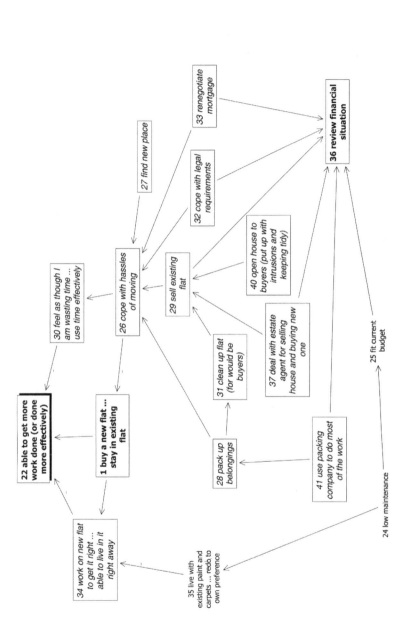

Map 4.3 *The downside.* This map concentrates on all the negative aspects of buying a new apartment and having to sell the current one.

a whole section of the map entirely devoted to the more negative aspects of moving. I was glad that I had **used a separate view in the software** to manage this sudden increase (doing it on paper would probably have required a second sheet).

I decided to call these negative aspects "constraints" and created a new style for them. One advantage of this category was that I could use it to identify negative statements quickly and then weigh them up against the positives, or benefits, to see if a move was worth it. Also, I could see in what way the negatives were coming up, and thought that might help me figure out what to do about them.

By considering some of the downsides, I also began to *surface dilemmas, particularly in relation to the short-term and long-term impact of the move*. The map was beginning to help me get to grips with the complexity of the issue. For example, "work on the new flat to get it right... able to live in it right away [34]" would *not* allow me to "be able to get more work done (or done more effectively) [22]", as I would not have time for both. On the other hand, if I were willing to "live with existing paint and carpets *rather than* redo to fit my preferences [35]", I would be able to "live in it right away", which would allow me to "get more work done". Similarly, "cope with hassles of moving [26]" meant that I would "feel as though I am wasting time *rather than* using time effectively [30]", which would make me less "able to get more work done (or done more effectively) [22]".

While there were many negatives, clearly all was not bleak (see Map 4.4). As I mulled over the negative aspects, new thoughts occurred. One was "stay in Glasgow for the next couple of years *rather than* move elsewhere [38]". *This insight was significant – until now I hadn't considered the future particularly*. This insight meant I should "stop looking for jobs [42]". Then more criteria popped up, such as "have a sports facility nearby [39]", which suggested a link to "meet new friends [43]", which in turn linked into "have a better social life [23]".

I focused again on having a better social life. How would I do that? (See Map 4.5.) The really big thing that came to mind was "get away from work dominating my life [47]". In turn, that prompted

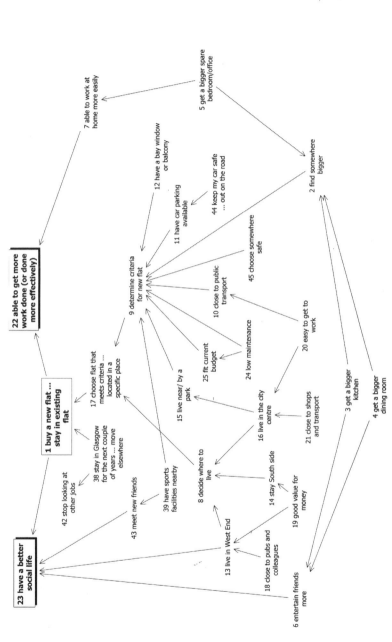

Map 4.4 *More detail.* With almost twice the number of statements, the map is being refined and the longer-term future is now a factor. Having a better social life is an important goal.

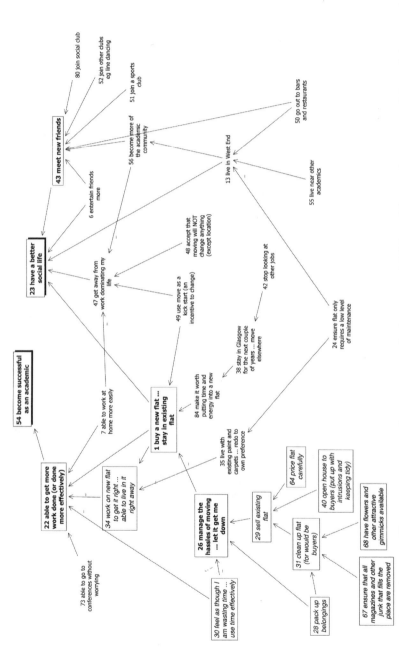

Map 4.5 *A new balance.* There are now two important goals, better social life and becoming successful, and they are in a sort of equilibrium.

additional insights. *One of these took a while to cope with emotionally, and that was that I needed to "accept that moving will NOT change anything (except location) [48]."* When I had fully grasped that fact intellectually *and* emotionally, a second insight occurred – that I could "use the move as a kick start or incentive to change [49]".

So I looked at "meet new friends" again and thought how nice that would be. How could I do that? That led to "go out to bars and restaurants [50]", "join a sports club [51]" and "join other clubs, e.g. a line dancing club [52]". I also could "become more a part of the academic community [56]", which would be easier if I were to "live near other academics [55]", which would imply I should "live in the West End [13]". I found this process of **cycling between generating new material and reflecting on existing material helpful in generating more material**. As part of this I worked to **link in the "orphans"** – the statements that were not yet linked into the map – as this too prompted new ideas.

Stepping Back and Looking at the Map – More Refining and More Elaboration

As a result of thinking about the negative aspects I began to focus more on why I should buy the flat. Was it going to be worth it? Was I simply indulging in a daydream? As a result, I entered "find somewhere I really like *rather than* move for the sake of it [61]"; see Map 4.6. This was to try to ensure I stayed focused on the real objective and didn't get caught up in the details of buying and selling. As a result of this, I decided that the concept "determine criteria for new flat [9]" would be replaced with statement 61 and linked "choose flat that meets criteria *rather than* one located in a specific place [17]" into it. Location thus became only one of the explanations of statement 61. Those statements that had linked into statement 9 were then reviewed and where appropriate either linked directly into statement 61 (e.g. "have car parking available [11]") or else linked through another statement (e.g. "low maintenance [24]" now linked to statement 61 through "fit current budget [25]").

I was now beginning to see natural clusters emerging. There was a cluster on what was required to "sell existing flat [29]", a cluster around "find somewhere I really like *rather than* move for the sake of moving [61]" and a cluster around "manage the budget *rather than* mess up my finances [36]"; see Map 4.7. I could now **examine the clusters to see if there were new aspects to add or missing links between them**. These clusters are areas of the map that are relatively tightly linked together (lots of intra-cluster links), with relatively few inter-cluster links. I had tended to focus until now on only the intra-cluster (within cluster) links. It was becoming rapidly apparent that none of these clusters was an island, but each had impacts on the elements of other clusters and was in turn affected by them. *This gave me some new insights as I began to realize how interrelated everything was and that I needed to consider the whole picture rather than merely a single aspect.*

This in turn prompted me to think "outside the box" of buying a house to identify some more significant issues. Doing so helped me build up a system of goals. I began to seriously ladder up the map; see Map 4.8. Exploring some of my objectives meant that two of the main goals – "become a successful academic [54]" and "become happier *rather than* see work as only objective [53]" – surfaced. They are related and affect each another; in fact, the former may have negative consequences for the latter. The earlier-identified goal "have a better social life [23]" remained, although it too was linked up through the insertion of "get away from work dominating my life [47]" to statement 53. Identifying statement 54, "become a successful academic", then triggered another area of development and statements, namely that if I "live near other academics [55]" then that suggested I "live in the West End [13]", which in turn meant that I would become "more involved with the academic community [56]" and therefore this would mean that I could "debate and review academic ideas [57]". From this point, "develop academic ideas [58]", "build up a network of colleagues [59]" and "ensure colleagues know of your work [60]" were the consequences. These all contributed to 54, "become a successful academic".

However, alongside supporting the academic goal, they both supported and detracted from the goal of having a better social

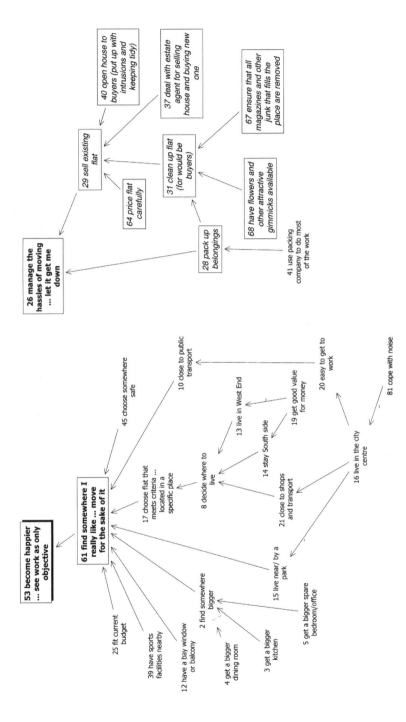

Map 4.6 *The big picture.* There are now so many statements it is possible to isolate clusters, like these two, and the money (in Map 4.7).

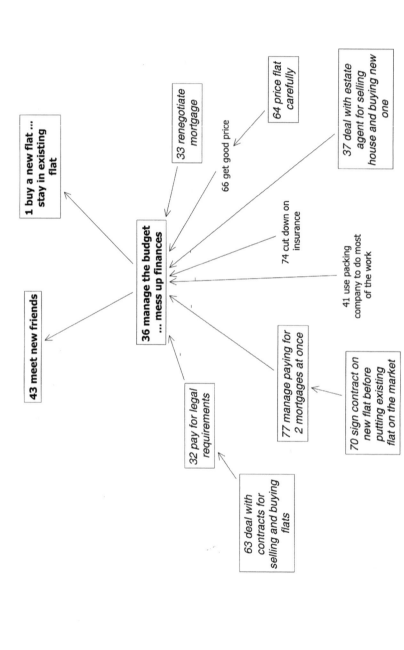

Map 4.7   *Look after the money.* The effect of concentrating on clusters was to direct my attention to the big picture. I realized that everything was linked together.

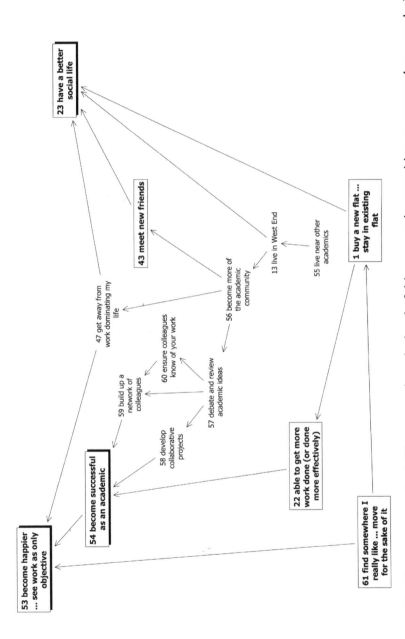

Map 4.8 *The dilemma rears its head.* The two goals at the head of this map are in opposition to one another – a solution is required.

life. On the one hand this would yield the opportunity to make friends, but on the other it would work against getting away from work dominating my life. *The map clearly revealed a dilemma – something I had to get to grips with.*

During this period I also began to pay more attention to the wording of statements and to the arrows linking them. Had I really captured the essence of the content and the structure of relationships among the statements? To clarify meaning, I began to examine the wording of the statements and the links between them. I tried to ensure that the links were hierarchically correct and I often changed the direction of the arrows as I began really to **test which was the option and which was the outcome**. An example of this was that previously I had "easy to get to work [20]" linking into "live in the city centre [16]". I suspect at the time I was trying to justify living in the city centre. However, on reflection I reversed the link, so that living in the city centre became only one means of getting to work easily.

I also began to work to **ensure that the statements were worded in an action-oriented mode**. So "low maintenance [24]" became "ensure flat only requires a low level of maintenance [24]". This attention to words and arrows helped me make sure that the meaning depicted in the map actually matched my thoughts. This process also helped me to question my assumptions and rationale fully.

Getting Comments from a Friend

I now decided to check my thinking by **reviewing the map with a friend**. I was worried that I had become very engaged with the content but was not really rigorously examining my logic. I wanted someone to challenge my thinking not only in terms of the direction and type of the relationships (were they negative or positive and had I missed an angle?), but also in terms of the consequences of various actions.

My map became elaborated as my thinking was scrutinized and I had to add more material to make it clear. The process of having to

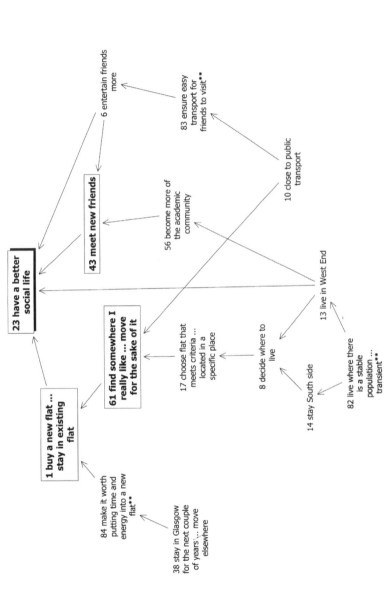

Map 4.9 *Another pair of eyes.* Reviewing the map with a friend helped to clarify ideas and statements and improved my understanding. (Statements with ** are new contributions.)

explain myself also triggered ideas I had not thought of. This was particularly true about two of the areas, "manage the budget (i.e. the mortgage) [36]" and "manage the hassles of moving [26]". My friend had moved recently and therefore was able to provide me with new information. Other areas of the map also benefited from his contributions. For example, he suggested I "live where there is a stable population *rather than* a transient one [82]", which made me reexamine whether or not I should live in the West End, which has a high turnover of population.

A final point is that I often had to make the language clearer before my colleague could understand some of the statements. This process created greater clarity for me too, and therefore enhanced my understanding.

Conclusions

In this chapter we have illustrated how mapping can first help you begin to understand what is driving a particular issue. Through exploring the consequences, it is possible to challenge thinking, particularly testing why something is considered to be important and worth doing. This scrutiny helps ensure that if the particular issue is acted on it is done in a logical and thoughtful manner, with clear expectations of what will emerge. As part of this process, values are surfaced, potential competing objectives considered and trade-offs made consciously. Likewise, thoughtful attention to the various options, assumptions, criteria and dilemmas can be undertaken.

Also revealed is how mapping helped explicitly in examining the issue, ensuring that, rather than taking a superficial view of the situation, as much as possible was taken into consideration in the time available, and a richer and more subtle understanding could be revealed. This was not always a comfortable process, as a number of emotional as well as cognitive insights were gained that took some time to deal with. However, the final decision was one that was robust.

Process guidelines

- Begin with the issue that is of concern.
- Capture the alternative aspect of a statement – the "rather than".
- Enter thoughts into the computer as they occur.
- Avoid spending too much time considering the position or wording of thoughts.
- Draw in the causal link.
- When a particular thought occurs, try to explore it further by "laddering up" to consequences, or by "laddering down" to causes or explanations.
- Capturing detailed options and linking them to the generic options helps flesh out the idea.
- Avoid getting worried about finalizing endpoints.
- By capturing the negative links as well as the positive links, you begin to identify some of the dilemmas/trade-offs.
- Give new categories a different style.
- Ask what the goals are.
- Use a separate view in the software for new areas.
- Cycling between generating new material and reflecting on existing material is helpful in generating more material.
- Link in the "orphans".
- Examine the clusters to see if there are new aspects to add or missing links between them.
- For each linked pair of statements, test which is the option and which is the outcome.
- Ensure that the statements are worded in an action-oriented mode.
- Review the map with a friend.

Learning points

This chapter has demonstrated some important learning points, both about mapping and about the specific case. The learning points about the specific case, however, are not unique, as similar "ahas" or "Eurekas" often emerge in other situations.

- Even early on it is possible to begin to gain a sense of control through getting to grips with the different components. This can help raise energy levels and encourage continuation of the process.

- Often emotional as well as intellectual insights can be gained when mapping and beginning to examine the issue. These are not always comfortable to deal with and may require some adjustment.

- It may be that what initially appear to be objectives or goals in fact end up being issues (or opportunities or threats) that *are means for achieving* (or not) a particular goal or objective. Recognizing that something is an issue rather than a goal can help clarify which goals the issue actually affects, along with the determining action needed to effect the goal.

- Mapping helps ensure that not only the positive or negative perspective is taken. Through considering both sides of the issue, a more balanced view can be attained. Through this process dilemmas can be surfaced. In particular dilemmas relating to the short-term and long-term impact, recognition of these trade-offs can be important.

- The process provides the means for understanding the conditions under which you are working. Being clear about how something might affect your future can often trigger revealing insights.

- One of the benefits of mapping is that it is impossible to keep "pretending to yourself". Through examining the map, illogicalities can be quickly identified and options that have been previously justified as achieving a particular outcome are revealed as being fallacious.

- Understanding the whole picture rather than focusing on discrete aspects of the issue can provide new insights. From this it is possible to see all of the consequences of particular actions (rather than those relating to one part of the issue) as well as identifying options that have more leverage (as they support a range of important aspects).

Postscript

I now have a new flat. Did the map help? Absolutely. I did not find a new home that met all of my criteria, which is not all that surprising, but I did find one that very nearly did. The map helped me make that final decision. Spending lots of money was daunting, but the map helped me realize that my new flat was probably as close to the ideal as I was likely to get. The map also helped me make a choice with which I was comfortable both intellectually and emotionally. I really like where I live now – and with good reason!

In addition, thinking about the negative aspects – the constraints – helped me plan around them. I was able to arrange matters so that they inflicted minimum hassle. My friends and family said that I appeared to have planned a military campaign, but the pay-off was that I had one of the most painless moves I have ever made.

Since I bought my new home, I have made some changes to it, like having some cabinets built and other furniture made. When I was constructing my map, I worried about the time that would take. However, rather than see these projects as taking time away from work, I have chosen to view them as interesting alternatives to work ("do not let work dominate"). Since I have been in control of these projects, I have been able to fit them in without any major hassles. And they have made my flat a more desirable place to entertain friends ("have a better social life"). Beyond that, my new home office has been a great success!

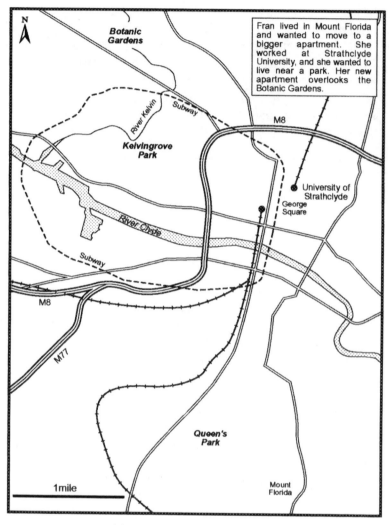

Fran lived in Mount Florida and wanted to move to a bigger apartment. She worked at Strathclyde University, and she wanted to live near a park. Her new apartment overlooks the Botanic Gardens.

Map 4.10   Map of Glasgow.

Notes

1   M. McCaskey (1974) A Contingency Approach to Planning: Planning with Goals and Planning without Goals, *Academy of Management Review*, **17**, 281–91.
2   The numbers are "tags" that the software allocates each node, allowing for greater manipulation of the material.

5

It's a Bummer to Be JB

IN THIS CHAPTER WE DO TWO THINGS. FIRST, WE PRESENT A situation in which a person needs to consider several possible options for dealing with a situation, but does not know how to evaluate them. In this case, the options focus on how John decided to deal with an unsatisfactory job. The options all involve thinking about personal aspirations and commitments, as well as those of a number of other stakeholders. But there are many other situations in which thinking about the options could be very beneficial. The options could concern career directions, investment possibilities, work choices for an organizational unit, make or buy decisions, retirement schemes and so on. Second, we show how to use mapping to conduct an interview.

Here is John's story.

In the mid-1990s I was very unhappy with my job. I was a full professor with job security in a major public affairs school at a major university in a great city. At least in terms of title, status and location, I had achieved my dream job. But in terms of job satisfaction, my situation was not at all good.

I had come to the university expecting to be part of two successful programmes: one in the management of public and non-profit organizations, and the other in urban and regional planning. The school claimed to be strong in both areas. At least in theory, that was true, or had been. Unfortunately, by the mid-1990s the programmes in management and planning had weakened and the prospects for change were dim. The situation was painful for me, since while I wanted to be connected to strong programmes, I also realized that any changes would depend in part on my leadership. The idea of having to lead when there was little hope was downright demoralizing.

While the situation was bad for me, it was also bad for our students. Management was the most popular concentration area in our curriculum, but was the least well staffed as a result of retirements, the extended leave of a key faculty member and an inability to garner new resources. In addition, there was only lukewarm support among the full faculty and the administration for rebuilding the faculty complement.

Meanwhile, the planning programme was still recovering from a bruising battle over whether to keep two young faculty members who did not have permanent jobs. In addition, the founding director had retired. Again, there was only lukewarm support among the full faculty and administration for rebuilding the programme.

Beyond those two programmes, I had long advocated the creation of a mid-career degree programme in public affairs. I thought that having such a programme was important for the school for a variety of strategic and pedagogical reasons. I was also interested because I particularly enjoy working with mid-career audiences. Unfortunately, as far as I could tell, there was little support for this idea either.

At the time – and this was a clear sign of how bad things had become – I had few real colleagues in the school. Chuck Finn was one. He had an academic title of Fellow and also served as the school's Chief Information Officer. In addition to Chuck, I was able to find a few like-minded people in the school's centre for leadership studies. Unfortunately, like everything else I cared about at the school at the time, the leadership centre was underfunded and understaffed. Building up the centre would take effort, and again there was little support among the faculty and administration for such an effort.

Finally, I found out that at the time I was the lowest-paid full professor.

So if I wanted to stay and be a part of thriving management, planning, leadership and mid-career programmes, it was clear I was going to have to exercise a great deal of leadership and do some serious "heavy lifting" as well. I wondered whether I should. I wasn't sure if the effort was worth it, given that across-the-board success was unlikely. And I have to admit frankly that being the lowest-paid full professor made me doubt whether I would get any direct benefit out of the effort. I didn't know if I would be better off simply focusing on my own teaching, research and service, and saying the heck with the school. Alternatively, I wondered whether I should cut my losses and search for a faculty position elsewhere. Emotionally, I moved back and forth between feeling hurt, angry and depressed.

Chuck knew I was unhappy. So one day he said, "John, you need to do something and I'm willing to help. I hate to see a good friend hurting so badly. How about we map your job options?" I had stewed about the situation long enough that I really appreciated Chuck's care and concern, and welcomed his offer to help by trying to **set up a time for an interview**.

"OK," I said. "When would you like to do it?"

"How about now?" he replied.

I gulped. I looked right and left and thought briefly about other things I might do. But since he was standing in my office with a writing pad and pencils in hand, and since I didn't really have anything else I absolutely had to do then, I agreed.

We cleared off a small table in my office and Chuck and I sat so **we both could see the map** that he would draw based on my answers to his questions.

As a kind of mental warm-up – and to help me get ready for something I had been resisting – we talked for about five minutes or so. Little time was really needed, since I had been thinking a great deal about what I might do, and since Chuck had already heard me complain *ad infinitum*. Indeed, he might have offered to map my thinking as a self-defence strategy! We also knew that **mapping should start quickly so that my thoughts would be captured, rather than lost**.

Chuck placed the writing pad sideways (long side on the bottom) on the tabletop, and then asked, "So, **what are the issues or options you have?**"

I thought about this for a while and then said, "I think I have three options that revolve around three different big possibilities: maintain the status quo; leave the school for another job as a professor; or stay, but renegotiate the terms." Chuck **wrote them with a mechanical pencil in three scattered positions across the piece of paper**.

He said, "Fine, let's **explore each of these in turn while recognizing that we might bounce between them**. I suggest we start with maintaining the status quo so we can figure out just how bad things really are for you. Then you'll have a better idea of whether you really do have to move, on the one hand, or whether there are ways to renegotiate the terms under which you would be willing to stay."

Maintain the Status Quo

Chuck, focusing on "maintain the status quo", labelled it statement 1. He then asked me, "What are the considerations around the status quo?", as this would allow me to **both ladder up to consequences and ladder down** to ways in which this might happen. My response was that I would have to "decide minimal writing was OK [2]." Chuck then said, "Really, and why is that?" I responded, "Maintaining the status quo takes incredible intellectual, emotional, and physical effort [3]. We are so understaffed in the areas I care about [4] that it takes a lot out of me just to keep things as they are [5]" (see Map 5.1).

"And what does deciding to do minimal writing mean?"

"It means postponing writing a book about mapping [6] (the book you are now reading!) and other books [7] I have wanted to write for quite a while, as well as several articles and book chapters [8]". Chuck got me to decide whether I saw each of these as a separate

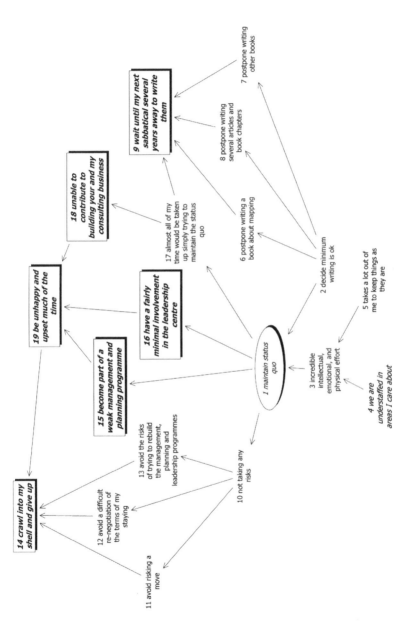

Map 5.1   *About as bad as it gets*. John's first option, maintain the status quo, has only negative consequences and leads to a situation no one would want. (Oval is the option; boxed are negative goals.)

project or as a single project, since **getting the right level of disaggregation** would be helpful to me. Previously I had told Chuck that junior faculty needed to have journal articles, but this was less significant for me as a full professor, so I could focus on books. "Anyway, I would have to wait until my next sabbatical several years away to write them [9]."

"And are there any other considerations around maintaining the status quo?"

"I'd end up not taking any risks [10], which means that I have to avoid risking a move [11]; avoid a difficult renegotiation of the terms of my staying [12]; avoid the risks of trying to rebuild the management, planning and leadership programmes [13]. I'd have to crawl into my shell and give up [14]."

I found the *discussion about what was a means and what was an end (or what was an option or outcome) particularly helpful*, and while at first I got a little frustrated with having to continue to think this out, the formality of mapping forced me to really understand how important these issues were.

"Are there any further considerations?"

"I'd become part of weak management and planning programmes [15]. And I would have a fairly minimal involvement in the leadership center [16], since almost all of my time would be taken up simply trying to maintain the status quo [17]. And I guess I'd be unable to contribute to building your and my consulting business [18] for the same reason."

"Which I guess means that in order to maintain the status quo, I'd also have to decide that being unhappy and upset much of the time is OK [19]."

I watched as Chuck drew the map, since he and I both wanted to make sure the map accurately reflected my thinking. **We would have to check with each other throughout the mapping process to make sure the map really was "my" map.** I mentioned to Chuck that I was "taken by the way in which the map was beginning to *reveal the interconnections between all of the* *things that I really didn't want as outcomes,* and also began to *clarify what it was I wanted, by considering contrasting statements.* For example, being happy and not upset all of the time – as opposed to their opposites – was starting to look like an important goal for me."

Chuck responded by asking, "Is happiness related to not crawling into your shell? If so, which is the more important of the two outcomes to you?" **Making me consider which of the two goals was the more important to me really forced me to think about my values.** I decided that being unhappy and upset would lead to what was more important in a negative sense: crawling into my shell and giving up [19→14].

As I reflected on the map, I realized that the mapping process was *minimizing my need to keep going over the same ground* – something I had probably done way too much of already! I was also prompted to say, "You know, *seeing this map is helping me tap into my real feelings, feelings I spend a lot of time denying*".

"Geez, John, when you see all those negative outcomes – negative goals, really – you are looking at a pretty bad picture."

I don't want to repeat what I said. Roughly translated, this was, "I feel awful." Chuck added these words (not shown) to the statement on the map "be unhappy and upset much of the time".

"What would other consequences be of maintaining the status quo?" he asked, in order to help me **ladder up to outcomes and ultimately purposes of the option.**

I indicated that a look at recent history was not encouraging, since "the faculty and administration are unlikely to change soon [20]" and "the prospects for improvement look pretty dismal [21]". "I guess I'd have to hope against hope that things would get better [22]." (See Map 5.2.)

Chuck responded, "You know, I know this situation about as well as you do, and I would have to say that you would have to win every battle for the next five years [23] in order to turn things around [24, 23→24]." "Yes," I said, "write those down." (Note that in Map 5.2

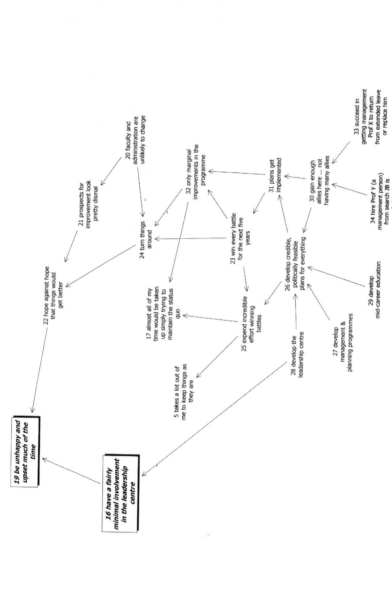

Map 5.2 *Huge effort for little gain.* Trying to make marginal improvements in the status quo means long and hard work for John with little hope of success. (Boxed are negative goals.)

there is a dashed line between 23 and 24 because, as you will see, it gets changed shortly.) "I'd like to link 24 in somewhere, too, at some point, since it is related to what 'hoping against hope' means."

Chuck said, "That's interesting. Presumably, the fact that the faculty are unlikely to change works against winning all the battles, or alternatively you would have to change the faculty and administration." (20→24)

"What else would it take to win every battle?"

"Well, it would take incredible effort [25], so draw an arrow from 'winning' [23] to that. I would need to develop credible, politically feasible plans for everything [26]: develop management and planning programmes [27], develop the leadership centre [28] and develop mid-career education [29]. Preparing them would take a lot of effort [25] and so would gaining enough allies [30]. With enough allies, the plans might be implemented [30→31], but my guess is the result of all that effort, as well as winning every battle, would be only marginal improvements in the programmes [32]."

Chuck was beginning to look puzzled. I noticed this and asked, "What is the problem, Chuck?"

"Well," he responded, "I am trying to sort out in my mind, and so on the map, what you have just said. First you mentioned that you needed to develop the leadership centre as a part of developing credible plans. But earlier you mentioned something about having a fairly minimal involvement in the leadership centre as something you didn't want to happen." Chuck pointed to this statement on the map [16]. "Presumably developing the leadership centre would mean that you would have a pretty extensive involvement in the centre?"

I nodded my head, and said, "Yes, 28 leads negatively to 16."

Chuck continued, "My bigger puzzle is that you think winning every battle only gains marginal improvements, but earlier, if I heard you correctly, you mentioned that winning every battle [23] would turn things around [24]. I guess on reflection, winning every battle isn't going to turn things around?"

I sighed, "I see what you mean. I guess in talking about it I realize that developing plans and gaining allies doesn't seem to be enough and it is going to take lots of effort to boot. So take out 23→24" (see Map 5.2).

"And as well as all that, we'd have to succeed in getting management professor X to return from his extended leave, or else replace him [33]. And right now I'm chairing a search committee for another management person, professor Y, and we would have to hire her as well [34]. Both X and Y are great, but they only help if they're here. If X were here, or his replacement was, he or she would be an ally [33→30]. If Y came, she would be an ally [34→30]. But right now I really don't have that many allies."

Chuck modified "gain enough allies [30]" so that it now reflected the conversation and read "gain enough allies here rather than not having many allies [30]".

"OK," said Chuck, "I can see this isn't looking like a very good situation right now."

"You're right," I said. "In fact, what is striking is how much work is involved in simply keeping things as they are. A lot of the so-called consequences of maintaining the status quo just involve more work for me with no guarantee of any pay-off at all [32→17, 25→17]. They are 'hows' or actions I have to take or be involved in. It all looks like a holding action, rather than any kind of broad-scale advance. And so I guess *I have to ask myself, why I would keep doing that?*"

Chuck looked at the map thoughtfully, and then looked at me. "Tell me what the other considerations around maintaining the status quo would be, besides 'hoping against hope' and 'you feel awful'.

"Since I am a tenured full professor [35], I would have a secure income and full benefits [36] as long as I continue to do a decent job in the classroom and behave respectably [37]. And I would maintain my status as a professor [38]. And those two things together would allow me to maintain my identity and security" [38, 35→36→38, 37→38]. (See Map 5.3.)

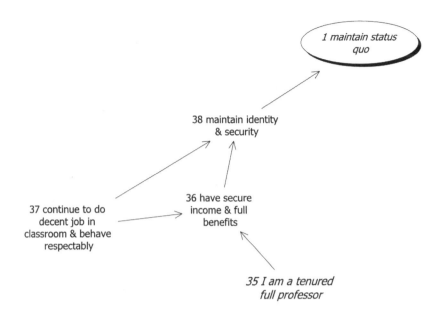

Map 5.3 *Just behave.* All John needs to maintain the status quo, and keep his job, is to do nothing wrong, but there would be other, personal consequences. (Oval is the option.)

"OK," he said, "but I want to know more about how you feel. You know, you have resisted creating this map for a long time, because – and I'm telling you this as your friend – I think you're afraid of how bad you would feel if you really faced what maintaining the status quo means to you emotionally."

I was quiet for a while. **Chuck pushed on the importance of exploring my emotions, but knew he had to give me time and space to let me give voice to them myself.** He knew that emotions are the real source of change, and in this case it had to be my emotions.

"I'm not very happy, particularly around the house [39]. The kids [who were 11 and 13 at the time] and Barbara rarely see me happy. I'm certainly not joyful [40]. One thing I'm afraid of is that the kids will think that work and being an adult is a drag [41]. I hate that thought. I actually love my work in general – it's practically a calling. I just hate my situation [42]." (See Map 5.4.)

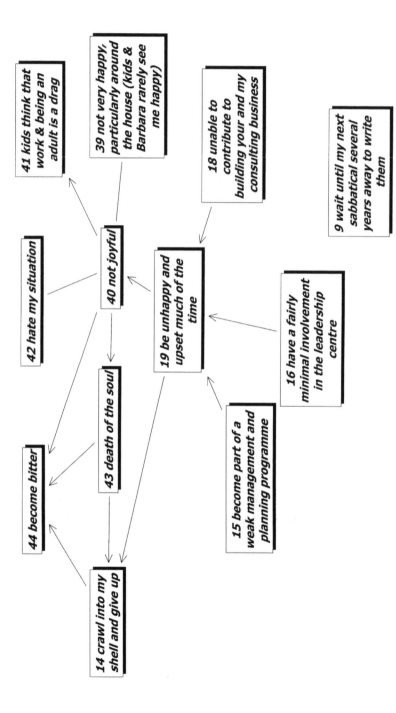

Map 5.4   *The shock of the bitter truth.* The consequences of merely staying in his job and doing nothing about it are really bad for John and his family. (All negative goals.)

"And..."

"And what?"

"What's really going on with you?"

I was again quiet for a while.

"Chuck, you know what it is? What I'm really experiencing is a death of the soul [43] [40→43]. I'm dying where I am right now. At least my spirit is. And if I don't do something to change my situation, I'll crawl into my shell and give up [43→14] and, worse still, become bitter [43→44]. I've seen that happen to other people and I'm not going to let it happen to me."

I reflected for a few moments on what I had just said and then turned to Chuck. "Thanks, Chuck – I guess! – for doing this. You're right, I was afraid to map my situation. I think I knew in my heart it just wasn't working and I was going to have to do something about it, like apply for jobs elsewhere, move or become much more political. And I just didn't want to face moving, because I really like Minneapolis and Minnesota and the university in general and all my friends here. And Barbara and the kids like it. They would hate moving and I would hate forcing the issue. And I also didn't want to face the fact that my spirit is dying where I am. My soul is shrivelling and I'm on the road to bitterness.

"You know, the odd thing is that *I feel a sense of relief from having it all out in the open and facing it. I also feel an energy surge*. Let's go on to the next option."

Chuck agreed, but before moving on, he insisted we do some quick tidying up, particularly around the emerging negative goals. First we linked my earlier statement about being unhappy [19] into not being joyful [40]. Then we linked crawling into my shell [14] and not being joyful [40] into becoming bitter [44].

Chuck then tore off the map from the writing pad and gave it to me. He reflected on the map and said, "You know, John, absolutely nothing good comes out of this option of maintaining the status quo." I said, "You're right, this map teaches me that *the status quo is untenable*."

"On the other hand," Chuck continued, "some good things do come out of creating the map. First, it is clear that creating this map has been a release for you. You have moved a long way emotionally by doing it. Second, the map at least shows you what you don't want, and therefore can serve as a kind of 'negative benchmark' against which to judge other options. So, for example, you don't want to put in a lot of effort for no gain. And you don't want to experience a death of the soul or become bitter. But the map also shows you by way of contrast a lot of what you do want. You want to be much happier than you are – in fact, you would like to be joyful. You want to be a part of strong management and planning programs, you want to be involved in a leadership programme and mid-career degree programme, and you want to write more. So when we explore other options, we need to find a way to include those goals – they're great goals for you and we need to figure out how to pursue them."

Leave the School for Another Job as a Professor

So we moved on to the next option, "leave the school for another professorial job [45]". Chuck began by saying, "You are, or were, really afraid of the consequences of leaving the school, so let's explore those first. **Sometimes it is best to ladder up to consequences first before laddering down to what it would take to pursue an option,** and this may be one of those cases."

"OK."

"So what would the consequences be?"

"Based on my first map, I guess I'd have to say that I would be walking away from a garbage can ['dumpster', a US term, in the map] load of %@#&!!! [46]" (see Map 5.5).

"Yes, assuredly. And what else?"

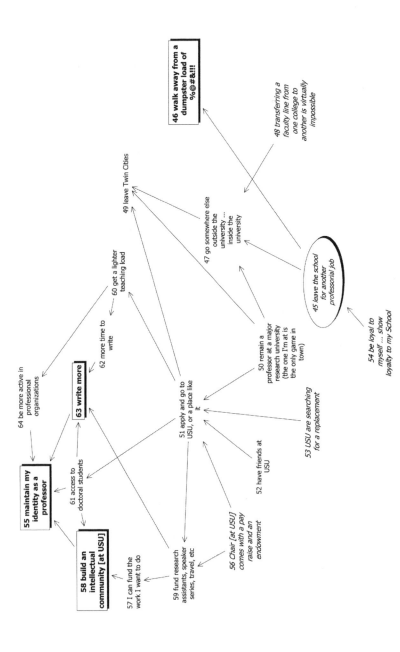

Map 5.5   *The grass is greener.* John's second option, find another professorial job, seems to lead to a much brighter future, but it would mean leaving the Twin Cities. (Boxed are goals; oval the option; and italics not boxed are assertions.)

"Well, I guess I'd have to go somewhere else outside the university [47]."

"What about somewhere else *inside* the university?"

"No, that's probably a non-starter. Transferring a faculty line from one college to another is virtually impossible [48]."

"OK, what else might leaving mean?"

"It probably would mean leaving the Twin Cities [49]."

"And why is that?"

"Because I want to be a professor at a major research university [50] and the one I'm at is the only game in town."

"So to go somewhere else outside the university would mean you would have to leave the Twin Cities," Chuck said, as he drew an arrow from "remain a professor at a major research university" to "leave the Twin Cities" and "remain as a professor at a major research university" to "go somewhere else" and therefore "leave the Twin Cities" [50→49, 50→47→49].

"Where would you like to go?" Chuck asked.

"Well, one place I'd certainly consider applying to is [Unnamed] State University (USU), or a place like it [51]. I have friends there [52] and for several years they've been asking whether I would be interested in a chaired professorship there when the incumbent retires. And now he has. They're searching for a replacement [53] and I'm certainly thinking about applying. In fact, having a live job prospect probably gave me the courage to do this mapping.

"Can we take a break from mapping for a while, so I can just talk?" I added.

"Sure."

"Thinking about leaving is really hard for me. I guess I'm old school, but I am very loyal. So here I'm not being treated very well, and thinking about leaving makes me feel like a traitor. That is probably nuts, but I have to say it."

"John, I've known you a long time and you are loyal. You believe in the school's mission and you keep thinking you can change the way things are done. But the map we just did shows there is very little you can do that would make much difference. And in the meantime, you are not happy, and staying is killing your soul.

"Forget loyalty to an institution that won't change," Chuck continued. "Be loyal to yourself. And realize that if you're not happy you are putting your marriage and family at risk. They're more important than any job.

"You gave it your best shot and stayed longer than anyone else would have. You know, a lot of your friends around the country wonder why you stay. *I* wonder why you stay. I'd hate to see you go, but I hate even more seeing you so unhappy and feeling trapped. So you don't have to worry about what other people think. You only have to worry about what you think."

"OK. I guess you're right. But you know, **occasionally it helps just to stop and talk without doing mapping. Sometimes things – especially when deep emotions are involved – are just too murky to map. You need to talk for a while in order to be able to map. And sometimes it is simply better to talk with a friend**. Anyway, let's keep going now."

"OK," said Chuck, "so we need to get loyalty onto the map as that seems to be something that is important to you. Let's add a statement saying 'be loyal to myself rather than loyal to the school [54]'. The status quo map has shown how important it is to focus on your goals, and the fact that you aren't coming close to achieving them is a driver for leaving the school [45]. So you're attracted to USU. What would you get out of moving there?"

"Well, I would maintain my identity as a professor [55]. The chair comes with a pay raise and an endowment [56] that can be used to fund anything, like research assistants, a speaker series, travel or whatever [59]. It could be used to fund the work I want to do [57] and build an intellectual community [58], which is something I don't have right now. I would get a lighter teaching load [60] and access to PhD students [61], which I don't have now, since we don't have a PhD programme. Having a lighter teaching load would give me more time to write [62] and that, along with doctoral students, would mean I could write more [63]. And the endowment would let me become more active in professional organizations [64], since I would be writing more and would have more research to present."

Chuck interrupted. "You have this valued outcome – maintain your identity as a professor [55] – unlinked at the moment. It seems to me that an intellectual community [58], doctoral students [61], time to write [62] and activity in professional organizations [64] are all about your identity, aren't they?"

"Yeah, that's a helpful summary," I replied. "Also, make 'write more [63]' a goal. It's apparent from the previous map [statement 9 – wait until my sabbatical several years away to write them: articles, book chapters, other books, book about mapping] that writing more is really important to me.

"I guess the really big thing is that I would get to be at a place where people value what I have to offer [65]. And that would mean I would no longer feel marginal, frustrated and impotent [66]. So I would be happier [67] and I'd have a renewed sense of excitement [68], which would also make me happier." (See Map 5.6.)

Chuck pencilled in a link from "walk away from a garbage can load of %@#&!!! [46]" to "be happier [67]" and looked for my agreement. I nodded.

He then said, "Early on, you made the obvious point that going outside of the university means leaving the Twin Cities. So what about your family, as a family, if you left the Twin Cities? Not just jobs for you and Barbara, but for your family in general?"

"The family would move away from close friends, attachments and familiar surroundings [69, 49→69]. And that would have a negative impact on Barbara's happiness [70, 69→70]. And the kids would be unhappy [71, 69→71]. And the kids' unhappiness would make Barbara unhappy [71→70].

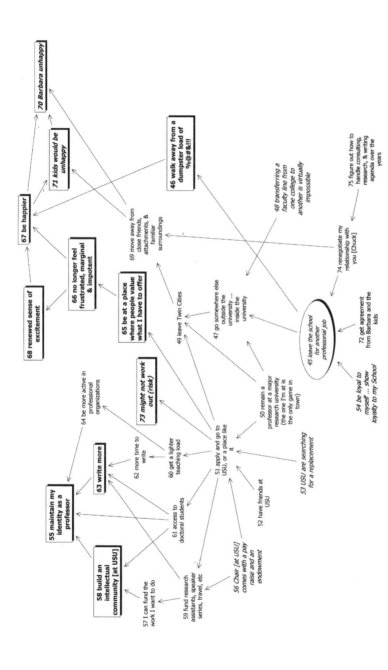

Map 5.6 *A wider view of the "greener grass".* All the immediate good outcomes are to John's benefit. Barbara, John's wife, and his children would not be as happy with a move. (Boxed italics are negative goals; boxed non-italics are goals; oval is the option; italics are assertions.)

"On the other hand, if I were happier, that would make Barbara happier [67→70], and if the kids saw me happier, that would make them happier, at least somewhat [67→71]."

"So there is some pretty complicated emotional stuff going on around leaving the Twin Cities," said Chuck. "I can see why you might not have wanted to open it up. But it also looks like there are things that would make everyone happy. And your children are young, they can adjust. Now let's see what it would take to leave [45]. What would you have to do?"

"I'd have to get agreement from Barbara, and the kids would have to agree [72], or at least be willing to go along. And I guess I'd have to decide to take a risk, since leaving might not work out [73]."

"And actually, I'd have to renegotiate my relationship with you [74], since you are a good friend and we wouldn't be living close to each other anymore. Part of that renegotiation would involve figuring out how to handle the consulting, research and writing agenda we have had over the years [75]. This just adds to what I said earlier about moving away from close friends etc. [69, 74→69]."

"Yes," Chuck said, "I was wondering where our relationship fit into all of this. I'd certainly miss seeing you frequently, but you haven't been all that much fun to be around lately, so moving might well be the best thing."

He looked at the map for a while and then added, "You know, the leaving option doesn't actually involve you doing very much early on, does it? Other than making this psychological leap to decide that being happy is OK and deciding to leave?"

"No, I guess not. ***The big leave-taking is in my head.*** I have to be willing to take a risk and I have to be willing to change my commitments. That's all, but it's actually a lot."

"Yes, I'm sure that's right," said Chuck. "I – and, in fact, a lot of your friends – have watched you struggle with your job situation for a long time. It is clear that it has not been easy for you either to leave or to give up and just be happy with what you've got. So let's look at what staying, but renegotiating the terms, might look like. First, we

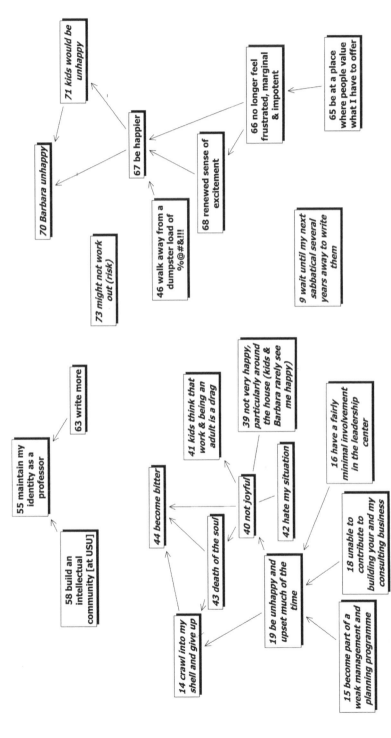

Map 5.7   *The good and the bad.* Here is an overview of the ups and downs if John moved to another professorial position in another state. (Boxed italics are negative goals; boxed non-italics are goals.)

probably should summarize this second map. Leaving for USU or a place like it would help you achieve all of your goals – exactly the opposite of what the status quo does for you. There would be disruption for you and your family, but there are ways to handle all of that." (See Map 5.7.)

Stay, but Renegotiate the Terms

Chuck tore the second map off of his writing pad and gave it to me. He wrote "Stay, but renegotiate the terms [76]" in the middle of the next page on the tablet.

"OK, John, so how would you go about staying under different terms?"

I exhaled. "I guess the only administrative vehicle in place that would help me do the work I want to do is the leadership centre. So that would have to be developed, which was 28 on the status quo map [see Map 5.2], so put that on this map too. The people associated with the centre, including you, are my only real colleagues at the school right now [77, 77→28]. But the centre is poorly funded [78]. And to have real standing in the school and university, it would have to be directed by a full professor [79], which it isn't right now" (see Map 5.8).

"So why don't you direct it?"

"I guess I could do that. The centre has an interim director right now who isn't a professor [80] and therefore she is unlikely to be appointed the director herself [81]. But she could be appointed associate director [82], the job she had before the previous director left, and she was really good at it [80→81→82]. I like her a lot and would be delighted to have her as associate director. For one thing, she is great at handling administrative details [83], which is not my strong suit to say the least, and that would help us develop the leadership center [83→82→28, 83→28].

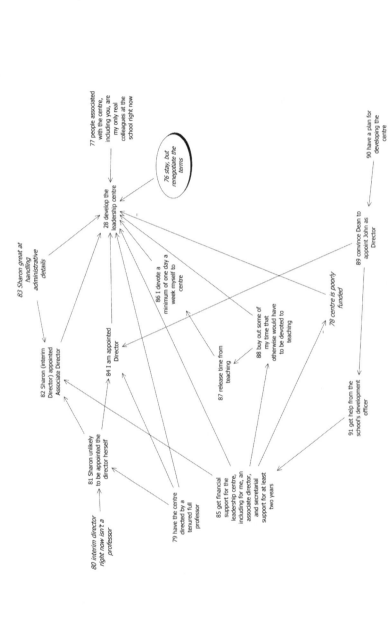

Map 5.8 *Stay, but on my terms.* John's third option revolves around the leadership centre, the one place where he could develop a focus for his work, but he needs a business plan for the centre that will convince the dean of its value to the school.

"OK, John, hold on, let me get some things down on the map. One part of being part of a strong leadership centre is you being appointed director [84]."

"Yes [84→28]. I'm also the only likely candidate!"

"And another part of staying is getting help with administrative details [83], which would meaning having Sharon be associate director [82]."

"Yes, you've got that."

"Now, you said the centre was poorly funded, so what would you have to do about that?"

"Write down 'Get financial support for the leadership centre, including for me, an associate director and secretarial support for at least two years' " [85, 85→78].

"And you would use some of that money to pay for Sharon?"

"Yes [85→82]."

"So what kind of time would you need to devote to the centre as opposed to teaching on centre programmes or researching and writing in that area?

"You mean how much time would I have to work on fundraising, relationship building, supervision and so on?

"Yes."

"I'd probably have to devote a minimum of one day a week myself to that [86, 86→28]."

"Would you have to gain some release time from teaching?"

"That would be nice [87]. And I guess if I were able to get financial support, one thing I could do with it is buy out some of my time that otherwise would have to be devoted to teaching, and I could spend that time on the centre [88, 85→88→87→86→28]. That would help the centre become self-sustaining."

"Who would have to appoint you as director of the leadership centre?"

I exhaled again. "The dean, which means I would have to convince him that it was a good idea [89, 89→84]."

"Right. And how would you do that?"

"Good question. I suppose a place to start would be having a plan for developing the centre [90]. He would want to see one [90→89]. And he'd have to agree with that plan before I could get help from the school's development officer to help with the fundraising effort [89→91→85]."

"You said earlier that the dean doesn't really care about leadership as a field. Does he care about you? **If you want someone to do something, you have to figure out what they care about.**"

"I don't know if he cares about me personally, but I do know he works to keep people he thinks help the school and are good at what they do, but are also ready to leave. He has worked pretty hard to keep high-quality faculty members, even when he didn't like them, like professor Z. The dean thought his area was very important.

"So I think the dean would work to keep me if I developed a good offer of an attractive job elsewhere [93] and could use that to convince him I was ready to leave [92, 93→92] [see Map 5.9]. For one thing, that would convince him I was an attractive property [94], even if he didn't understand or appreciate my area very much [93→94]. And besides, he has all but told me the only way I'll get a significant salary increase is if he has to put together a retention offer to counter an offer from some well-known school. So getting an offer from somewhere else and convincing him I was ready to leave would at least result in me getting paid more money for all the aggravation, even if it didn't help the centre [96, 92→96]. But I think it would convince him to appoint me as the director [94→89]."

"Hang on," Chuck said. "Let me get some arrows in here. **I was too busy getting your ideas down to have time to do any linking, so now let's go back and figure out the structure of the argument.**"

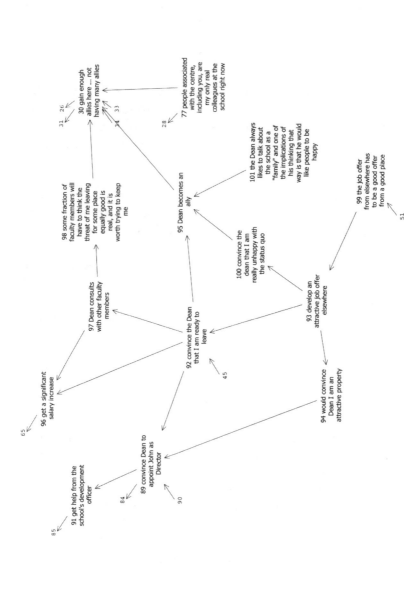

Map 5.9 *In order to stay, be ready to leave.* To prove his worth to the school, John has to get an attractive offer that would convince the school he is worth keeping. (Map shows links to other parts of the whole map.)

After putting all the arrows in and checking them with me, Chuck said, "Convincing the dean that you're ready to leave [92] is starting to look like **a pretty important construct, since it connects to so many crucial items.**"

"Yes, it is. And that is a depressing thought, because leadership, management, planning and mid-career education are not very high on his agenda. So I guess I can't convince him directly about the worth of what I care about. It looks like my only viable option is to get a good offer from somewhere else and see if that will convince him to respond favourably. If he does, that's great. If he doesn't, then I guess I either have to leave, or else accept all of those negative consequences of the status quo."

"So let's assume you get a good offer from somewhere else," Chuck said. "What would that do?"

"If the dean is to put together a retention offer, he will consult with other faculty members [97] and some fraction will have to think that the possibility of me leaving for some place equally good is real too [98] and support an effort to keep me [30 (from Map 5.2), $92 \rightarrow 97 \rightarrow 98 \rightarrow 30$]. It means that the job offer from elsewhere has to be a good offer from a place that everyone thinks is a good place [99, $99 \rightarrow 93$]."

"I also think that to get the dean as an ally I need to convince him that I am really unhappy with the status quo [100]. He always likes to talk about the school as a 'family' and one of the implications of his thinking that way is that he would like people to be happy [101]. I think he is genuine about wanting that, even though he realizes some people are going to be unhappy no matter what."

"So 'developing a good offer to leave' might indicate you were unhappy," Chuck commented.

"Yes, so link $93 \rightarrow 100$."

"**Let me summarize here,**" said Chuck. "In order to stay, you have to convince the dean that you are willing to leave. To do that, you have to develop an attractive job offer [93] from elsewhere. If you can convince the dean that you are ready to leave [92], that will help him think it is a good idea to have you direct the leadership centre [89], which will help persuade you to stay and will also lead him to help you with the development effort [91]. Getting help with the development effort will help you get the time you need [89] to develop the centre [28]."

"That's right," I said. "It is kind of amazing that in order to stay on renegotiated terms I have to be ready to leave, which ties two of my main options together. *The previous option and this one are in some ways the same option. Either I go or stay, but to stay I have to be willing to go.*"

"You're right, John. But in some ways that should make your choice of options easier. *You have to pursue both options!*"

"To tell you the truth, that is a real eye-opener. Surprisingly, I don't think I ever put that together before."

"So, John, if you stayed but under different terms, let's see what you would get out of that. Maybe we should try doing a check against all the negative goals you mentioned on the status quo map [Map 5.4] with all of the positive outcomes of leaving [Map 5.6], and see how the renegotiating option fares against them." (See Map 5.10.)

Chuck reminded me that the status quo option map suggested that even if you "won every battle" there would still only be "marginal improvements [32]" and so things "would not get turned round [24]". "So what's different here?" he asked.

"As you pointed out, the most crucial difference is what comes from getting the dean on my side. This would mean that we would win close to every battle and turn things around in a major way." So Chuck crossed out "marginal improvements [32]" and put in $23 \rightarrow 24$ [on Map 5.2] to show the link between winning every battle and turning things round.

"But," he commented, "what about the problem of the incredible effort it will take [25]?"

"Oh, with the dean's support the effort will much less, as the new map [Map 5.4] shows, so we can cross out 25."

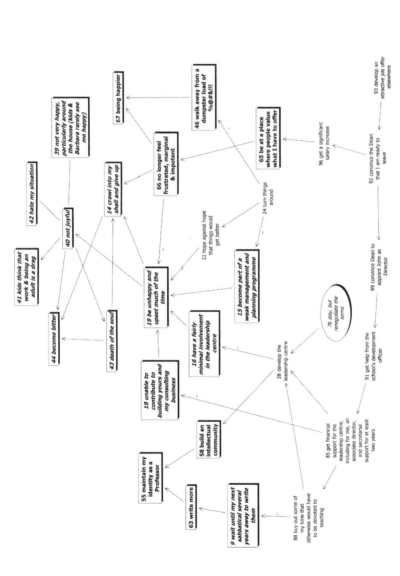

Map 5.10 *The worst of times, the best of times.* This map compares the effects on John of the status quo and the renegotiation of his position at the school. (Boxed italics are negative goals; boxed non-italics are goals; oval is the option.)

Chuck started checking against the negative goals by pointing me to the bottom level of negative goals. He said, "If we can see how your new plan rates against these, then we will have a reasonable check against the higher goals."

So I started looking at those negative goals. "If we get the centre running, that could strengthen the management and planning programme [15]. Obviously I will play a role in the centre [16]. And I guess I stand a reasonable chance of getting writing done [9] if I can buy out some of my time [88].

"I suppose the most important thing is that I would stay excited and involved and vibrant, rather than crawling into my shell [14]. And I wouldn't be in a garbage can load of %@#&!!! [46].

"Building the centre would mean I could build an intellectual community here [58]. And if my colleagues give me a vote of confidence and the dean gives me a decent salary [96], I would begin to feel valued again [65]. It all seems to check out. There would still be a lot of work, but at least there is hope."

Concluding the Session

"OK, John, we've been at this for about two hours. **Let's look at your three maps and see what you think**."

"I guess the most obvious thing is that I need to quit procrastinating and do something. I need to work on figuring out how to build up the centre. I need to go on the job market. And I need to talk with Sharon and Barbara. They need to understand why I need to go on the job market in order to stay. They are good friends and colleagues – and Barbara is my spouse – and I need to be honest with them, in order that they don't feel so betrayed if, down the line, I actually do decide to go. I need to be both ready to go and ready to stay."

Chuck jumped in, "Which do you actually want? I'm asking as your friend and also as a very interested party. I have a real stake in the answer!"

"I'd rather stay. But that first map has shown me that the status quo is horrible for me. If I stay with things as they are, it will be corrosive to my spirit. So while I do want to stay, this mapping exercise has convinced me I really need to be prepared to go. If I stay the way things are, I will experience a death of the soul. I'll be unhappy and miserable and embittered and neither you nor anyone else will want to be around me. So I need to get moving on the insights these maps have provided.

"Thank you, Chuck. You've helped me get out of a hole I'd put myself in. If I stay in the status quo, I stay in that hole. And that is no good for me or my family or anyone else I really care about."

Conclusions

In this chapter we have done two things. We have shown how a person can use mapping to understand the options they face. *Option exploration* involves elaborating each option in terms of what it would take to pursue the option, and in terms of what would happen if the option were pursued. Option exploration can be applied to an almost infinite array of topics; indeed, anytime there is an array of options that might be pursued.

We have also demonstrated the use of *interviewing* as a mapping technique. In this case, Chuck helped John clarify his options through interviewing him and mapping the responses. John had three options and Chuck and John worked together to produce a map for each option. All of the content was John's, but Chuck's questioning helped draw out the content and clarify its structure. Interviewing also can be applied in an almost infinite set of circumstances; indeed, anytime it makes sense to help an individual understand their own thinking, as in this chapter, or to gather information from an individual in order to understand how they see things, for example, for research purposes.

Process guidelines

- Set up a time for an interview.

- Create a workspace in which the interviewee can watch
  as the interviewer creates the map of the interview. Have
  all of the appropriate mapping materials present (e.g.
  flipchart sheets, pencils, erasers, coloured pens or stick-on
  dots).

- Some introductory conversation can be quite helpful, but
  mapping should start quickly so that the interviewee's
  thoughts are captured rather than lost.

- Begin by first listing the big options that the interviewee
  thinks he or she has. List them in small print in the upper-
  left-hand corner of the paper, or spread them across the
  paper.

- Build a map around each option.

- Typically, the interviewer should start by prompting the
  interviewee to ladder down into the "hows" of the first
  option.

- Then ladder up to outcomes and ultimately to the purposes
  of the option, the "whys".

- Sometimes it is best to ladder up to consequences first
  before laddering down to what it would take to pursue an
  option.

- The interviewer and interviewee will have to check with each
  other throughout the mapping process to make sure the map
  really represents what the interviewee thinks.

- The interviewer will need to work with the interviewee to get
  the right level of disaggregation of ideas, so that the resulting
  map is as useful as possible.

- The interviewer should push on the importance of the
  interviewee exploring his or her emotions, and has to give
  the interviewee time and space to do so.

- Sometimes it helps to stop and talk without doing mapping.
  Sometimes things are just too murky to map, especially

when deep emotions are involved. In these circumstances, you may need to talk for a while in order to create enough structure to be able to map. And sometimes it is simply better to talk with a friend.

- Look for constructs that connect to many crucial items. They are likely to be especially important and time should be spent exploring them in detail.

- Remember that if the interviewee wants someone to do something, he or she will have to figure out what that person cares about.

- If the interviewee is rattling off a long list of concepts, it is often best to get them down without worrying about the connections among them. But at some point it will be important to stop and go back to have the interviewee explain the connections among them; that is, to articulate the structure of the argument.

- At natural stopping points it is important for the interviewer to summarize what he or she has heard in order to make sure that the map is accurate, or perhaps to prepare for the next stage of the mapping exercise.

- Towards the end of the exercise, the interviewer should have the interviewee reflect on what the map or maps are saying. This will help ensure that any important learning points are drawn out and remembered.

Learning points

- This chapter has demonstrated some important learning points both about mapping and about the specific case. The learning points about the specific case, however, are not all that unique, as similar "ahas" or "Eurekas" often emerge.

- When the interviewee faces a troubling situation, getting started with mapping helps minimize his or her need to keep going over the same ground mentally.

- Seeing his or her map unfold can help the interviewee tap into his or her real feelings, feelings that he or she may have spent a lot of time denying.

- Getting a problematic situation out in the open can prompt the interviewee to explore exactly why he or she stays in – or is stuck in – the situation.

- Getting a problematic situation out in the open can help an interviewee experience both relief and a surge of energy to move on to next steps in dealing with the situation.

- More often than not, the big changes an interviewee has to make are in his or her head. In other words, the big changes are often internal rather than external. The map helps clarify that.

- Exploring options often indicates that options that were initially thought to be different are not, and options initially thought to be the same are not.

- Often options are not mutually exclusive and you may, or sometimes must, pursue more than one option at a time.

Postscript

The story had a happy ending for John. He did go on the job market and applied for the job at USU. He was on the short list of candidates invited to interview, which he went and did, and was really attracted to the school and the city in which it is located. He took Barbara and his children to look at houses. Since the city was in the Deep South, all of the houses they looked at had really nice swimming pools, which attracted the whole family. John was excited about moving and the family was willing to move, too, albeit rather reluctantly. In the end, however, USU offered the job to another person, who took it, which was very disappointing to John.

Nevertheless, the strategy worked – at least in part – as it had been mapped. John was appointed director of the leadership centre with Sharon as deputy director. Another major plus was that John and Sharon, along with Barbara, received a grant from the university's central administration to set up a cross-university working group on issues related to leadership research, teaching and service. John was able to work with colleagues he valued on many research, writing and teaching projects. He stayed excited, involved and vibrant, and was not embittered. It truly was the case that in order to stay under renegotiated terms he had to be willing to leave. And the mere fact of being willing to leave freed him and energized him. He also got a substantial pay raise.

Professor X did leave, Professor Y was hired, and some efforts were made to strengthen the management programme. The dean also supported a major cross-university effort to strengthen the school's planning programme. John played a role in that effort, though not a major one. Nonetheless, one of his desires – to be part of a strong planning programme – was on its way to happening once again. The new programme is now touted as a model for the rest of the university about how to organize and manage an interdisciplinary cross-college programme.

Not long after, the dean stepped down and a new dean was appointed. One of the first things the new dean did was ask John to lead an effort to create a new mid-career degree programme, which he did with Barbara and Sharon's help. The three of them worked hard to create a wonderful new programme that filled a real market need, brought them into contact with many new and fascinating participants, and very quickly generated a major portion of the school's teaching income. The new dean and his associate dean also worked to further strengthen the management programme.

The leadership centre continued and celebrated its twenty-fifth anniversary. A cross-university undergraduate leadership minor was created and is thriving. Centre staff produced numerous well-regarded publications. Mid-career education, which the leadership centre pioneered, was central to the school. There were losses as well, the biggest being Chuck's departure for an academic post in New York – which was ironic, given that John thought he was the one who might be leaving. But on balance, things were much better.

Now that dean has stepped down and a new dean is in place. He has made it clear that a top priority is further strengthening the school's emphasis on leadership and management of public and non-profit organizations. The leadership centre ceased to exist as such, but was folded into a new centre incorporating a broader agenda and many more members of the school's faculty and staff. The leadership centre in a way had succeeded itself out of a job: leadership and mid-career education were now central to the school and needed a new vehicle to go to the next stage.

So all of the programmes John had wanted to be part of are now in place and thriving. Certainly not all of these good things were a direct result of a two-hour mapping exercise, but the exercise obviously helped. John knew clearly what he wanted and, as Louis Pasteur once observed, chance favours the prepared mind. In other words, if you are ready for change, you just might get the changes you want!

Part III

What Do We Think?
A Guide to Oval Mapping

6

To Merge or not to Merge – That Is the Question!

IN THIS CHAPTER WE REPORT ON A SITUATION WHERE A GROUP of people have a range of choices open to them regarding a particular strategic issue. They think they know which direction or choice they want to make, but would prefer to explore all the ramifications of the issue before committing themselves. The decision will affect their futures and the futures of others. In fact, there are a number of other interested parties to consider. In addition, they want to be sure that all of them are happy with the direction taken and understand its rationale.

This situation is typical of many at work, at home or in the community. Frequently we find ourselves responding to issues, sometimes proactively, other times in a more reactive manner. To help us move forward, we need to understand the context of the issues, what options are open to us, what other issues might be related and what is the best route given the circumstances.

In the previous part of this book we used examples that focused on individuals – ourselves – and what we should do in different situations. In the chapters in this part, the authors worked as facilitators of mapping by a group. In the current chapter, Fran helped a group determine the best way forward.

When working with a group it is important to use mapping to draw out the range of views that need to be expressed, integrated and evaluated. While Fran did not have in-depth knowledge of the issue this group was facing, she did have mapping and facilitation skills that could help them explore the issue.

Getting Started

The client was Ros Micklem, who was Principal of Cardonald College, a publicly funded College of Further Education (CFE) in Scotland. (CFEs are similar to community or technical colleges in the US.) The college catered to 17–30-year-olds studying in the areas of design, fashion, journalism, pottery and jewellery, as well as other more "traditional" subjects, such as business and finance.

The college is one of 10 in Glasgow, Scotland, and was faced with a serious issue. The funding body responsible for allocating monies to colleges in Scotland was seriously considering whether it would be more effective if there were five colleges rather than ten (one for roughly each point of the compass plus one for the centre of the city) or three instead of ten (roughly north, central and south). If the funding body decided to implement either of these changes, the colleges would be under serious pressure to merge. The big problem was that most colleges believed merging would have a huge impact on staffing, curriculum (there was some overlap between colleges) and the general culture of each college. The impacts would cause major disruption and be very difficult to manage. However, if they did have to merge, being proactive and choosing with whom to merge might make the transition a little less traumatic. Thus the issue that needed to be explored was whether to merge or not to merge.

Since Cardonald is situated in the southwest of Glasgow, one of the options facing the principal and her staff was to position themselves as the college for the southwest. The college currently has around 11 000 students, which makes it the largest in Glasgow. Because of their size they could perhaps stand alone and not have to experience the trauma of merging. However, before committing themselves to this direction, they needed to consider the ramifications of this choice. For example, how might it:

- affect their funding levels?

- make them vulnerable in terms of student numbers?

- affect staffing, perhaps because the merged colleges could pay staff more and therefore tempt the good staff to leave Cardonald?

Thus there were many issues to consider and little time in which to decide whether or not to merge, as the funding council would be making its decision soon and they needed to be in a position to capitalize on the situation. Ros needed to find a way of exploring the issue as thoroughly as possible within a tight time span. In addition, she wanted to involve her senior management group (SMG), as they would need to buy into whichever option was chosen; and she was also keen to involve the Board of Management (board) of the college. This meant involving around 16 people. How could she capture everyone's views, make sense of them and help the group go forward while also getting the chance to participate herself?

As Ros was considering this problem, Fran was exploring a challenge of her own. She was associated with a group of former Strathclyde MBA students interested in the mapping process who were looking for opportunities to practise their skills and she had agreed to help them with this. Fran and Ros had worked together on a number of projects and so they regularly kept in contact. During one of their conversations, Ros mentioned the issue of working on the potential merger. It occurred to both of them that there was a definite potential here for the MBA group and Fran to work with the board and SMG using the group-mapping process.

What was the next step?

Fran mentioned that before starting a group-mapping workshop there were a number of items they needed to consider. These included:

- Determining the venue and timing for the meeting.
- Agreeing on the issue question that would provide the focus for the meeting.
- Reviewing the nature of the participants and formulating subgroups.
- Marshalling the equipment.
- Agreeing on a plan for the meeting.

She and Ros agreed to meet for an hour or so in the near future to tackle these items.

Starting with the first item, Fran asked Ros whether it was possible to **find an appropriate large room with plenty of flat wall space away from the distractions of day-to-day business**. Fran knew from past experience that getting a good room was critical. The last time she had carried out a meeting of this type she had had to work in a narrow L-shaped room with poor ventilation. This meant that participants were forced to sit in a line rather than a semi-circle and so couldn't see one another or all of the material. Ros suggested that the group might use a large room in their New Technology Business Centre (on the Cardonald site). This would mean the group would not have to travel far and would be away from all of the distractions of their offices. Exploring this option further, it emerged that one of the rooms in the centre could be divided in half with a folding door. Each side of the door provided an excellent wall surface on which to create maps. There was also plenty of room in the hall for coffee and refreshments and restrooms were near by. It seemed ideal.

Next Fran and Ros discussed the focus question. They wanted to **produce an unambiguous 10-15-word focus question for the group that provides sufficient direction (while not closing down fruitful discussion)**. The question needed to give the group plenty of room to consider all of the issues surrounding the possible choice of "going it alone". Ros also wanted to ensure that the risks were surfaced, because she knew the group would be tempted to consider only the benefits. After trying a number of alternatives, the final wording of the focus question emerged as: "In the context of the current review of FE provision in Glasgow, what would be the strategic implications for Cardonald College of choosing not to engage in discussions about merger?" While they were both aware that it was a lengthy question and was worded in the negative, they felt that it both clarified the context within which the group was to work and emphasized the need to consider the negative issues as well as the positive ones. Ros realized that *spending time getting the issue question right can clarify the purpose of the workshop considerably*.

Agreeing on the focus question led naturally to a discussion about the participants. Fran wanted to **explore who the participants would be, as this would help in anticipating potential conflicts and planning the meeting more effectively**. Through knowing a little about them – what they were like, their backgrounds, their major concerns etc. – Fran felt she would have a better sense of what to expect during the meeting. In addition, as there were potentially 16 participants (they weren't sure how many of the board would attend), they needed to create two subgroups of eight members each in order to **allow lots of potential airtime for the participants to ensure that all could contribute**. The make-up of these groups would require some careful consideration, as Fran and Ros wanted to ensure that there was a mix of perspectives, personalities and board and SMG.

Finally, Fran discussed the equipment she would need to **ensure that all the necessary materials were available**. As they were going to use the group-mapping technique, the first item they required was some oval Post-its.[1] Providing the participants with ovals would allow them to capture their contributions and stick them up on a wall covered with flipchart paper. Doing so in front of the group would allow others to "piggy back" on the material and provide additional ideas. Using ovals would enable the group to move the ovals to form clusters (see Chapter 3).

In addition, Fran would provide two sets of pens with reasonably thick tips, one set for her (different colours to signal different categories) and another for the participants (all the same type and colour). Giving participants all the same type of pens helps **provide a degree of anonymity**. Fran and colleagues had found that once the group gets into the process they take little account of who wrote up items unless they are in a distinct pen colour or type. In addition, providing pens with reasonably thick tips helps ensure that the participants write on the ovals in a text size that is readable from several feet away. Fran then asked Ros to provide flipchart paper and masking tape[2] so that the walls could be protected.

The equipment thus included:

- Packs of oval Post-its.

- Pens for participants.

- Pens for the facilitator.

- Flipchart paper and masking tape.

- Optional: camera (digital if possible) to take pictures of the group working as an aide mémoire.

Now that they had gone through the practicalities, they began to review how the meeting should unfold. Fran had already facilitated a meeting with Ros's SMG using the group-mapping technique, so Ros and the group were familiar with what would unfold. However, in this case there would be two subgroups. How would this be managed?

Fran and Ros carefully considered how they would introduce the session. Fran suggested that they **start with an introduction from Ros as the client** (since she would be inviting everyone and it was for the college's benefit), before handing over to Fran to explain what the meeting would involve. Fran would **explain to the entire group the process to be followed and the meeting's objectives**, before asking them to break into two designated subgroups. Fran plus one of the former MBA students – Rob – would facilitate one group, with Steve and Ian (the other former MBA students) facilitating the other.

Because she had a great deal of experience with the technique, Fran would manage the process on her own, working to get the ovals into clusters and beginning to establish the relationships between ovals. Rob would work to the back or side of the group using a portable computer to capture the material in *Decision Explorer*. The material on the wall would thus be available for future reference. On the other side of the room divider, Ian and Steve would both work on prompting the participants to surface material, help them structure it into the clusters and begin to elicit the linkages. They would put the material into the portable computer at the end of the meeting. The outcome would be the same for both subgroups.

The session would aim to start at 9.00 a.m. Coffee would be provided at 8.45 a.m. to try to ensure that people arrived early so that a prompt start could be made. As all of the participants were very busy, Fran and Ros agreed that the session would finish at 12.30 p.m., with lunch being provided as a reward for those who could stay. There would thus be about three hours of working time.

Fran thought it was important to meet with Rob, Ian and Steve to inform them of what she and Ros had agreed, and to provide them with as much context as she could. None of the past MBA students knew much about the situation, but, like Fran, what mattered most was their mapping and facilitation skills. Using the group-mapping technique would allow them quickly to gain an understanding of the issue and their lack of knowledge meant that they wouldn't fall into any traps created by making incorrect assumptions. During this facilitator meeting, they agreed that they would **arrive early so that all the necessary preparation could be carried out before participants started to arrive**. Preparations would include getting the flipchart paper put up, making sure that the agenda, focus question and participant groupings were written on flipchart sheets and posted on the wall, and making sure that the furniture in the room was organized to facilitate the mapping process.

The day began with Fran, Steve, Rob and Ian arriving at 8.00 a.m. ready to prepare the room. The folding wall was moved into position, with just the last section remaining open so that the facilitators could check the progress of the other team. Each side of the wall was covered with 18 sheets of flipchart paper, two rows of nine sheets each (see the photograph in Figure 6.1), as this would **allow lots of room for the participants' contributions to be captured and structured**.

Fran wrote up the focus question twice (once for each subgroup), as well as an agenda and list of the members of the two groups. Ros arrived at 8.15 a.m. to check everything was OK and to review her and Fran's introductions. By 8.30 a.m. all was ready and the participants were starting to arrive.

At 9.10 a.m. (only 10 minutes behind schedule) Ros kicked off the meeting and started by thanking people for attending, particularly the nine board members. She then spent time reviewing the situation regarding the merger discussions and asking everyone to contribute to the morning's discussion, as it would form the basis of the decision that had to be made within the next two weeks. She finished by asking everyone to introduce themselves in a "round robin" (particularly for the facilitators' benefit).

Figure 6.1   *Setting up the room.* The focus question placed above the
flipchart paper and a semi-circle of chairs.

Fran thanked the group again and started to explain the process. She
noted that the group-mapping technique had been used to support
many different groups working on all sorts of issues and problems,
and that it had proved to be useful and usually enjoyable. She
described it as "brainstorming with a difference" (i.e. it would allow
the group to surface opportunities and benefits, ideas and
suggestions, actions, difficulties, issues and context in an effective
and efficient manner). To help make the point, she reflected on how
most meetings result in some members getting little or no airtime,
and that in many circumstances participants think the meeting is
"going round in circles". Fran explained that the process allowed
everyone to write up their ideas as and when they thought of them,
essentially getting the chance to speak simultaneously. She also
noted that the capturing and structuring process helped build a
shared understanding and helped avoid going over old ground. The
process would help the group manage the complexity of multiple
inputs and move forward based on a shared understanding.

Fran then spent time carefully **explaining what the meeting's
tasks were and why they were being carried out**. Working

through the agenda (written up on a flipchart so that everyone could see it easily), Fran explained that the two subgroups would first surface their views relating to the issue. Then each subgroup would begin to explore the clusters created by the facilitators – first to check that the facilitators had done a reasonable job, and second to begin to clarify how each "oval" contribution related to those around them. As a result of this structuring process, more material might be surfaced, gradually moving the group to a shared understanding of the issue. Finally, the subgroups would finish by prioritizing the clusters according to their importance and urgency.

On completing this part of the introduction, Fran went on to **review the "ground rules"**. The first "rule" (and the one that always gets a chuckle) was "**if there is something that you don't agree with written up and posted on the wall, you are not allowed to remove it**!" Instead, think about why you disagree (or agree) with the statement, write a comment down on an "oval" and post it next to the "offending" statement. This way the group can understand the rationale behind your response and build on it. **The only time an oval statement can be removed is when there is direct duplication, and removal will be done with the agreement of the entire group**.

The next rule requested that participants "**keep oval statements to around 7-10 words**." This was partly to facilitate the structuring process and partly to ensure that everyone could read the contribution from where they sat. The final rule related to stockpiling, "if contributions are sitting in a pile then it is impossible for others to build on them! Instead, **once two or three ovals are written up, get up and place them on the wall**."

Once again, Fran reinforced the purpose of the meeting: to surface and structure as much material as possible. She therefore strongly encouraged participants not to "self-censor". It was important to **write up everything that you can think of in relation to the issue, as this way there is a greater "wealth" of material to work from and less chance of something being missed**.

The group split into their two subgroups, with one subgroup working on one side of the folding wall and the other subgroup on the opposite side. Once again, the purpose and rules were reviewed

Figure 6.2   *Putting up the ovals.* This group is starting to put their ovals up
on the wall (note: this is not the Cardonald College Group).

and participants were asked if there were any questions. Fran then
handed ovals and pens out to her group and asked them to get
started. At first the group felt a little uncertain, which is typical.
Someone had to be first, and participants are sometimes tentative
and self-conscious to begin with. What should they write? How
much? Who was to be first to put something on the public wall? (See
photograph in Figure 6.2.) Fran **encouraged the group to start
writing and then post the ovals on the wall**. She also spent time
helping those who weren't sure what to do.

Once the first ten or so ovals were posted, the participants got the
idea and oval statements began to emerge quickly. Examples of ovals
placed were:

- Competition from others.
- Make best use of resources.
- Avoid threat of losing advanced classes.

During this process, Fran began to **move the ovals into clusters of
apparently related material** to the best of her ability. Before

doing this, she reassured the participants that they would get a chance to work through each of the clusters once the flow of ideas had died down, so they could check to make sure that the right material was in each cluster. Putting the material into clusters helped the group manage the mass of information more effectively. Rather than becoming overwhelmed with the amount appearing in front of them and therefore being hesitant to contribute more, participants could keep raising material, often surfacing previously unconsidered options and constraints. When a cluster began to become very large, meaning more than 30 statements, Fran **explored whether there were two clusters embedded in the material**. For example, initially she had a cluster on staffing. Closer scrutiny, however, revealed that there were two subclusters – one focusing on providing career opportunities and the other on ensuring a good working culture. While these were related, they appeared to be separate clusters in their own right.

While moving the ovals around and putting them into clusters, Fran also **numbered each of the ovals (using a red pen)**. This was to help Rob, who was putting material into the *Decision Explorer* software package. If Fran hadn't numbered the ovals, he would not have easily known which of the statements he had captured and which were missing (see the related point in Chapter 3). The numbering process would also help later on, when the participants began to explore how the various contributions related to one another. Numbers are particularly helpful when one contribution is in one corner of the wall and the other is diametrically opposite. In this case, instead of drawing a lengthy and messy arrow all the way across the map, a small arrow can be drawn from the oval of origin and at the arrow's tip can be written the number of the oval to which it points.

Finally, by numbering the ovals Fran was able to let the group know how many contributions they had surfaced, allowing them to feel good about their progress and also to compare how they had progressed compared with the other group. To keep an account of where she was with the numbering, Fran **wrote the last number used on the edge of the flipchart paper**.

Along with continually asking participants to consider issues, constraints, options and outcomes, Fran began to ask them to

word the contributions in an action-oriented manner. For example one participant had written on an oval "small is beautiful". Fran gently enquired if the proponent could explain a little more about this. After some discussion, he reworded the statement to read "Exploit advantages of small is beautiful." Others had written questions, such as "What are the effects on funding?" When this contribution was converted to an action "explore what are the effects on funding", it in turn gave rise to a range of options that would help achieve this, as well as clarity regarding the consequences. One of the participants commented that this process of incorporating an action orientation encouraged them to *be clearer in their own mind what the statement comprised rather than just offering some vague concern*.

In the first part of this session, it was almost all Fran could do to understand the ovals being posted and get them roughly into clusters. But she also tried when she could to **ensure that all were contributing**. When people were not writing on ovals, Fran would unobtrusively chat with them, asking them what they thought of the process, finding out their views and prompting them to write them down on ovals. This way those who were the quiet ones of the group began to surface material, ensuring a wider range of alternatives and potentially more ownership of the outcomes.

Before calling a break for coffee, Fran **did a quick review of the clusters**. She highlighted what each cluster was about by reading aloud a selection of contributions and attempting to summarize the content. She tried to make sure in this summary that there was a contribution from each person by quickly examining the various styles of handwriting.

This review helped the group make sense of what they had surfaced, consider whether they had missed any key areas (indicated by the clusters) and begin to get some "added value" as they could see what the emergent issues were. Fran also commented that in the 30 minutes that had just elapsed, the group had generated around 80 contributions. Finally, she **outlined what the next steps would be**. Participants went off to coffee feeling pleased with their productivity and *surprised at the extent of the material surfaced. There was more to the issue than they had realized*.

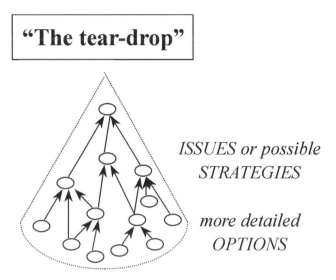

Figure 6.3   Positioning the ovals.

While the participants were relaxing with coffee, Fran and Rob **used the coffee break to tidy up the clusters.** First, they **made sure that there was lots of room between each cluster so that the separation (and therefore categorization) could be easily seen.** This helps participants work with the richness of the material. Next, they checked each cluster to ascertain that the material in each was as appropriate as possible. Finally, in the last few minutes of the coffee break they tried to **position the ovals so that those that were superordinate outcomes or issues (broad motherhood-and-apple-pie statements) were at the top of the cluster and the more detailed options and assertions were at the bottom.** (See Figure 6.3.)

For example, the following statements appear in the cluster relating to "impact on staff":

- 14 Communicate with staff and other stakeholders regarding the process.

- 49 Salary levels affected by others are becoming larger.

- 53 Uncertainty about the future.

- 54 Job security for staff (five years).

- 56 Ensure funding of staff.

- 57 Consider attrition of staff through mergers.

- 121 Maintain staff confidence and morale.

- 127 Consider response if asked to take on redundant staff from merged colleges.

- 135 Loss of staff to merged colleges who headhunt.

- 137 Recruit good staff for merged college.

- 155 Determine the effect on the career path for staff.

On reviewing these, it seemed that "121 maintain staff confidence and morale" was quite broad and could be affected by "uncertainty about the future", which in turn could be affected by "job security for staff" ($54 \rightarrow 53 \rightarrow 121$). There also seemed to be a second chain of argumentation relating to staff levels due to the merger, starting with "consider attrition of staff through mergers" to ovals 137 and 127 ($57 \rightarrow 137$, $57 \rightarrow 127$). The cluster, once structurally "tidied", showed several potential chains of argument to be worked through by the participants. Map 6.1 shows the tidied-up version of this cluster. The tidying up was to help with the next step. Fran and Rob's 15-minute coffee break had sped past.

Having had a break, the participants returned to the room refreshed and interested to see what the next steps might turn out to be. Fran quickly reviewed the clusters again for the group (just to act as a memory jog), before asking them which cluster they would like to start examining in more detail. Not surprisingly, they chose the cluster relating to funding, a subject very close to their hearts. Fran **started by reading out all of the contributions in the cluster**, partly so that participants knew what was in the cluster and partly to check that all the components were in the right group. Then together they began to **develop the chains of argument within the cluster**.

Starting with the oval "research what will the effect of funding be", one of the participants noted that progress might be made if they "understand the attitude of the funding council if we don't change", another oval in the cluster. Fran moved this oval to just beneath the other. Another of the participants commented that the oval dealing

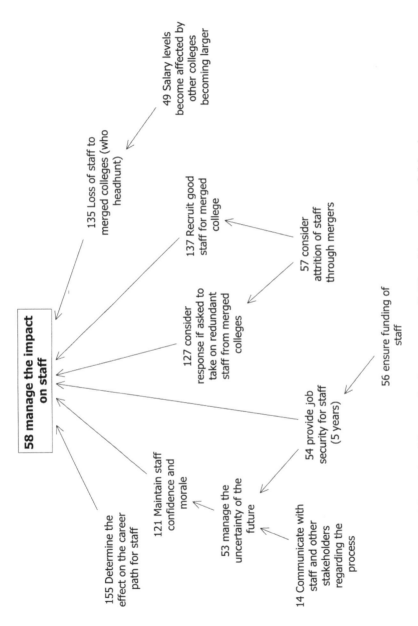

Map 6.1 *Manage the impact on staff*. The tidy version of this cluster.

with "relationship with the funding council may be weakened because we are less engaged with them" would also have an impact on funding. Again, Fran moved the oval to adjoin the others, but this time she noted that **there seemed to be two statements embedded within the oval and it is a good idea to separate them so that they can be explored fully.** Thus, the first might be "weaken relationship with the funding council", while the second, which supported it, might be "Cardonald College is less engaged with the funding council". Before making these changes, she checked with the contributor to make sure he was happy with this. She then drew an arrow from the latter statement to the former statement.

One of participants noted that the college needed to work actively on maintaining a strong relationship with the funding council. As this was new material, Fran **requested that the new contribution be written up on an oval so that it could be included in the cluster.** The participant was happy to do so. It is always a good idea to get participants to write up the new material, as new contributions can often come quickly and it is important to make sure they are captured in the proponent's handwriting rather than the facilitator's.

Once the oval had been placed on the wall, another participant noted that working on the relationship would help the college "get its share of investment in the estate (or physical plant)", another of the ovals in the cluster. Fran asked, "Why is it important to 'research what the effects will be of the funding council's decision'?" Virtually everyone answered her with comments relating to "have a clearer idea of the amount of grant in aid", which is the amount of financial support they would receive from the council. Knowing the amount would help them "determine whether or not to merge", which would contribute towards "maximize resources for students". Fran made sure that both of these contributions were captured and the links between them drawn into the developing map. Fran **continued the process of laddering both up and down the chains of argument, continually asking the group about options and constraints as well consequences.** This process of structuring and elaborating the cluster resulted in one member of the group commenting, "*The structuring process shows that there is a lot more to this issue than I had realized and a lot* *more options open to us.*" The process had helped her feel more in control.

During this discussion, it became clear to Fran that there were some contributions that were beginning to sound as though they were key issues and possibly goals. For example, the statement "maximize resources for students" was definitely important to all those attending the workshop, and sounded to Fran like a key issue. She began to **build up the hierarchy, putting potential goals at the top with key issues supporting them, then options/assertions and context supporting them**. To do this, Fran flagged the potential key issue "maximize resources for students" with an asterisk, noting her action to the group and explaining why she had done this. They immediately caught on and demanded that two other ovals in the cluster be similarly marked. One of these, "research what will be the effects on funding", they commented was more short term, but still very important and therefore key. The other, "penetrate communities and work places more effectively", was more long term and reflected the values held by many of the group.

Fran continued to work through the contributions in the cluster, moving the ovals so that those supporting another oval were lower down the wall than the oval that appeared to be a consequence. Once she felt that she had moved and structured the ovals into the desired hierarchy, she began to **draw in all the links between these different contributions**. As she did so, participants added more comments, both to alternative links between the material and new contributions that helped create other links. This process continued until the group was satisfied with both the completeness of the contributions and their linkages.

This process of beginning to link material together was interesting to the group. They began to see how differently various people perceived the situation, and through the discussion gained a much wider perspective. A buzz of energy ensued.

As they worked through the material, it became evident that some of the ovals in the cluster related to ovals in other clusters. For example, the oval stating "get our share of investment in estate [physical plant]" was linked to "maintain high and positive public profile" in the cluster about public relations, and to "penetrate communities and work places more effectively" in the cluster on increasing access in the community. Fran **made sure that these cross-cluster links were captured, since they helped reveal how the decision areas were interconnected; that is, how decisions in one area have an affect on another area.** In addition, rather than spending too much time debating which cluster an oval should be placed in, using small arrows to indicate cross-cluster links helped Fran move the group forward. It became clear to the group that *dealing with the issues in isolation (i.e. not looking at the cross-cluster links) would not only reduce the effectiveness of the action but also potentially result in unsustainable outcomes.*

As a final step, Fran **reviewed the material in the cluster for a last check.** In doing so, she pointed out which were the key issues, how the various ovals supported one another, and how various contributions supported some of the material in other clusters. One of the participants noted, "I've never considered this issue so fully and *spending all this time developing it means I have a greater understanding and feel more confident about handling it.*"

To signal the cluster's boundaries, Fran drew a rough line around the cluster (see Figure 6.4), clearly illustrating which of the ovals were within the cluster and which were part of a different cluster. She also gave the cluster a label (e.g. funding, student/learners). However, partly due to the lack of time and partly to the number of key issues identified, these labels were short and not action oriented (which is the preferred mode).

The subgroup continued to work through the clusters, adding new material (the wall map finally totalled around 120 contributions), exploring how the ovals related to one another and building a sense of shared understanding. While they worked through more of the material, the process of making cross-cluster links became easier. As each cluster was completed, the participants had a greater under- standing and awareness of the material on the wall.

However, some participants were a little concerned that time was passing and they were unsure whether all the clusters would be covered within the time available. Fran **reassured the group that the first cluster usually takes quite a long time**. This is because participants need to become familiar with the process of structuring the ovals. In addition, as they work through each of the clusters they will also become more familiar with the content of the other clusters, and therefore be able to make the cross-cluster linkages more efficiently. *The process of linking statements in one cluster to statements in other clusters also began to give the group some idea of which of the options were most potent –* something they found very useful.

By 12.20 p.m. all the clusters had been reviewed, the contents elaborated, links drawn in and key issues noted (see Figure 6.4). Fran reminded the group that the final task before lunch was prioritization. **Getting participants to reveal their preferences about which of the issues they felt deserved the greatest priority provides useful feedback.** Knowing the participants' priorities would also help the college make sure it dealt with most important issues before the final deadline. In addition, **carrying out the prioritization task would give the participants a sense of closure**, an important part of facilitating groups.

To perform the task, Fran used self-adhesive "dots" as indicators of preferences. To determine how many of these preference indicators (sticky dots) each participant should have, she employed the rule of thumb that participants should receive two dots for every three clusters. By using this ratio, there was a greater likelihood that every participant would place at least one of his or her preferences on at least one of the clusters that received the most preferences and was therefore considered a priority. This allocation process helps build ownership and commitment, as participants feel their views have been taken into account, while at the same time reducing the number of issues on which to focus.

Fran in fact gave each participant two sets of dots – green and red. While both were to indicate importance, the red dots signified urgency, whereas the green ones were to identify important areas of a more long-term nature. She explained that participants could, if they wished, **place all of the preference indicators (of either or both colours) on one of the clusters, if they felt it was so important it demanded the entire allocation, or scatter them**

**across the different clusters near to the labels. She made sure
that the prioritization explanation was very clear so as to
avoid mistakes and misunderstandings.**

Participants quickly got the hang of the task and began to scrutinize
the clusters, watching where others placed their dots and placing
their own. Some carefully considered all of the clusters, made a
mental note where they wanted to place their dots and then got up
and did so; others wandered up and down the wall slowly, sticking a
dot here and a dot there before moving on. All of the participants
appeared to be completely engrossed with the task.

Finally, at 12.30 p.m. all the participants had used up their dots and
Fran was able quickly to calculate the results. Not surprisingly, the
cluster around "funding" received the greatest number of red dots,
followed by the cluster relating to "looking after staff". The cluster
depicting "meeting business needs" and the cluster "keeping up
with different modes of learning" received the greatest number of
green dots.

Following on from this review of the results, Fran returned to the
agenda that had been announced at the beginning of the session.
She **revisited each of the tasks, reflecting on what had been
achieved, giving participants a sense of achievement**, as well as
promising to **provide a report comprising the maps and other
details within the next two weeks**. In doing so, she was able to
note that the participants had surfaced and structured a considerable
amount of information and had therefore comprehensively
addressed the issue "What are the consequences of not merging?".

Finally, she asked Ros to lead a final review of the morning's effort,
which included **providing a brief explanation of what the next
steps would be,** then thanking all the participants for their hard
work and inviting them to lunch. Before heading off for lunch, many
of the participants came up to Ros, Fran and the other facilitators
and noted how much they had enjoyed the process, and how it had
helped them with their thinking. Ros, Fran, Rob, Steve and Ian were
pleased. Members of both the SMG and the board also commented
that they were pleased that they (both constituencies) now **shared a
common view**.

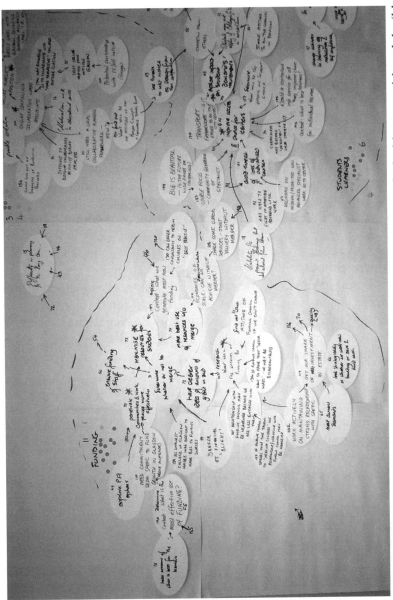

Figure 6.4 *Identifying clusters.* The dotted line shows a cluster. Key items are marked with an asterisk and the 'blobs' show the results of the prioritization exercise.

Postscript

The second group finished 10 minutes later with a similar amount of material. Interestingly enough, while there was obviously some overlap between the two groups' efforts in terms of the issues addressed, there were also a number of differences. Fran's group had addressed more issues than Ian and Steve's, whereas Ian and Steve's had considered some of the issues in more depth, particularly concentrating on an interesting feedback loop.

Following the meeting, Steve and Ian worked to capture their material in *Decision Explorer* and Fran then worked to merge the two subgroups' efforts together. She analysed the resulting map (see Resource B in this book) and presented the results, along with the merged maps, to Ros in a report. On the basis of what they produced, the college decided to "go it alone", a decision it has not regretted.

Moreover, although Fran was a little apprehensive about letting loose a group of relatively inexperienced "mappers" on a real group with a significant issue, all who attended considered the meeting to be very productive. Subsequently, when the SMG and board wanted to do a major review of the college's strategy, they asked the team back – much to the team's delight.

In reviewing the exercise with her three colleagues, a number of other interesting learning points emerged. First, Rob observed that *providing a confident sounding introduction to the technique appeared to instil a sense of trust in the process and therefore encourage participants to be more open to the process.* Once progress was being made participants quickly got into the swing of things, but getting started required care. Another insight came from Steve, who commented that *keeping the clusters tightly formed spatially (rather than scattered across the wall) helped participants manage the extensiveness of the material.* Participants were able to work on clearly defined "chunks" one at a time (while capturing cross-cluster impacts).

Finally, Ian commented that *it was really useful having some members of the groups who had previous experience of the process – they could help others, giving the facilitators more time to focus on structuring the material.* Unfortunately, as he reflected, this wasn't always going to be possible.

Conclusion

As noted earlier, organizations frequently experience situations in which an opportunity or threat emerges and they have to make a decision about how to act. In order to do this as comprehensively and quickly as possible, a three-hour meeting can be very effective when it involves those who have knowledge on the area, who will be expected to implement any decisions, and who will be affected by the consequences (particularly if they are powerful people).

The group-mapping process not only allows a considerable amount of information to be elicited, but does so in a way that allows everyone to speak, rather than having to wait for a gap in the conversation. In addition, it helps the group move from a position of divergence to one of convergence, as they begin to understand how differently they view the situation, how the contributions of one can affect the contributions of another and how their preferences coincide. Thus a more sustainable outcome is developed.

In addition, participants usually say that this form of group mapping is fun. Group mapping works best when the issue is one that is not highly interpersonal. For example, it works well on such questions as how best to capitalize on the benefits of e-commerce, how to manage a new competitor or collaborator, whether to move to a new location and so on. An alternative approach to group mapping is presented in Chapter 8, in which a series of interviews of individuals was carried out first by using cognitive mapping. The cognitive maps were then merged and the group worked on the merged map.

Process guidelines

Preparation
- Find an appropriate room with plenty of flat wall space away from the distractions of day-to-day business.

- Produce an unambiguous 10–15-word focus question for the group that provides sufficient direction (while not closing down fruitful discussion).

- Explore who the participants will be, as this helps in anticipating potential conflicts and planning the meeting more effectively.

- Allow lots of airtime for the participants to ensure that everyone can contribute.

- Ensure that all the necessary materials are available.

- Be sure to provide participants with a degree of anonymity.

- Arrive early so that all the necessary preparation (flipchart paper put up and the agenda and focus question written and ready to use) can be carried out before participants started to arrive.

- Allow lots of space on the flipchart paper for the contributions to be captured and structured.

Beginning the session

- Start with an introduction from the client.

- Explain to the entire group the process to be followed and the meeting's objectives.

- Note that the capturing and structuring process helps build a shared understanding and, importantly, avoids going over old ground.

- Review the "ground rules".

  - If there is something that you don't agree with written up and posted on the wall, don't remove it. Add your own oval that points out why you disagree.

  - Keep "oval" statements to around 7–10 words.

  - Once you have written two or three ovals, get up and place them on the wall.

- Get group members to write up everything that they can think of in relation to the issue, as this way there is a greater "wealth" of material with which to work and less chance of something being missed.

- Encourage the group to start writing on ovals with a coloured felt-tipped pen and post the ovals on the wall.
- Help those who aren't sure what to do.
- Number each of the ovals using a coloured felt-tipped pen.
- Write the last number used on the edge of the flipchart paper to keep track of the numbering.

Clustering the ovals

- Move the ovals into clusters of apparently related material.
- When there are many ovals in a cluster, explore whether there are two or more clusters embedded in the material.
- Word the contributions in an action-oriented manner.
- Ensure that everyone has been contributing. One way to do this is by checking the handwriting for a quick review of the clusters.
- Outline what the next steps will be.
- Use any breaks to tidy the clusters.
- Make sure that there is lots of room between each cluster so that the separation (and therefore categorization) can be easily seen.

Structuring clusters

- Position the ovals so that the superordinate outcomes or issues (that is, those that are broad motherhood-and-apple-pie items) are at the top of the cluster, and the more detailed options and assertions are at the bottom.
- Start by reading out to the group all of the contributions in the cluster.
- Develop the chains of argument within the cluster.

- Where there seem to be two statements on the oval, it is a good idea to separate them by making two ovals so that they can be explored fully.

- Request that new contributions be written on an oval so that they can be included in clusters.

- Continue the process of laddering both up and down the chains of argument, continually asking the group about options and constraints as well as consequences.

- Build up the hierarchy by putting potential goals at the top with key issues supporting them, and options, assertions and context supporting the key issues.

- Draw in all the links between these different contributions.

- Make sure that cross-cluster links are captured, as they help reveal how the decision areas are interconnected and how decisions in one area have an affect on another area.

- Review the material in the cluster for a final check.

- Reassure the group that the first cluster usually takes quite a long time.

Attaching priorities to clusters

- Get participants to reveal their preferences concerning which issues they feel have the greatest priority provides useful feedback.

- Carry out a prioritization exercise gives participants a sense of closure.

- Make sure that the explanation about how to indicate priorities is very clear so as to avoid mistakes and misunderstandings.

- Place all of the preference indicators (of either or both colours) on one of the clusters, if participants feel the issue is so important that it demands the entire allocation, or scatter them across the different clusters near to the labels.

Providing closure to the session

- Revisit each of the tasks reflecting on what has been achieved, giving participants a sense of achievement.
- Produce a report comprising the maps and other details within the following two weeks.
- Provide a brief explanation of what the next steps will be.

Learning points

The group

- Spending time getting the issue question right can clarify the purpose of the workshop considerably.
- It is worth working hard to be clearer regarding what the statement comprises rather than merely noting some vague concern.
- Be prepared to be surprised at the extent of the material that is surfaced. There may be more to the issue than the group realizes.
- "There are a lot more options open to us than we initially believed."
- Avoid dealing with the issues in isolation from one another, as this not only reduces the effectiveness of the action but also potentially results in unsustainable outcomes.
- Spending time developing the "picture" means that you have a greater understanding and feel more confident about handling it.
- The process of linking statements in one cluster to statements in other clusters gives the group some idea of which of the options would be most potent if resources were infinite.
- The two constituencies appreciated sharing a common view.

The facilitators

- Providing a confident-sounding introduction to the technique appeared to instil a sense of trust in the process and therefore encourage participants to be more open to the process.

- Keeping the clusters tightly formed spatially (rather than scattered across the wall) helped participants manage the extensiveness of the material.

- Having some members of the groups who have had experience of the process before is helpful – they could help others, giving the facilitators more time to focus on structuring the material.

Notes

1   The oval mapping technique was developed by Eden in the 1970s. The original cards were based on 80-column computer cards rather than the current oval cards. Through time, the cards were trimmed and transformed into ovals. Our view, after 20 years of exploration and use, is that ovals are both theoretically sound and practically more effective. The use of rectangular Post-it pads suffers from "rectangular thinking" where structures are inclined to rows and columns, and the use of hexagons encourages "six-sided thinking". Although neither is as effective as ovals for generating free-form causal map structures, we would encourage everyone to try oval mapping even if oval cards or oval Post-it pads are not available.

2   While Blu-tac® (a specific form of self-adhesive putty) is recommended as the best option for attaching flipchart sheets to the wall, it is not always available outside the UK and therefore masking tape works as a viable alternative.

7

Small College Hoping *not* to Get Smaller!

IN THE PREVIOUS CHAPTER, OVAL MAPPING WAS USED TO address an important strategic issue involving a number of related sub-issues. In this chapter we show how the oval mapping technique (OMT) can be used to guide overall strategy development for an organization – in this case a small, not-for-profit college in the US named Hope College – including helping it focus attention on its purpose, goals and the strategic issues that need to be addressed. But the general approach could be used with many different kinds of public, for-profit and not-for-profit organizations – indeed, with any organization wishing to attend to its purpose, goals, issues and strategies.

The story we present is a composite of several different cases in which John and Chuck have been involved. That way we are able to reveal more of the content of the map than would be the case otherwise, because anonymity can be preserved. Fifteen people participated in a single mapping episode designed to help articulate the basics of a strategic plan (mission, goals and basic strategy areas) for the small college. Normally, we suggest that no more than ten people be involved in constructing a single map, but having more people seemed to work in this case, in part because a facilitator – rather than the members of the group – was placing the ovals on the map and linking them with arrows. This approach is different from the more typical use of the OMT, but helps manage and reduce the complexity of a large group.

John and Chuck took turns being the "up-front" facilitator working with the map – a fairly intensive process – and the person entering the map into the *Decision Explorer* software and reflecting on the group's progress. **Using two facilitators in this way is similar to the Cardonald College case, although one facilitator would have been enough, and the process would have worked well without using the software.** In this case, two facilitators were used because John and Chuck were working with the organization on its broader strategic planning process, and the software made it easier to keep and use a record of the work.

Presenting the Cardonald College and Hope College chapters side by side allows for some important comparisons and contrasts, and therefore we hope some meaningful learning for you, the reader. There are a variety of ways to approach mapping. By presenting the two fairly similar, but also different, chapters we hope to help you think more carefully about how to apply mapping in your own practice. The Hope College case differs from the Cardonald College case in the following ways:

- The intervention took place over a day and a half rather than a half day, and used a hotel away from the college rather than a meeting room on site.

- Hope College is a non-profit organization that is more reliant on a broader range of funding sources than the public-sector Cardonald College, most (though not all) of whose income comes through a government grant.

- The mapping process focuses on developing an overall organizational strategy that considers a broader range of issues.

- A broader range of stakeholders is involved in the mapping process, many of whom did not know one another when the exercise began.

- The up-front facilitator is more actively involved in putting ovals on the wall.

- There is an agenda with approximate times attached to it, whereas in the Cardonald case there were only start and finish times listed. This was in order to keep participants from getting attached to breaks at particular times instead of focusing on completing a task.

- The process begins not with mapping, but with an "ice-breaker" exercise designed to help build relationships and set the stage for mapping.

- Additional alternatives are offered for how to use the mapping surface and sticky dots while mapping.

- There is additional discussion about how to preserve an oval map.

- There is additional discussion about map content because the case is a composite, and therefore confidentiality will not be breached.

The mapping episode focuses on articulating a way forward for a college in serious trouble. Hope College is a small undergraduate liberal arts college located in the Appalachian mountains of the southeastern United States. It was founded as a non-profit organization in the late 1940s with the support of a Protestant denomination. Its purpose was to provide local students with an opportunity to gain a college education with an emphasis on liberal arts and teacher preparation.

Until 1990 enrolment was approximately 500 students per year, but then a new president arrived and began a major expansion programme. Enrolment increased dramatically to over 1500 students per year. A major building programme was also begun, with financing expected to come from increases in tuition and fee revenues. Faculty teaching loads were greatly increased and the morale of both faculty and students declined. The debt undertaken to finance the new buildings was difficult to service. A number of new continuing education and service initiatives were begun to bolster revenue, but the college was not equipped to deliver them well. Fundraising efforts faltered. Enrolments began to decline as well, while faculty unrest increased to the point that some were calling for the president's resignation. Unexpectedly, the president did resign in early 2000. The board appointed an interim president and offered her its support for the necessary changes.

The interim president decided that she had to initiate and lead the college through a major strategy change effort. She hired John and Chuck to help. After consulting with them, she decided that several things had to occur early in the process. First, a quick assessment was needed of the current situation to demonstrate that change was being initiated and thus ensure that the demotivated staff did not leave. Second, a representative group of key stakeholders needed to be assembled for a retreat to review the assessment and to figure out a rough outline of the goals and strategies that might be used to improve the college's situation. She thought the group should include representatives of the board, faculty, administration, students, alumni, potential donors and townspeople, among others. Third, the group's sense of what needed to be done should provide key inputs to the job description for the next president, inform the search committee's efforts to recruit and evaluate candidates, and guide the new president during his or her first months in office. The job description and conversations with involved stakeholders would also help candidates decide whether they were qualified for the job and interested in taking it. This chapter reports on the stakeholder retreat held after the assessment process, reported on next, had been carried out.

An "assessment committee" comprising selected board members, faculty, administrators, students and alumni was given six weeks to produce a report on the current situation. Committee members spoke with a number of others via interviews and focus groups, and also engaged the services of a consulting firm specializing in higher education to help them gather information on other colleges. In brief, they found the following facts:

- Enrolment is down to 1200.

- Student morale is very low and instances of vandalism by students are on the increase.

- The college does not have an effective enrolment management system.

- Faculty members are over-extended and often have to teach courses outside of their area of expertise. There is little or no time for faculty to update existing courses or for professional development. Faculty morale is quite low, in part because they have not received a raise in three years.

- The average age of faculty members is 50 and a number of retirements are expected soon. There might be more retirements if an attractive early retirement package were offered.

- The college is in a small mountain community of 5000 that is also a popular tourist destination. The closest major town is 25 miles away and has a population of 50 000. There are three other small, private colleges in the area, and a popular state college is 50 miles away. There are possibilities for collaboration and programme differentiation among the colleges.

- There is probably a market for major continuing education and service initiatives, but the college lacks the capacity to deliver them.

- The college has a reputation within the community for being poorly managed and for having more than its share of unruly students.

- The college still has a large capital debt due to the building expansion programme.

- There are some wealthy alumni and other potential benefactors who might be tapped for major financial contributions, but only if the college can make a persuasive case on its behalf.

Preparing for the Retreat

With the quick assessment done, the interim president invited a group of 15 stakeholder representatives (many of whom had been on the assessment committee) to a one-and-a-half day retreat to "map out" a potential future for the college, to discuss next steps in the process and to explore how to search for a new president.[1] The retreat was to be held in a resort hotel located not far from the college. The interim president worked out the agenda and the details of the various exercises with John and Chuck in advance. Getting this right is crucial, as was noted in the previous chapter.

The agenda for the retreat is presented in Figure 7.1. It starts at 4.30 p.m. on the first day with an "ice-breaking" exercise, followed by dinner and a discussion. The second day is devoted to an oval

Day	Time	Topic
One	4.30–4.45 p.m.	Introduction to the retreat
	4.45–5.45 p.m.	Introduction of participants and hopes and fears exercise (see chapter text for a description)
	5.45–6.00 p.m.	Adjourn for dinner
	6.00–7.00 p.m.	Dinner
	7.00–9.00 p.m.	Discussion of assessment Report and further reflection on hopes and fears
Two	7.30–8.30 a.m.	Breakfast
	8.30–9.00 a.m.	Further discussion of assessment report
	9.00–Noon	Begin oval mapping exercise, with break in the middle
	Noon–1.00 p.m.	Lunch
	1.00–2.30 p.m.	Finish oval mapping
	2.30–2.45 p.m.	Break
	2.45–4.00 p.m.	Implications of oval map for further strategic planning
	4.00–4.30 p.m.	Discussion of implications of the map for the presidential search
	4.30–5.00 p.m.	Responses from the interim president and closing thoughts from participants

Figure 7.1   Agenda for the Hope College retreat.

mapping exercise, further discussions and development of recommendations for next steps. The scheduled finish time was 5.00 p.m. John and Chuck had previously **made sure the site would work well and agreed to assemble all of the necessary equipment and materials,** in the same way that Fran had done in the Cardonald College case.

Two of the most important preparation tasks were to **decide on the** *purpose* **of the mapping session and what the** *focus question* **would be** (in a manner similar to the previous chapter). The purpose of the mapping session – as determined by the client, the interim president – was to articulate a draft mission and set of draft goals and strategic concerns that might guide the college over the next one to three years on its way to a longer-term future. In other words, the session was to go a long way towards developing an

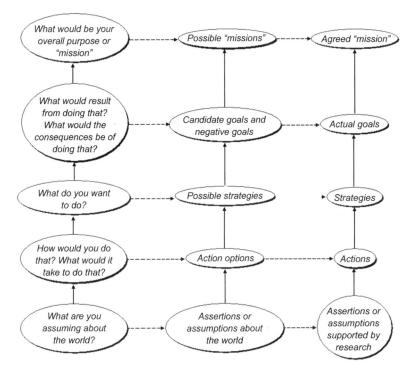

Map 7.1   *An action-oriented strategy plan.* The structure that lies behind all the maps in the book. The refinement of the statements and the analysis moves from left to right and top to bottom – or from bottom to top.

action-oriented strategy map. (See Map 7.1 (previously Figure 2.1) for the basic structure of an action-oriented strategy map.) After the map was completed and discussed, the group was to consider and suggest next steps in the strategy change process. They were also to prepare a set of recommendations to guide the search for a new president.

Once the interim president had clarified the purpose of the mapping session, it was very important to decide what the focus question would be. In other words, what question would the participants be asked to answer through mapping? The decision was made by the interim president, in consultation with John and Chuck and some key advisers, that participants should be asked: "What do you think Hope College should do over the next one to three years to assure its future?" This question was chosen because it was not clear what the college's mission, goals and strategies should be, nor was a well-articulated and credible vision available. This meant that a productive course was probably to ask participants to focus on actions that they thought Hope College might take in the next one to three years. The resulting bundles of possible actions would help identify key strategic issues that the college as a whole and the new president would need to face, and strategies would emerge from the resolution of the issues. Candidate goals could be expected to emerge by inference from the bundles of actions the college might undertake, and a candidate purpose or mission and vision would then emerge from the candidate goals. Goals, mission and vision developed in this way – by teasing them out from what people could imagine doing – are more likely to be realized because of the heightened understanding of what they might mean in practice, as well as the greater commitment to them, than if they are invented in a more abstract, ungrounded way with little direct connection to action.[2]

In other circumstances, a different focus question might have been chosen. For example, if a vision or mission statement were available to which people subscribed, the focus question might be: "What could or should Hope College do in the next several years to realize its vision (or achieve its mission)?" Or if a set of agreed goals was available, the starting question might be: "What could or should Hope College do in the next several years to achieve its goals?"

Of course, it was entirely possible that there was no viable future for the college, but that was not the assumption guiding the session. Instead, it was to begin by assuming that there was a promising future and the group's task was to discern or create it. The interim president hoped the group's thinking might reveal a powerful mission, vision or set of goals that could lead to a more promising direction than the path the college was on at present.[3]

Note how the focus question contrasts with the focus question in the Cardonald College case. There the question was: "What would be the strategic implications for Cardonald College of choosing not to engage in discussions about merger?" That question directs attention to a specific issue and its ramifications, rather than to a set of actions Cardonald should take over the next one to three years. The key point is that mapping facilitators should make sure they work with the client to **formulate a focus question that takes the context for mapping and the purpose of the session into account.**

The Hopes and Fears Exercise

The first half-day began at 4.30 p.m. with a welcome from the interim president and the chair of the board. While many of the group members knew each other, the tensions leading up to this meeting had put most people "on edge" to say the least. In addition, some group members were acting somewhat as representatives of campus constituencies and their role as a representative was not clearly understood. The session therefore began with a "hopes and fears" exercise designed to accomplish two important objectives. The first was to ensure that the issues important to the group members were immediately put "on the table" to allay any suspicions regarding hidden agendas. The second was to surface issues that were of common interest to the group. The exercise proceeded as follows:

- Before stakeholder representatives introduced themselves, they were asked to write down on separate large Post-it notes *one hope* for the college and *one fear*.

- As they introduced themselves, in addition to saying who they were and what their connection to Hope College was, they read out their hope and fear.

- As they did so, they gave the "hope" Post-it to John and the "fear" Post-it to Chuck.

- John organized the hopes into clusters sharing a common subject matter or theme, just as would be done in the early stages of oval mapping, while Chuck did the same for the fears.

The hopes essentially captured an initial sense of what some of the *key issues and implicit goals* for the college might be, while the fears captured *negative goals*. The exercise helped people get to know one another and also helped give voice to their concerns for the college. The group discussed the hopes and fears briefly and then adjourned for dinner, where the introductions and conversation continued. After dinner, the assessment report was discussed and the issues and negative goals were revisited. **The hopes and fears would be looked at again towards the end of the OMT session as a check on progress and a way of fostering a sense of accomplishment**.

The clusters of hopes (an amalgam of issues and implicit goals) included the need to:

- get more students;
- get more and better teachers;
- raise student and teacher morale;
- increase revenues;
- collaborate with other institutions of higher education;
- consider closing down the school;
- find an outstanding new president and provide the necessary support to him or her;
- reconsider the school's mission;
- maintain the physical plant;
- create better relationships with the town;
- increase revenues.

The clusters of fears focused on:

- continued decline and increasing despair;
- failure to fulfil the mission;
- unemployment and major personal disruptions for staff;
- students left stranded in their academic careers;
- a severe blow to the economy of the area.

The hopes and fears were clearly concerns that would have to be addressed, and the group agreed that they would use the retreat to figure out how to do so. ***Group members were surprised to see*** *the amount of agreement regarding both goals and problems raised by the hopes and fears exercise. Recognizing common concerns and goals helped the group begin to trust one another.*

The Oval Mapping Exercise

The next morning began with breakfast and continued briefly with dialogue focused on the assessment report and the issues identified the night before. By 9.00 a.m. the group was beginning to gel. **People had now had time to start building a relationship with one another, and to establish the beginnings of a sense of common understanding, concern, connection and trust**. The group was starting to develop a common language and a shared sense of the situation the college faced. **Since they were likely to be involved at various points in the overall strategy change effort, spending time developing an effective group early on was likely to pay off later**.

Earlier, during the time allotted for breakfast, John and Chuck had created the mapping surface in the same way that Fran and her colleagues did in the Cardonald College case. That is, they attached 18 sheets of flipchart paper to the wall in two rows of nine sheets each. There was room for additional sheets if they were needed.

They next **drew a dashed red line horizontally across the mapping surface with a marking pen, about one-third of the way down from the top. The line would be used to separate goal- and mission-related ovals above the line from strategy- and action-related ovals below the line**. The line was used to ensure that adequate space was left for goals, because they would be developed in the latter part of the mapping exercise. (A similar line was not used in the Cardonald College case because it wasn't really needed.) The group was now ready to create an oval map.

At 9.00 a.m. the group began the oval mapping exercise, which occupied them until 2.30 p.m., with about an hour out for lunch and some fresh air. In other words, the mapping exercise itself took

about four and a half hours, or about an hour longer than the
Cardonald College groups took, but a number of additional tasks
were also carried out.

The session began by asking the group to assemble in chairs in a
semi-circle around the mapping surface. Each member of the group
was given five ovals. (The number was somewhat arbitrary, but 5
ovals times 15 participants would equal 75 ideas for action,
assertions, assumptions etc., a substantial number to begin with.
More ovals could be added later as more ideas surfaced.) Then each
participant was asked to answer the focus question: "What do you
think Hope College should do over the next one to three years to
assure its future?" Material from the hopes and fears exercise
was left on the wall and so might serve as a prompt for responses,
but participants were encouraged to engage in broad-range
brainstorming.

As in the Cardonald College case, participants were asked to use the
marking pen they had been given to write their answers on the ovals,
one answer per card, written legibly and so they could be read from a
distance. Statements were to be no more than 7–10 words long.
Participants were also asked to put their answers in action terms by
beginning each with the imperative form of a verb; for example, *get,
buy, hire, create, do, analyse* and so forth. Finally, participants were
encouraged not to use the words *and, or, in order to* or *so that,* since
the presence of these words usually indicates that there is more than
one idea per card.

Once they had filled out their cards, **each participant was given a
small wad of self-adhesive putty and asked to attach a small
piece no larger than the size of a split pea to the back of each
oval in the middle towards the top**. The ovals could thus be
attached to the mapping surface. They could also be moved from
one place on the mapping surface to another without damaging the
surface, because the dab of putty was not large enough to pull the
flipchart paper apart. Tape rolls made of masking tape, or preferably
drafting tape, which is not as sticky, would also have worked.
However, if tape is used to attach ovals to the surface, the surface is
more likely to tear when an oval is moved than if self-adhesive putty
is used. Note that in the Cardonald College case oval Post-it notes
were used; they are more expensive, but do work very well.

After participants had filled out their five ovals, John **collected two (of the participant's choice) from each of the 15 participants, for a total of 30 ovals, about all he could physically hold in his hands. He then asked the group to help him place the ovals one at a time on the mapping surface in clusters held together by a common theme or subject matter. He began each cluster below the dashed line,** since answers to the question would in all likelihood be possible strategic issues, not goals or mission, as most people tend to start with the issues that are bothering them. As ovals were placed on the map – and numbered sequentially – Chuck entered them into the software. (Note that in the Cardonald College case Fran asked participants to attach their own ovals to the wall. Either approach can work, but in this case John attached the ovals himself to make arranging ovals into clusters more efficient, rather than having 15 people work on it, which would have taken more time and there might have been less overall understanding. Also, this way it was easier for Chuck to keep up with entry into the *Decision Explorer* mapping software.)

Several clusters resulted. The clusters identified *issues*, in that they outline areas of concern and possible *options* for addressing the concerns. The clusters did not represent actual *strategies*, because the group had not agreed which options to select. That would be a task for a future group or groups. These future groups would propose actual strategies once they had explored and evaluated integrated packages of options. The issue areas were:

- Refocus mission of school.

- Boost teacher morale.

- Boost student morale.

- Enforce rules of conduct.

- Increase academic standards.

- Redesign recruiting and marketing strategies.

- Increase student enrolment.

- Improve management.

- Generate more income, e.g. tuition and fees.

With these clusters in place, John collected the rest of the ovals, one card at a time in round-robin fashion, and asked the group to help him place them in the appropriate clusters, or else start a new cluster. In this case, no new clusters were created. When placing ovals on the map, he tried to make sure that the more abstract and general ideas were placed at the top of the cluster and the least abstract and most concrete ideas towards the bottom. Doing so was a way of working on building up the hierarchy of ideas. This was done to facilitate the linking of ideas in the next step. **A blue stick-on dot was placed on the most general idea in each cluster to indicate that it identified a strategic issue, defined as a cluster of related possible actions**. Fran had used a purple asterisk to identify hers.

After this was done, **additional structure was added to the clusters by pencilling in links in the form of arrows representing the causal links**. In other words, the next step involved figuring out what led to what. In order to ladder down from a strategic issue label, the facilitator kept asking "What would it take to do that?" or "How would you do that?" Pencil was used to allow the group to change its mind easily later. This is different from the Cardonald case, where Fran used a flipchart pen to draw in the links. However, she needed to be careful to get the links right. While pen can be seen better by the participants, it is harder to erase than pencil. *When John was actively engaging the group in placing ovals and drawing links, he was ensuring that they "knew" the map in such a way that they could actively work with and identify with it. As the group develops an understanding of the content within the process, they begin to see the map as "theirs" rather than the facilitators' or the administration's*.

For example, in the case of the strategic issue area "generate more income, e.g. tuition and fee income [2]", three main bundles of actions were structured or developed (see Map 7.2): "increase tuition and fee income [45]", "cut expenses [56]", and "engage in fundraising campaign [50]". Increasing tuition and fee income might occur through "increasing tuition and fee levels [45]". This would have to be done carefully, or it could lead to a decrease in student enrolment and hence a reduction in income. Cutting expenses might entail "closing the college [62]", "mothballing some buildings until finances and enrolment improved [58]", "vacating

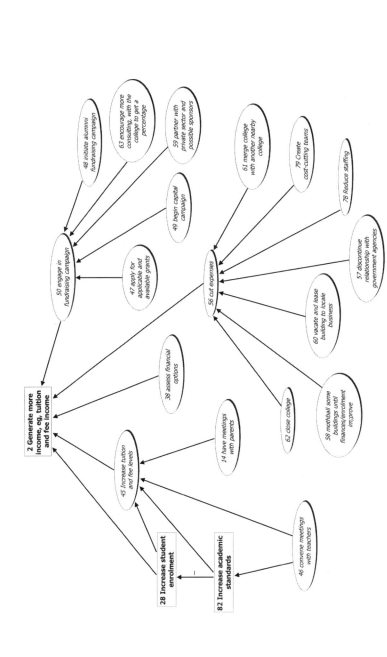

Map 7.2   *Generate more income.* This is one of the nine issue areas that the group from Hope College identified. The issue is directly affected by another issue, "increase student enrolment" (which is itself affected by five other issues) and by eighteen actions arranged in four groups.

and leasing buildings to local businesses [60]", "discontinuing relationships with government agencies [57]", "reducing staffing [78]", "creating cost-cutting teams [79]", and "merging the college with another nearby college [61]". Fundraising might involve "applying for applicable and available grants [47]", "beginning a capital campaign [49]", "partnering with private sector and possible sponsors [59]", "encouraging more consulting with the college to get a percentage [63]", and "initiating an alumni fundraising campaign [48]".

Another example of strategic issues is presented by "increase student enrolment [28]" (see Map 7.3). Effectively resolving this issue will depend on addressing five other issues, as well as figuring out what to do about the likely negative impact of "increasing tuition and fee levels" on student enrolment. "Increasing academic standards [82]" may also lead to a decrease, rather than an increase, in student enrolment. On the other hand, perhaps having "more remedial work [11]" and "partnering with local high schools [32]" could remove the minus sign (because the link is negative) between "increasing academic standards [32]" and "increasing student enrolment [28]". In addition, "refocusing the mission of the school [7]", "redesigning recruiting and marketing strategies [3]", "boosting student morale [31]" and "beginning to enforce rules of conduct [70]" may all have a positive effect on student enrolment. It could be that Hope College might have to change its target market and the way it approaches the preparation of potential students. A similar kind of structuring was done for each of the other strategic issue areas.

When completed, the issues were related in the way shown in Map 7.4. Note that in this map a really central issue appears to be how to increase student enrolment, but effectively addressing that issue depends on how the rest of the issues are addressed. Improving management is also a potent issue because it is linked to every other issue.

Once the strategic issues had been structured, the next task – which Chuck led – was to develop a set of possible goal and mission statements for the school. Specifically, the next task was to tease out the goals and mission implicit in the strategic issues. In order to do

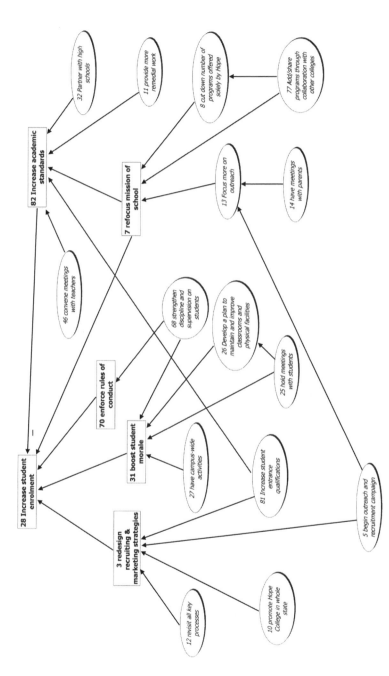

Map 7.3 *Increase student enrolment.* This issue has fifteen actions in five groups with one action from the previous map, "increase tuition and fee income", likely to have a negative impact.

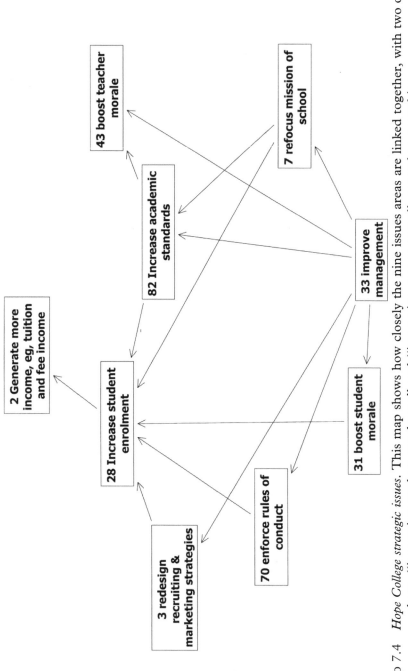

Map 7.4 *Hope College strategic issues.* This map shows how closely the nine issues areas are linked together, with two of them, "increasing student enrolment" and "improving management", central to everything.

this, Chuck gave each participant more ovals, saying that they could have even more if necessary.

He then asked the group to answer the following questions: "What would the consequences be of successfully addressing these issues? In other words, if you successfully refocused the mission of the school, boosted teacher and student morale, enforced rules of conduct, redesigned recruiting and marketing strategies, increased academic standards, increased student enrolment, improved management and generated more income, what would happen? What would result?" Through this process, he was hoping to elicit the goals that would really move the organization forward, since they emerged from what people really cared about.

Participants again filled out ovals, just as they had when creating the strategic issues. Chuck then started taking ovals from each participant and, with the help of the group, **created groupings on the mapping surface above the dashed red line**. Duplicates were eliminated by group decision once it was determined that they were in fact the same. While eliminating duplicates seems like a simple step, it does require close attention, since we have often found when exploring apparently similarly worded statements that new meanings can emerge that provide valuable insights. Then the group worked to identify the links between the issues and the statements above the line, adding ovals and changing links where necessary to complete a chain of argumentation. This approach was different from the Cardonald College case, in which Fran laddered up directly from the issues towards goals, without asking the group first to brainstorm and cluster a set of potential consequences. Either approach can work, but in this case the brainstorming and clustering approach was used to get a contribution quickly from each of the 15 participants as a way of maintaining their attention and involvement.

Once the appropriate links were made from the issues to the consequences and among the consequences, Chuck asked the group to identify which of the ovals above the line really were goals, rather than connecting statements. **Group members were each given several red dots and asked to use them to identify the statements they thought best articulated desirable goals for the college. To help the group, Chuck noted that goals were those statements that were "good in their own right".** After the pattern of dots was examined and discussed, the group agreed on the draft goal system presented in Map 7.5. As stated, the goals do not have a great deal of "zing" and sound more like somewhat flat assertions. But when compared with the present reality they certainly are aspirational, and with appropriate word-smithing they could be turned into a potential vision for the school. *Also, this represented the first "official" agreement by the group. Because they were agreeing on goals and common purposes, the process built additional trust among group members.*

The map shows a rather tightly interconnected set of candidate goals, which is often typical of goal systems. The overarching goal is simply to "improve Hope College", which was taken as the draft mission for this stage of the mapping exercise, though it hardly could be the mission for the school. It simply was not specific or inspiring enough. Everyone therefore realized that the statement would need further work, probably by clarifying what they would hope to achieve as a result of improving the college. In other words, the consequences of improving Hope College would need to be articulated through further laddering up. But for the time being all agreed that what they were trying to do is figure out how to improve Hope College so that it might survive and prosper.

Before moving on to clarify the mission, Chuck asked the group to check their map against the results of the previous day's hopes and fears exercise. Recall that the hopes included get more students, get more and better teachers, raise student and teacher morale, increase revenues, collaborate with other institutions of higher education, consider closing down the school, find an outstanding new president and provide the necessary support to him or her, reconsider the school's mission, maintain the physical plant, create better relationships with the town and, last but certainly not least, increase revenues. All of these showed up on the full map except for finding and supporting a new president. Addressing how to do this was to be the next agenda item for the retreat. The group did observe, however, that collaboration and cooperation with other institutions probably did not receive the attention they deserved. The group decided to recommend that a special task force be convened while the presidential search was underway to look at the possibilities, advantages and disadvantages of collaborating with other institutions.

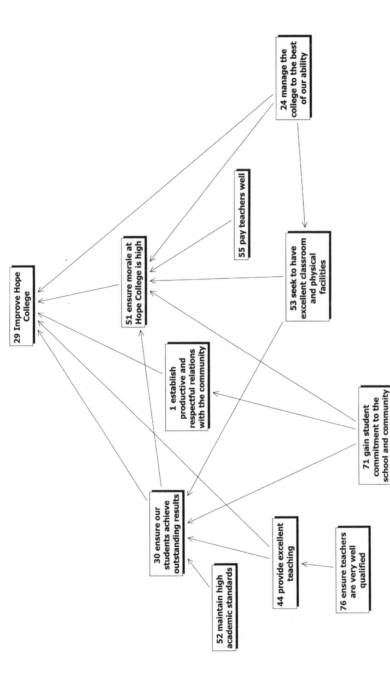

Map 7.5 *Hope College draft goals.* These candidate goals emerged from considering the consequences of successfully addressing the nine strategic issues. All of these would improve Hope College.

The clusters of fears focused on continued decline and the death of Hope College; failure to fulfil the mission; unemployment and major personal disruptions for staff; students left stranded in their academic careers; and a severe blow to the economy of the area. The group felt that the map did outline a rather hopeful future for Hope College, and thus provided a way to avoid most of the fears coming to pass. Seeing that the map checked out well against the previous day's exercise provided the group with a real sense of accomplishment.

Chuck next asked the group to refocus on the question of mission. In order to clarify what the group would recommend as a mission, he asked them to consider the following questions: "Why would you want to improve Hope College? What benefits would flow from doing so? And what would be lost if Hope College were not improved?" Responses from the group were recorded on flipchart sheets and hung on the walls. After considerable discussion, the group concluded that they thought Hope College's real mission was: "To make lasting positive educational and civic contributions to our students, partners and the community." *The group felt pride in the statement and a sense of accomplishment at having crafted it. They also knew what it would mean in practice to work towards it, as the map they had created was behind it.* A member of the group wrote: "The mission of Hope College is to make lasting positive educational and civic contributions to our students, partners and the community" on a new oval and posted it directly on top of "improve Hope College".

By now it was 2.30 p.m. The group took a short break and then resumed work on the last two agenda items: providing advice on next steps for the strategic planning process and on the search for the next president. The group discussed the fact that it would take a minimum of six months and perhaps as much as a year to hire a new president. In the meantime, it would be very unwise for Hope College not to begin addressing its most pressing issues. The group therefore urged the interim president to launch a formal strategic planning process and to appoint a strategic planning "process champion" to guide the effort on a day-to-day basis.[4] She readily agreed. *By doing so, the president was able to coalesce some powerful interests around a positive message for the college community. In essence, this overt act signalled the official "turnaround" from beleaguered victims to hopeful actors.*

John and Chuck then advised the group to reflect on the goals and issues they had identified (see Map 7.6) and to appoint a series of task forces to outline in more detail the options for achieving the goals through addressing the issues, as this would assist in the strategic planning process. After discussing both the goals and issues on the map and talking through various possibilities, the group suggested creating five task forces. These would focus on developing options and recommendations for:

- improving relations and cooperation with neighbouring institutions and the community;

- generating additional revenue, including through tuition and fee income;

- improving student enrolment and campus life;

- improving teaching and student achievement;

- improving physical facilities, including classroom and lab facilities.

The group suggested that each task force have co-chairs, one from the Hope College board or staff and the other from an external stakeholder group, as this would be likely to increase the ownership and political feasibility of the outcomes. This approach would help keep the thinking process open, improve relations with neighbouring institutions and the community, and build a larger coalition for change.[5] The co-chairs from the five task forces would also act as a strategic planning steering committee, perhaps along with some additional appointees from the college. When the task force reports were done, or even while they were still in draft form, the steering committee would review them, reconcile them and prepare a final draft strategic plan for consideration by the interim or new president (depending on when the report was done and the new president hired), the board and other stakeholders.

With this discussion out of the way, the group spent 30 minutes talking about the search for a new president. They believed that the draft mission, goals and issues on the map should help inform a draft job description. All agreed that the college should seek a president with a proven ability to achieve improvements in student achievement and enrolment, teaching excellence, physical facilities,

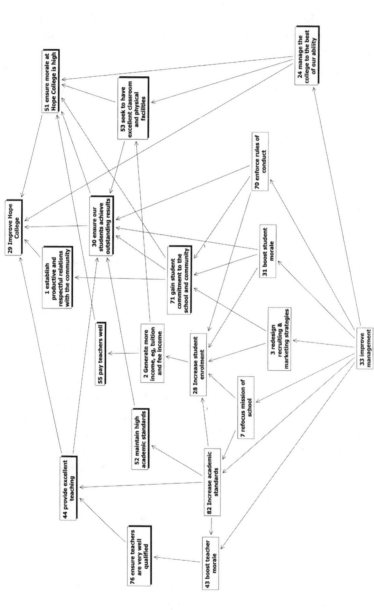

Map 7.6 *Hope College goals and issues.* After considering this map, the Hope College group created five task forces to carry forward the college's strategic planning process towards achieving its mission: "To make lasting positive educational and civic contributions to our students, partners and the community".

collaborative relationships with others and revenues. This would mean that the president should have demonstrated experience both as a leader and as a manager. Given the need to develop a broad coalition and base of support for change, the new president should also have excellent interpersonal and political skills. The points were recorded on a flipchart sheet to be typed up and reviewed by the interim president and the board.

Ending the Retreat

The president called the meeting to a close shortly before 5.00 p.m. She noted how productive it had been and thanked everyone for actively participating. She said that the group had made a major contribution to assuring the future of Hope College. She commented that this truly was a profound gift, given the despair that many throughout the community felt with regard to the college's future. She reviewed what the group had done and the recommendations they had made. She reiterated what she understood the next steps to be and made commitments for further action. And she also expressed the hope that she could call on participants in the future as the college pursued the next steps. All agreed that they would be willing volunteers. *By officially agreeing to specific recommendations, the president was able to encourage even more trust and hope. The combination of the two leads to commitment and dedicated volunteers.*

As the group was disbanding, Chuck and John took the final step in the mapping exercise, which was to **preserve the map**. This was done in three different ways. First, digital images were taken of the map as a whole and of each individual flipchart sheet. These images could be used to show what the session was like to those who could not attend, and also could be used to reconstruct the map if need be. Second, the ovals were secured to the mapping surface with long strips of tape and all of the seams were also taped. The map could then be taken down all at once and folded up into a neat package for transportation back to the president's office. The interim president intended to tape the map to her office wall and describe its importance to any and all visitors. That way the spirit of the exercise could remain alive and the excitement of a new and better future communicated to others. Finally, the map was captured in the *Decision Explorer* mapping software so that it could be reproduced and worked on in the future.

Conclusions

The Hope College experience shows how a group can use mapping to prepare a draft mission, set of goals and strategic issues quickly and easily, as well as articulate the logic linking each. There were approximately 125 concepts on the map, all linked with arrows showing what influenced what. The map took about four and a half hours to create and discuss, which is a quite an efficient use of 15 people's time. The case also shows how mapping can be used as a support to an overall strategy change process.

Process guidelines

- Make sure the site will work well and assemble all of the necessary equipment and materials.

- Decide on the *purpose* of the mapping session.

- Using two facilitators in this way is similar to the Cardonald College case, although one facilitator would have been enough and the process would have worked well without using the software.

- Decide what the starting question should be. Work with the client to formulate a focus question that takes the context for mapping and the purpose of the session into account.

- If it is important, make sure that people have enough time to start building a relationship with one another and to establish the beginnings of a sense of common understanding, concern, connection and trust.

- If a group is new and will be working together for a long time, spending time early on developing an effective group will pay off later.

- Draw a dashed red line horizontally across the mapping surface with a marking pen, about one-third of the way down from the top. The line can be used to separate goal- and mission-related ovals above the line from strategy- and action-related ovals below the line.

- Give participants a small wad of self-adhesive putty and ask them to attach a small piece no larger than the size of a split pea to the back of each oval in the middle towards the top. The ovals can then be attached to the mapping surface and easily moved around.

- The facilitator can collect two ovals (of the participant's choice) from each of the participants. The facilitator can then ask the group to help him or her place the ovals one at a time on the mapping surface in clusters held together by a common theme or subject matter. If the clusters will be identifying issues, begin each cluster below the dashed red line.

- Additional structure can be added to the clusters by pencilling in links in the form of arrows representing the causal links. The advantage of using a pencil is that links can be erased easily if need be; the disadvantage is that pencilled links are not as easy for the group to read.

- A blue stick-on dot can be placed on the most general idea in an issue cluster to indicate the name of the strategic issue, defined as a cluster of related possible actions.

- Ovals representing consequences of addressing the issues can be placed in groupings on the mapping surface above the dashed red line.

- Group members can be given several red dots and asked to use them to identify the statements that they think best articulate desirable goals for the organization.

- Preserve the map by using digital photographs, by taking the physical map away or by using *Decision Explorer* software, or some combination of the three.

Learning points

- Group members were surprised to see the amount of agreement regarding both goals and problems raised by the hopes and fears exercise. Recognizing common concerns and goals helped the group begin to trust one another.

- When John was actively engaging the group in placing ovals and drawing links, he was ensuring that the group "knew" the map in such a way that they could actively work it and identify with it. As the group developed an understanding of the content within the process, they began to see the map as "theirs" rather than as the facilitators' or the administration's map.

- Agreeing on goals represented the first "official" agreement by the group. Because they were agreeing on common purposes, the process built additional trust among group members.

- By agreeing to move ahead with a formal strategic planning process, the president was able to cement together a potent coalition of powerful interests with a positive message for the college community. In essence, this overt act signalled the official "turnaround" from beleaguered victims to hopeful actors.

- By officially agreeing to specific recommendations, the president was able to encourage even more trust and hope. The combination of the two leads to commitment and volunteers.

Postscript

As noted in the introduction, the Hope College case is a composite of several change efforts in which Chuck and John have been involved. In the cases, the mapping exercise resulted in guidance both for the organization in the near term and, in some cases, for its search for a new leader. Strategic planning task forces were used to help flesh out the options for dealing with the strategic issues the organization faced and to make recommendations on how to proceed. Each task force was co-chaired by an outsider and an insider and the co-chairs of all of the task forces served as a strategic planning coordinating committee. In the relevant cases, a job description for the new chief executive was prepared and reviewed by the board and representatives of other interested stakeholder groups. A search committee was appointed and began looking for a chief executive who could help the organization pursue its mission, achieve its goals and deal with its issues. A new sense of inspiration and collective commitment to the organization pervaded the whole community. The mapping exercise certainly did not ensure a desirable future for the organization, but it did play a key role in galvanizing collective action around pursuit of the common good.

Notes

1   For more on how to organize retreats in general, see Carol Weisman (2003) *Secrets of Successful Retreats*, St Louis, MO: F. E. Robbins and Sons.

2   For more on this point, see Colin Eden and Fran Ackermann (1998) *Making Strategy*, Thousand Oaks, CA: Sage, pp. 79–112.

3   For more on this point, see John M. Bryson (1995) *Strategic Planning for Public and Nonprofit Organizations*, revd edn, San Francisco, CA: Jossey-Bass, pp. 111–21.

4   For more on the process champion, see Bryson, *op. cit.*, pp. 215–17.

5   For more on stakeholder identification, analysis and involvement, see F. Ackermann and C. Eden (2003) Powerful and Interested Stakeholders Matter: Their Identification and Management, *Best Paper Proceedings*, Seattle, WA: Academy of Management Conference; and J. M. Bryson (2004) What to Do When Stakeholders Matter: Stakeholder Identification and Analysis Techniques, *Public Management Review*, 6(1): 21–53.

8

Making the Most of Our Assets

IN THIS CHAPTER WE DESCRIBE A CIRCUMSTANCE WHERE A "new practitioner" uses mapping to help him support others in developing a coherent plan to capitalize on an organizational opportunity. We are including this chapter as a means of illustrating how someone who is relatively new to the process is able to use the technique and gain benefit from it, as well as presenting both learning points and process guidelines that reflect this position on the learning curve.

Francis, having come across mapping and its application to strategy, was interested in trying it out for "real". He had tried mapping with friends (on their personal issues) and on his own and now wanted to further his experience. Around about this time his organization was considering how to provide a "total solutions" service to customers. This service would traverse a number of different departments and would need to be set up carefully so as enhance the organization's capabilities to customers rather than detract from them. To this end, the organization was keen to ensure that a coherent plan was developed and that those who would be key to its implementation were involved. A possible application had been found. Nevertheless, while being keen to apply the technique, Francis was also wary of doing so in his own organization, in front of his peers (and seniors). Careful design was therefore paramount.

Thus the case sets out something that is common in practice: an issue or opportunity emerging that requires consideration, negotiation and planning to ensure a sustainable future.

The company was considering setting up a new business stream, which would enable a number of skills and competencies pertinent to monitoring the integrity of assets to be integrated, and which it was anticipated would yield higher-value services. However, to do this the business stream would require the cooperation of a number of departments within the organization. Thus, attention would not only have to be focused on ensuring that as wide as possible a range of views was collated (so as to avoid missing opportunities or risks), but at the same time also ensuring that those who would be necessary to deliver the service were committed to its purpose.

What follows is Francis's story.

Getting Started

I had been interested in mapping for some time and was looking for a chance to try it out in the organization. When the business stream was being considered I thought that this might be an appropriate opportunity. I therefore spoke with the sales and business development manager – Derek – as he would be responsible for the new stream. Derek appeared interested in trying out the technique: he was conscious of the need to gain commitment from all the departments and it sounded as if the mapping process might help. I had achieved my first objective, to **find a client willing to support the process**, ensure that the outcomes would be realized and provide the resources. This was necessary, as what I was proposing was after all a departure from typical approaches used in the organization.

Together Derek and I began to **consider who should be involved**, as it was important to consider those who have vested interests, power and knowledge. This proved to be less straightforward than we thought, as we wanted to **ensure that everyone will have sufficient airtime** (the ability to contribute); cover the major technical areas; and through their support, increase the chance of successful implementation. In addition, I didn't want to start too ambitiously – this was after all my first attempt at mapping in public with a group (particularly as I was not entirely a neutral party and might be regarded with a little scepticism). We finally agreed on six participants.

I now had to decide whether to start with interviews or go directly to trying group mapping. While I was sure that the participants would not feel uncomfortable with working together using the oval mapping technique (see Chapter 6), I was conscious that there were other considerations. Given the wealth of expertise held by the participants, I was keen to **provide interviewees with the time and space to reflect on their experience, allowing me to elicit a richer map**. Supporting this approach was the view that one of the managers was known for dominating meetings and I wanted to avoid this happening.

Moreover, using one-to-one interviews would not only enable me to **familiarize interviewees with the mapping technique**, but also reduce the load put on me. I felt I could cope with capturing the contributions from one person, but was less sure about capturing them from the energetic debate I felt would unfold if we were to use group mapping.

Once I had completed the interviews I could take the individual maps, weave them together and present the results (and stimulate further debate) in a group workshop – something I felt was necessary, as we had to ensure that a sense of shared understanding and ownership for the outcomes was attained. I was also hoping that by stimulating their thinking about the business stream, participants would be curious about how others perceived the situation and therefore encouraged to attend the group workshop.

While talking about the design, Derek and I were aware of the need to **sort out what the outcomes from the mapping process might be**. Derek was keen to get some clarity on the objectives for this new business stream, a set of goals that everyone would sign up to. However, in order to ensure that these were realizable, we would also need to consider what strengths existed. Thus, we would start by surfacing issues, ladder up to goals and then consider what strengths the organization held that would support the goals.

We had a plan . . .

I now had to sort out where I was going to do the interviews, in what order, and how much time I would need/could get for each interview. I felt that it was important to **find somewhere to do the interviews that reduced the probability of interruption and allowed people to concentrate on the issues.** (We do our everyday work in open-plan offices where disruptions were routine – not ideal for interviews!) However, I didn't want to make too many demands on Derek or those being interviewed. I therefore settled for booking a conference room in an adjacent office block, near enough to get to quickly but sufficiently distant to avoid "easy" interruptions.

Next I considered whom to start with. The mapping literature recommended starting with the most powerful stakeholder, as this gets a broad and holistic view early on. However I wanted to **gain some confidence in my mapping.** I decided that rather than go with the recommendations (made in the mapping literature[1]) I would start with someone who, while having a wealth of knowledge and interest in the subject, was not the most senior manager (and therefore less of a risk to me). I ended up choosing Les, who would not only provide me with a good overview of the material, but was also reasonably senior and therefore would provide a good overview. Finally, I decided that an hour would probably be a good balance between managing the demands on staff who were to be interviewed and being able to get into the detail and subtlety of the situation. I would also **build in time between interviews, first to allow the interview to continue should the group member want it, and second to allow me to "tidy up" the map while it was still fresh in my mind.**

All this worked out. I informed those selected about the process and its purpose and began getting times in diaries. I also spent some time thinking about what I might say in terms of an introduction and assembling the appropriate equipment.

Doing the Interviews

The first interview started well. I outlined the purpose: "to explore issues facing the development of the new business stream." Wow, there was no shortage of contributions – my worry about the interviewees saying nothing was needless. Les started fluently and I was hard pressed to keep up.

To avoid missing things, I made sure that as soon as possible I would **use a break to review what had been said**. This would allow me to check my understanding and reassure Les that I had been listening and capturing what he had said or meant. However, it also gave me an opportunity to capture some of the material that I could remember but hadn't yet managed to get on the map. As I did this, I began to notice that Les (and many of the others later on) *started with a flurry of statements regarding what might hold back development – taking the negative position first* before moving on to discussing more positive themes (see Map 8.1).

Once Les had exhausted all of the things he wanted to say – about ten minutes into the interview – I could **begin the process of laddering up and down the chains of argument**. By asking "Why do you think this is important?" I was able to tease out what Les saw as the consequences. What was interesting to me was that in a number of instances it felt as though this "so what" type of question resulted in Les taking a "step back" and having to consider more carefully his assertion – something he too said he found useful. He reported that he had got so used to expressing his views about what should be done that he had lost sight of the reasons for doing it. It was obvious that at times *we make assertions about what should be done without considering why*. This process helped both of us not only to identify the issues facing the new business stream but also to begin to surface the goals.

We also spent time on surfacing organizational strengths and the inter-relationships between them. It was interesting to note that this process started with many technical strengths (no doubt reflecting Les's engineering background) and I had to work quite hard to surface some that were not technical. Moreover, Les (and others) found it really *difficult to get to grips with the notion of strengths as a linked system and struggled to put forward links*. I would need to find some way of helping the group in the workshop identify links between the strengths and the goals.

Due to my wish to capture all of the material Les was providing, I found myself continuously writing and not spending as much time as I would have liked laddering up and down, exploring any statements that were currently unlinked, and checking whether there were links between the different clusters of material. *Mapping a messy and complex organizational issue like this was a completely different experience from practising on a personal map.* I therefore asked Les whether it would be possible for me to review the material with him once I had had a chance to tidy it up. He readily agreed – in fact he said he was looking forward to seeing what I'd made of his thoughts.

Over the course of the next five interviews, I found myself getting more and more confident in my mapping abilities. By the time I got to the last interview I was able not only to capture what was being said but also link it appropriately, ask the laddering questions and feel as though I was getting a good map – one that reasonably represented the views expressed and that the interviewee found added to their thinking. By building in time at the end, I was able to give feedback on what I had captured and get agreement for the final map (as a representation of their current thinking). What did fascinate me was that *the participants used a variety of interview styles* – some came with mind maps of their own, some with a focus on issues and others started directly with statements about the goals. There were obviously different preferred ways of thinking through proposals; I would need to consider this when designing the workshop. I also made sure that immediately after the interview I tidied up the maps (in my case using the mapping software *Decision Explorer*). This process allowed me to *ensure that all of the aspects that were still in my head but not yet on the map could be added.*

The process of feeding back the interviews during a second feedback interview was also interesting. I noticed that the **interviewees directly engaged with the maps through adapting and adding material**, thus gaining further ownership as well as building their own thinking. Interviewees added new material, changed the wording of some statements, added or altered links and generally "bought into" the process. Unfortunately, I did not get the chance to spend a second block of time with all of the interviewees. It became obvious that simply letting them have their maps and

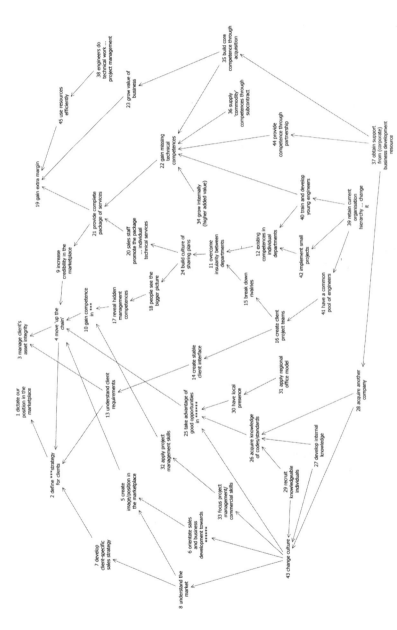

Map 8.1 *Accentuate the negative*. In this first map, with Les and with all six colleagues, Francis found that the negatives had to be aired before more positive views could be introduced.

expecting comments back didn't work: I had to *use the second session as an interview and be actively involved*. I suspected that people who had never come across maps before needed help in interpreting them the first time they saw them.

Integrating and Analysing the Maps

I now had six maps – one for each participant – which comprised around 240 statements and 300 links. I could begin to weave these together to produce a single map (model). Although I hadn't managed it with the feedback interviews, I really wanted to try to **run the workshop within a "psychological week"**[2] **– the beginning of one week to the end of the next – to keep the memory and enthusiasm fresh**. This was to prove a challenge, as Christmas was arriving and diaries were full. Although I used the *Decision Explorer* mapping software to do this, it is possible to do all of the following manually.

There appeared to be some common themes that emerged from the interviews. Starting with these themes, I began to examine how the six different participants had viewed each of the themes and, where appropriate, began to add in links or merge contributions so as to integrate the different views into one picture. I was very careful here to avoid doing violence to members' views – I changed the wording in some cases, but tried to keep the meaning instantly recognizable. Unless I could **be sure that the two statements meant the same, regardless of whether they used the same words**, I did not merge. Instead, I entered a link illustrating that they appeared to have an impact on one another. I did this by examining each statement's context (that is, the statements that either directly linked in or out of the two being considered). To ensure that I could see which links I was adding, I used a different style of link (a dotted line rather than solid). Moreover, I did try to be very careful to **avoid duplicating chains of argument**, as there was always the danger that a more extensive chain of argument existed. For example, it might be that I thought A linked to D and therefore considered inserting the link. However, on further examination it became apparent that while A did link to D, it did so via B and C. Therefore

I would simply be creating a "short cut" and so a redundant link. This would only complicate the model and add little if any value.

Next, I looked at "heads" (those statements that didn't have any arrows out of them). My first question to myself was were they goals or had I missed a link from them to another statement (and thus they would no longer be a head). I began to review each map, identifying the heads and asking myself "Was this a 'good outcome in its own right' rather than a means to an end?" – the definition of a goal that I was using. It was interesting to note that Jim's map had started with the goals as he saw them and so it was easy for me to identify his; others' maps were less straightforward. To help quickly re-identify the goals I decided to **colour all of those that were goals a solid bold black, giving them a particular style**.

As I identified a statement that I felt was a goal, I would then **ladder down from the goal to determine whether the statement(s) immediately supporting it were also goals (albeit subordinate ones)**. Once I felt I had identified these, I collated all of the candidate goals onto one map. This might be one possible starting point for the workshop.

Next, I began the process of identifying the many key issues that had been raised by the group as a whole. Here I began to **look for busy points**.[3] Where a statement had many links going in and/or out of it, it seemed likely that it would represent important parts of the map – a possible key issue. I also took into account those issues that had had a lot of emotion behind them (based on the non-verbal behaviour demonstrated by interviewees). Again, I wanted to be able to distinguish these possible key issues easily and so coloured these statements purple. What I was seeking to do was to ensure that there was at least one key issue for every theme identified, although I did recognize that there may be some key issues and themes I had missed and that these would be revealed by carrying out this and subsequent analyses.

However, I was finding this hard work. I had originally budgeted for one day but it was beginning to look as if I would need more. Part of this was due to my need to keep tidying up the maps. The process of carrying out the analysis meant I was **able to highlight further inconsistencies with the mapping guidelines**. Part of it was also

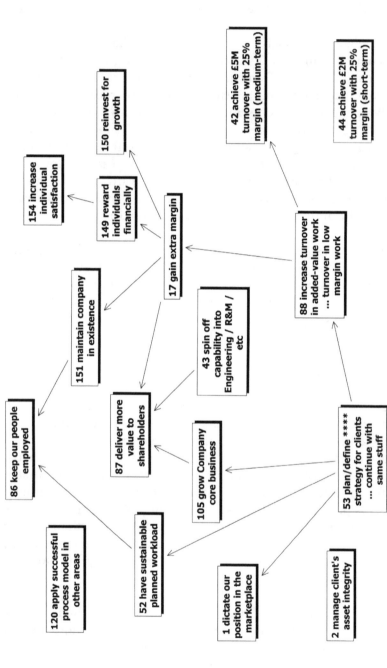

Map 8.2 *Starting point.* Having identified goals – good outcomes in their own right – Francis developed a set of candidate goals for his first workshop.

due to my need to remember not only how to do the analyses but also why. I reflected that this would probably *get faster as I got more experienced, both in mapping and its associated analyses*.

I prepared the merged map ready for the workshop. The first thing I did was to **check that the goal system map contained at least one contribution from each member**. This would ensure that their attention would be retained, as the first thing they would look for would be their own contributions. Second, I wanted to make sure that this starter map would not be too complex or busy. I knew that if I had too much material on it, participants would **experience a sense of cognitive overload as they would not easily be able to assimilate all of the information**.

Last, I created a number of maps that depicted the context of the key issues identified, looking at the wealth of material supporting each key issue. These would allow the group to explore more of the detail, but again manage the complexity (rather than reduce it). To help participants **make the connections between goals and the issue maps**, I included the goals on these maps.

The Workshops

The first thing I had to think about was how was I going to run the workshop. I decided to do two short sessions (of about three hours) rather than a single one-day workshop. This idea had already occurred to me when I was endeavouring to get at the strengths, as it would allow me to use the time between workshops to tidy the combined map and begin the process of mapping strengths to goals. Additionally, the thought of having to get a whole day in people's diaries was a little disconcerting. As this was going to be my first time at facilitating a group, two short interventions seemed a much better idea!

Next was the problem of choosing a room. I wanted a location where all of the participants could see one another as well as the computer-projected map. I thought the best thing to do was to **visit the**

different workshop room options to help make a judgement. This was vital! None of the rooms was ideal but one, with some ingenuity, could work. Now I had a room and two planned workshops, I thought carefully about the introduction I would make and how I would set the scene.

Everyone arrived on time, commenting on how they were interested in what others had said, and appeared to be relaxed and ready to start. Once I had gone through the brief introduction, we started with the goal system map. Immediately there were comments regarding the goal system's comprehensiveness. However, after some debate the participants agreed that there weren't any missing goals, although they did think that some of the links needed to be rearranged. I immediately worked to **make the changes that workshop participants suggested, as doing this would reflect the system's development and help gain ownership** (see Map 8.3). The changes were not too drastic, so my initial stab, based on the interviews, seemed a good starting point. In a few cases there was important argument about which way the arrow should be – which was the means and which was the end.

We next moved to the issue maps. To help participants get an idea of the entirety of the model, I thought it would be best to start with a quick **run-through of each of the issues (providing an over-view) before exploring the detail of each issue map**. This proved useful, as it enabled the group to confirm to themselves that the issues they had raised had been captured and would be discussed.

To my surprise, considerable debate arose around one particular map focusing on the key issue regarding "culture". As a result of the discussion, a distinction was made between internal and external culture – one focusing on how people acted and interacted within the organization, the other related to the image of the culture of our organization that is presented to the customers. This debate highlighted how *the map helped the group members begin to develop a sense of shared understanding and realize that until then they had been at cross-purposes*. This was quite an eye-opener for the group as well as me. The insight meant that a number of changes needed to be made and the group worked hard to get them resolved.

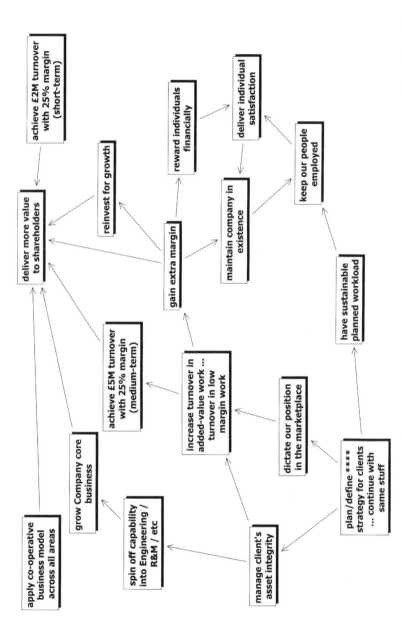

Map 8.3 *Gaining ownership.* As the discussion developed, Francis amended the goal system to reflect his colleagues' thinking.

I was now running out of time and was conscious that we were not going to be able to review all of the issues. I realized that I needed to *appreciate how engaged the group could become in the mapping process*, and how this should be taken into account when planning a workshop. A quick check with the group resulted in them selecting (through a simple voting process) a subset of issues to concentrate on and, with the group's agreement to work an extra half hour (they really were keen to keep going), these issues were developed. We finished the workshop with a quick review of the progress made, clarification of the purpose of the next workshop and general thanks. All felt the time had been well spent – in fact, two them came up to me afterwards and said it was the most productive meeting they had been to in the organization!

I spent some of the next day tidying up the combined map, making the changes suggested by group members and analysing the map to see if there were any new emerging properties. I also used this time to get ready for the "strengths workshop". Maps were made and again checked to ensure that there were contributions from all.

On the morning of the second workshop, I discovered that Les and David were unable to attend. Disaster – these were the two most senior members of the team. What would this mean for the outcomes? Given that the other four participants were very keen to continue, we started the workshop, albeit with some misgivings on my part. I realized that in future I should *have a contingency plan for dealing with the loss of key participants*.

Despite the set-back from losing two participants, those remaining quickly got into the strengths task and began to add further strengths and suggest links. I was a little surprised by this, given the reluctance in the interviews to link strengths. Was this because the **group members were able to use their experience in mapping to work more effectively, the familiarity making it easier**? As links and new strengths were suggested, one member commented that the organization appeared to be missing some key strengths. These "missing" strengths were quickly added to the map, which was fast becoming an organizational memory or "minutes". As more progress was made on the linkages, participants were able to determine the emergence of some interesting patterns of strengths –

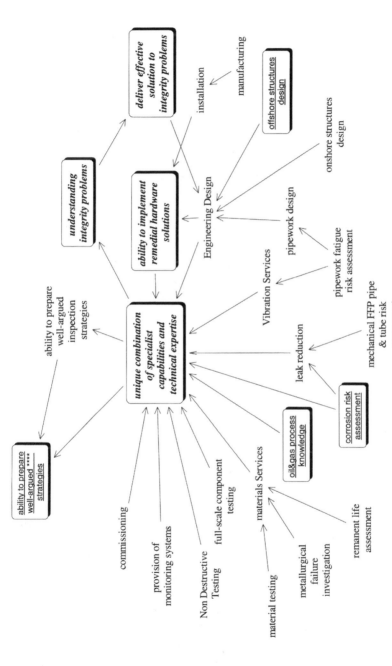

Map 8.4 *Developing distinctiveness.* As links and strengths were added, the map began to show how the organization was distinct from its competitors.

particular portfolios of strengths giving rise to distinctive characteristics of the organization in relation to competitors (see Map 8.4).

The final stage of mapping the strengths onto the goal system went
remarkably quickly.

Postscript

Those attending felt that they had made good progress and now had
a clearer idea of the goals of the business stream. They had seen how
existing organizational competencies formed patterns that added
distinctiveness and would support the goals. On the other hand, they
had also seen how adding further competencies would strengthen
the existing structure, and the discussions had highlighted some key
issues that would need to be resolved before implementing the new
stream. Although the resultant business plan did not provide as
much depth as was available in the combined map, it did contain a
number of the key actions for taking forward the work of the group,
including exploring approaches to change both the internal culture
and projected image of the company and seeking out ways of adding
competencies.

Conclusions

This chapter illustrates that mapping is a way to enable a range of
different perspectives to be brought together in a way that is both
efficient and effective. Instead of arguing over material or feeling as
though the group is "going round in circles", the material is
captured, structured and can therefore be built on, suggesting new
options rather than fighting over old ones.[4] As most of us are not
able to hold more than 6–8 pieces of information in our heads at
once, and most of the issues we have to deal with are a great deal
more complex than 6–8 statements, some means of managing this
complexity is required. Mapping provides that means. As a
consequence, a wider range of views can be worked with, increasing

the depth of consideration along with increasing the ownership of outcomes – what could be described as "procedural justice".[5]

Moreover, through the interviews Francis was able to surface a wealth of material, which when viewed in the workshop was considered for its content rather than its proponent, something that often gets in the way of considering alternatives and potential ways forward. The maps enabled participants to read the contributions and consider them before replying, allowing further consideration and avoiding the need for physiological responses.

This case is not untypical of many business opportunities, being able to surface a wide range of views, understand how they relate to one another and begin to agree a way forward that will help the organization develop a plan that is both coherent and owned. After all, as noted by Machiavelli (1514):

There is nothing more difficult than to achieve a new order of things, with no support from those who will not benefit from the new order, and only lukewarm support from those who will.

Process guidelines

- Find a client willing to support the process.
- Consider who should be involved.
- Ensure that everyone has sufficient airtime.
- Provide interviewees with the time and space to reflect on their experience, allowing a richer map to be elicited.
- Familiarize interviewees with the mapping technique.
- Sort out what the outcomes from the mapping process might be.
- Find somewhere to interview that reduces the probability of interruption and allows people to concentrate on the issues.
- Gain some confidence in mapping.

- Build in time between interviews, first to allow the interview to continue should members wish it, and second to allow the map to be "tidied up" while it is still fresh in the interviewer's mind.

- Use a break to review what has been said.

- Begin the process of laddering up and down the chains of argument.

- Engage interviewees directly with the maps through adapting and adding material.

- Run the workshop within a psychological week – the beginning of one week to the end of the next – to keep the memory and enthusiasm fresh.

- Be sure that two statements mean the same, regardless of whether they use the same words.

- Avoid duplicating chains of argument.

- Colour all statements that are goals solid bold black, giving them a particular style.

- Ladder down from the goal to determine whether the statement(s) immediately supporting it are also goals (albeit subordinate ones).

- Look for busy points.

- Highlight further inconsistencies with the mapping guidelines.

- Check that the goal system map contains at least one contribution from each member.

- Avoid participants experiencing a sense of cognitive overload, as they are not easily able to assimilate all of the information.

- Make the connections between goals and issue maps.

- Visit the different workshop room options to help make a judgement.

- Make the changes that workshop participants suggested, as doing this will reflect the system's development and help gain ownership.

- Run through each of the issues (providing an overview) before getting into each map's detail.
- Group members are able to use their experience in mapping to work more effectively, the familiarity making it easier.

Learning points

- Interviews often start with a flurry of statements regarding what might hold back development, taking the negative position first.
- We make assertions about what should be done without considering why.
- Groups may find it difficult to get to grips with the notion of competencies as a system and struggle to put forward links.
- Mapping a messy and complex organizational issue like this is a completely different experience from practising on a personal map.
- The map helps the group participants begin to develop a sense of shared understanding and realize that until then they have been at cross-purposes.
- There can be a variety of interview styles used by the participants.
- Ensure that all of the aspects that are still in your head but not yet on the map can be added.
- Use the second session as an interview and be actively involved.
- You get faster as you get more experienced – both in mapping and its associated analyses.
- Appreciate how engaged the group can become in the mapping process.
- Have a contingency plan for dealing with the loss of key participants.

Notes

1 For example, Eden and Ackermann argue that it is important to seek out the views of the power brokers early in the interview cycle, so that their views can be tested against those of others by using some of the views as prompts. See C. Eden and F. Ackermann (1998) *Making Strategy: The Journey of Strategic Management*, London: Sage, p. 301.

2 A psychological week is the period between the beginning of one week and the end of the next.

3 Resource B (p. 311) discusses different forms of analysis that are used in these circumstances.

4 R. Fisher and W. Ury (1982) *Getting to Yes*, London: Hutchinson, p. 1342.

5 W. C. Kim and R. A. Mauborgne (1995) A Procedural Justice Model of Strategic Decision Making, *Organization Science*, **6**, 44–61.

9

A Question of Turning Around

I N THIS CHAPTER WE PRESENT A STRATEGY-MAKING CASE. Most organizations, including departments of large organizations, operating companies, community groups, small or medium-sized enterprises as well as large multinationals, want to consider their own strategic future and make plans about how they might better control it. Sometimes it is assumed that only large corporations undertake strategic planning, whereas in practice all organizations do it in some way. Here we describe the strategy making of a relatively small organization with limited resources, meaning no planning department or manager responsible for strategy, other than the chief executive. The senior management team needed to formulate their strategy over a weekend. The part of the strategy making reported here considers the first day of a two-day workshop that used mapping as the core technique. The second day focused on the details of strategy implementation and so is less relevant. The case described has been authorized by the chief executive as an accurate record of the weekend.

The case presents the use of computer-based methods – specifically, *Decision Explorer* and *Group Explorer*.[1] Computers were employed to make quick progress possible. However, every aspect of the mapping process could have used the oval mapping technique, although to do so would probably have taken twice as long. Throughout the case, differences and similarities between the use of computer-assisted methods and the oval mapping technique are noted in italic.

The case is a very good example of what can be done by a small group of managers to create a realistic basic strategy for their own department, unit or group, or in this case a small organization. There is nothing particularly unique or unusual about the circumstances or process used. The case introduces concepts from strategic management such as distinctive goals system, distinctive competencies and core distinctive competencies, business model and mission statement. However, we hope that these concepts are introduced in a manner that clarifies their practical significance for moving an organization forward. In this case presentation, when these concepts have particularly important process implications they are marked as process guidelines with **[Strategy]** added, to indicate their importance for strategy making.

Getting Started

Neil was new to the company, but not to the industry. He had recently been appointed as chief executive with responsibility to turn around the company over the next three years. The company was extremely short of cash and so was finding it difficult to find the time to develop a sound strategy for the future. It was relatively small, with just over 200 employees, and was privately owned. Neil had bought into the company to the extent that he had a small shareholding. Other members of the senior management team also had smaller shareholdings.

Neil was keen to take a completely fresh look at the strategy of the organization, but could not afford to spend too much time or money on doing so, given the organization's precarious position. A meeting with Neil in a café in the centre of London led to an agreement that only the senior management team would be engaged in a strategy-making workshop. There was some conversation about involving other key players beyond the management team because of the significant role they would be expected to play in the implementation of any new strategy. However, it was decided to restrict the workshop only to the most senior managers who were also shareholders. This would mean that all those attending would have the same focus on a three-year time horizon. At that time the organization was involved in publishing magazines, running conferences and organizing exhibitions, which meant that it operated against a continuous set of deadlines. As a result, even given the importance of a strategy-making workshop, senior managers could not take any time out of the normal working week. The workshop was planned to take place in a local hotel over a weekend.

Most senior managers, in most organizations, spend most of their time fire-fighting and dealing with the issues rather than opportunities. Therefore, strategic thinking tends to be set within the context of burning issues. In this particular case it was even more so: the everyday operations of the organization were not running easily or successfully and stress levels were high. In addition, the arrival of a new chief executive was stressful for other senior managers in the organization. All this meant that there were likely to be tensions within the management team. Therefore, the strategy-making workshop needed be about team building as well as strategy. The thinking of the senior management team certainly mattered for the future of the organization.

The objective for the workshop was to develop a sound strategy for the organization, tested through the creation of a business model. The business model needed to show with some degree of confidence that within the three-year time horizon the fortunes of the company could be turned around. Doing this over a weekend was not going to be an easy task. In addition, it was essential that at least half of Sunday be spent discussing the immediate plans for the delivery of the strategy and what was to be said to all other employees of the company. As planning for the workshop continued, all the other staff became aware that the strategy workshop was happening and that it was significant for the future of the company. So they were keen to hear about outcomes first thing on the Monday following the workshop. Testing out the strategy through developing a rough business model was likely to take at least half a day and, given that there would be some cycling between a statement of strategic intent and its implications for cash flow and profits, this meant that the equivalent of one long day remained for the strategic thinking.

Colin and Fran, who had been asked to facilitate the strategy making, had worked with Neil ten years before when he was in a different organization. Neil had experienced the oval mapping technique and *Decision Explorer* at that time. He was keen that a

Figure 9.1   A group working through networked computers (*Group Explorer*).

mapping approach be used on this occasion and, anyway, knew that Colin and Fran would expect to use some variety of mapping as a part of their approach to strategy making. *Under less tight time constraints they would have been inclined to use oval mapping in the first instance and then move to a more thoroughgoing strategy map through the use of Decision Explorer interactively with the group.* This would have enabled the group to become accustomed to a "simple" hand-mapping process before being faced with computer technology.

However, given the time constraints they persuaded Neil that it would be necessary to use a more efficient method for capturing the maps in real time by using a system of networked laptop computers, linked directly to the public *Decision Explorer* display. The system would improve the productivity of the group, but *replicate the principles of the oval mapping technique.* Participants are able to write the text that they would have otherwise written onto an oval directly into a laptop computer. After they hit the carriage return their text is sent to the *Decision Explorer* public display so that all members of the group can see the statement. Figure 9.1 shows the type of arrangement that is expected. Each statement appears on the screen within an oval shape and the leader of the group, or facilitator, is able to use his or her computer (which is running *Decision Explorer*) to *move the statements to different positions on the screen in the same way that ovals are moved around a wall surface.* However, by using *Decision Explorer* directly instead of wall space, each participant can also use their own laptop to instruct the display to show arrows to link statements and produce a causal map.

Usually such workshops only require one leader or facilitator. In this case it was important to ensure that there was one facilitator available to work directly with the group and another to think, as an outsider, quite carefully about the material coming forward. In this way some short cuts could be taken, but with the risk that the workshop might move too fast for members of the group. Experienced facilitators can sometimes use their experience to move a workshop along quickly, but risk losing participants for whom the process begins to become opaque.

Thinking through the Workshop

How to get at different views of what is
important for the future of the organization

As indicated above, the senior management team were under significant pressure. Unless the first part of the workshop paid due attention to the urgent strategic issues facing the team, these issues would be a continual background of worries as other tasks were attempted. The workshop was therefore planned to start with an explanation of the strategic issues facing the organization that were expected to have an impact three years into the future. With the networked computer system to help, and only five members in the group, it seemed likely that half an hour would be enough time to get these out onto the public screen and do some rough structuring of the statements into a map.

It is usual for managers to have some important and urgent items they wish to air early on in a meeting. Unless these important and urgent issues do get aired, the participants often become more focused on finding the space to "grind their own axes" than they are on listening to others or making other contributions. The half-hour time frame was thought to be enough to **get urgent issues "out on the table" early in the workshop and make sure that there was clear acknowledgement of their having been stated**. Their presence on the public screen was planned to give comfort to those wishing to be sure that their concerns were not "glossed over".

This would be followed by the need for the group to make sure they understood all the material surfaced. *Unlike the traditional oval mapping session, the contributions made using the networked system are completely anonymous.* This has both disadvantages and advantages. It provides a licence for extreme, or blunt and honest, comments (sometimes these helpfully declare embedded frustrations that should be surfaced), participants are able to disagree with statements without disagreeing with the person connected to the statement, and participants can more easily and deliberately launch a discussion topic. However, participants have no responsibility, at this time, for defending or elaborating their views. *Full anonymity (as compared to the partial anonymity of oval mapping) can help break down the tendency of a group to suppress important views in order to maintain the social well-being of the group* – a phenomenon known as "group-think".[2]

Full anonymity, at this stage, represented an effort to balance the positive outcome of getting "honest" statements surfaced with the risk of irresponsible statements arising that won't need to be explained. **A facilitator must watch for scurrilous contributions, and when they arise carefully manage their impact on the group – while also noting that sometimes humorous statements, and deliberate typing errors, can help a group move forward.** *As with traditional oval mapping, clustering similar topics or themes is likely to be helpful as a starting structure to the map.* Given the action orientation of a serious strategy workshop, the more important clusters would come from consideration of the causal links between statements. The next stage, following queries about potential misunderstandings, was planned to involve each of the participants adding causal arrows to introduce links across all of the material (not merely between statements they had contributed).

Given that the group was inexperienced in mapping, it seemed likely that, at least to start with, the linking process would be less than perfect. While the facilitator working with the group would be attending to the positioning of material on the screen, the second facilitator would be able to monitor potential problems with links. For strategy making, it is crucial that causal links are believed to be accurate by all members of the group, as these linkages might have a profound impact on strategy implementation at a later stage. It seemed likely that this stage could take up to an hour.

It is always important to **pay attention to both content management and process management**. Attention to content can guide the management of process, and attention to process issues can guide the order in which content is addressed by the group. When there are two facilitators, it is usual for one to be primarily attending to process and the other primarily attending to content.[3]

Typically groups rarely map out the interaction between all the issues the organization faces. In this case it seemed likely that the anonymity feature would be particularly helpful, and that the issue map would reveal something new to every member of the group. It was expected that 50–70 issues would be surfaced during this stage. It was therefore going to be important to establish some draft priorities – both as a consequence of the statements themselves, but more importantly from a simple analysis of the structure of the map on the screen facing the group. This might take about half an hour and should provide the group with an important milestone. The milestone was expected to be an identification of central issues, of those issues that were a significant driver of many other issues, and of those bundles of issues (clusters) that were relatively separate from one another.

How to gain an understanding of the implicit strategic direction of the organization

With many strategy-making groups, this process of surfacing issues of importance to the group is used to provide clues about the implicit, taken-for-granted purposes or goals of the organization. When an issue is identified, it is put forward as an issue for the organization because it is implicitly, or sometimes explicitly, presumed to be attacking something that it is important for the organization – a goal. In this instance, some of the goals were inviolable: there were set targets established by the organization's major shareholders. The task of the senior management team, also shareholders, was to show how a resolution of what they regarded as important issues would drive through to these targets via some business outcomes or goals.

Issues or problems that managers actually attend to give a good indication of what goals are really driving the organization forward. Seeking to understand what outcomes are expected from dealing with issues begins to identify these goals. They should be the link between issues and ultimate outcomes such as shareholder value (in the private sector) or meeting the mandate of a public-sector organization.

How to surface and reach agreement
on a draft statement of strategic direction

The next task for the group was expected to be a ratification, or otherwise, of why the issues were important for the future of the company. The group would be asked to identify the outcomes and goals that would be attained by addressing the important issues suggested by the previous task of issue identification and structuring. In doing so, the process of laddering upwards towards increasingly higher-order outcomes would be expected to show a linkage between the resolution of the issues and the inviolable goals. The objective of the task was to articulate some draft goals that were expected to drive the organization towards meeting shareholder requirements. In addition, it was anticipated that some of the important issues might be re-evaluated because they did not address these requirements in a clearly articulated manner. It was expected that this process could take up to one and a half hours.

The completion of this task would also represent a significant milestone for the group. They should have a much clearer view of a (possibly) distinctive set of goals for their organization, in which the goals should be represented as a network – where each goal helps sustain another goal and is in turn sustained by the resolution of an issue or a goal. It should then be possible for the group to construct a draft statement of strategic aims for the organization. The statement should be a narrative that fully expresses the network of goals. It is likely that the statement would primarily be an expression of what should be driving the operational activities of the organization's managers in meeting the needs of shareholders.

A statement of strategic aims is powerful when it represents the interaction between all of the goals [Strategy]: the goals are seen as a system where each goal helps deliver other high-level goals and may in turn be helped by the delivery of subordinate goals.

The power of the emerging goals should be tested by examining the extent to which they are different from those of competitors[4] [Strategy]. If they are the same, the group is choosing head-on competition, where the winner will be determined only by the different quality of the organization's competencies. Delivering shareholder value through a *distinctive* system of goals is likely to more sustainable over a long period of time.

How to explore what the organization is really good at

To some extent, for many years the company had been plodding along in the same business, and with the same products presented in the same way. There was an implicit assumption that the delivery of these products was the best exploitation of the competencies and particularly the distinctive competencies of the company and its staff. However, in order to deliver shareholder needs, it seemed likely that the company would need a tighter focus on exploiting its distinctive competencies. Where distinctive competencies were being sustained and yet did not significantly support the required strategic future reorganization, effort on sustaining them should be reduced. Therefore, the next planned task for the workshop was to be the explication of distinctive competencies within the context of the draft goals. Once again, *these could have been surfaced using the oval mapping technique, to ensure that the inter-relationship between competencies and distinctive competencies could be identified through a map*. By using the networked computer system, the map of competencies can be created faster, anonymously and with the ability to create a continually updated computer-based record.

How to test whether there is a viable business[5]

A successful and robust strategic future for an organization is dependent on its being able to deliver its goals. If the goal system is distinctive, the organization will be separating itself from the competition in terms of its aspirations. However, it is most important that the organization separates itself from the competition through its unique ability to deliver the distinctive goal system. To do so, it must demonstrate to itself that it has distinctive competencies that support the goals. The mapped linkages between distinctive competencies and goals represents the logic of a viable business – the business model. Distinctive competencies must not only be unique but capable of retaining their distinctiveness if they are to sustain a robust strategic future. Testing for a viable business was important for Neil.

When taken together, the previous tasks allow the development of a qualitative business model. This process seeks to test the distinctiveness of the draft distinctive competencies, to be discussed below; and demonstrate that the exploitation of the distinctive competencies can resolve the important strategic issues and help achieve each of the goals within the draft goal system.

Typically, this task can be difficult for the group. With a management team of 8–10 people, usually a two-day workshop would be required to reach the stage of a well-constructed qualitative business model. With five people it might be possible to complete this task in three hours.

Neil mentioned that this group knew the language of core competencies, but was not clear about what one was. It was therefore going to be necessary to ensure that they knew the difference between a distinctive competence and a core competence: core competencies only emerge after the link between all distinctive competencies and the goals of the organization have been established. **Core distinctive competencies are those that are "at the core" of the business model (delivering a successful and realistic strategic future)** [Strategy].

In thinking through this workshop, we were hoping to get to this stage by the end of the first day. It seemed just possible...

The plan

The planned timetable for the workshop at this stage therefore looked something like:

- 9.00–10.30 a.m. – Issue surfacing and mapping

- Issue prioritization = milestone

- 11.00 a.m.–12.30 p.m. – Explication of outcomes and goals that are linked issues to shareholder needs

- Drafting of a distinctive network of goals and draft mission statement = milestone

- 1.30–3.00 p.m. – Explication of and network of competencies and distinctive competencies

- 3.30–5.00 p.m. – Drafting the business model: linking the exploitation of distinctive competencies to have the resolution of that issue and meet the draft goal system

This schedule was a deliberate **attempt to build a workshop timetable,**[6] **even though it is rarely possible to stick to it precisely.** However, an initial schedule would give form to the workshop and permit contingencies to be dealt with in the full knowledge of the consequences of changes to the plan. Of course, the participants must be told that the plan may be adjusted to deal with unforeseen contingencies.

This timetable therefore left the following tasks to be undertaken during Sunday:

- Reviewing issue prioritization and goal system.

- Quantitatively testing the business model against shareholder needs.

- Drafting a statement of strategic intent.

- Considering immediate implications for strategic action priorities.

- Agreeing the way forward.

- Agreeing what to tell staff on returning to the office.

Given the amount of work that ought to be completed on the first day, it was felt that detailed planning of Sunday should be left until the end of Saturday. Nevertheless, it was important to establish that it was at least just possible to manage all these tasks on Sunday, or at least without the rough proportional breakdown of time to be allocated to each of them.

The final plan suggested the following: three-quarters of an hour on reviewing issue prioritization and goals; an hour and a half on quantitative testing; half an hour on drafting a statement of strategic intent; an hour and a half on immediate implications for strategic action priorities; two hours on reaching agreement on the way forward; and half an hour on reaching agreement on what to tell staff. This suggested about seven hours of work on Sunday, which was agreed to be just possible.

The Workshop

Arrivals

Neil, Colin and Fran arrived on Friday evening to ensure that the hotel room was adequate and to set up the networked computer system. The hotel room was disappointing, as the standard hotel boardroom-style meeting room was wholly inappropriate for a team-building and strategy-making workshop. The room was cluttered with too much furniture, pictures and wall lights. Two hours later, most of the furniture had been removed, pictures were taken off the wall and the room layout was completely changed. The process facilitator was to be seated at the front on the side, so that he or she could be an integral part of the group, and a small table and chair were set up at the back of the room for the content facilitator. Colin and Fran planned to exchange these roles after each task. The remaining furniture was set up as a semi-circle of small tables and chairs, with a laptop computer on the table in front of each chair.

The five participants arrived on time on Saturday morning to an inadequate supply of coffee and stale pastries! While waiting for more coffee to arrive, the conversation made it clear that, as expected, although some of the group were able to work together on operational issues of mutual interest, their conversations and thinking about the nature of the organization and its future differed markedly. Other than Neil, no participants had experienced a serious strategy-making workshop, and none had experienced an approach to group work using a high-productivity computer-based group support system.

Personal introductions to Colin and Fran occurred over coffee. Then to start the workshop, Colin introduced the objectives, rough agenda and time allotments for the day. Colin made sure that **the explanation used no jargon and made it clear why each of tasks was important and how they fitted into the whole work programme for the workshop**. Fran went on to introduce the processes that would be used, including the way the computer system would work. As none of the group, other than Neil, had experienced mapping, their introduction to it had to be exceedingly transparent and incremental. The intention was to **provide the group with realistic expectations about objectives and timing of the workshop, and to indicate some clear milestones**.

Fran explained some of the reasons why it was helpful for a group to get out on the table the issues they felt were important for the strategic future of the organization.

The "issue dump"

She introduced the standard oval mapping conventions – as conventions, not rules:

- It does not matter whether the issues stated are set out in detail or are set out to be "bigger and possibly more ambiguous".

- Issues may be those that relate to your own responsibilities or to other parts of the organization.

- They do not have to represent issues that have been regarded as important in the past.

- Each statement should represent one issue – if issues are linked to one another, this can be acknowledged during the next stage.

- If possible, try to characterize the issue in six to eight words – more than eight words usually means that there is more than one issue and it will help to decouple them.

- Just agreeing or disagreeing with issues already on the screen is not permitted – however, alternative views and additional commentaries are encouraged.

- An issue is something about which somebody needs to do something – if nothing is done, then the successful future of the organization is at risk.

- Quality of typing and spelling is absolutely unimportant, as long as we all know what is meant.

It was important to **make sure that participants knew what was expected of them**. They usually want to make sure they are not making fools of themselves. To lighten up participants' concerns, don't make the conventions sound too much like rules.

There was no hesitation among participants about contributing issues. Sometimes there are some participants who are unhappy about their computer skills or their competence in selecting good issues. However, full anonymity reduces some of these risks.

After about 20 minutes the group had produced the work output shown in Map 9.1, with 52 issue statements. Fran had been moving the issues around the public screen so that they appeared to her to be in rough clusters according to themes or topics. The **topic labels for clusters provided a useful way of summarizing** this first stage. As Fran attached labels, she checked with the group to make sure her impressions of the emerging themes were accurate.

Interesting features of the "issue dump" are that it is dominated by internal issues; there are many issues about

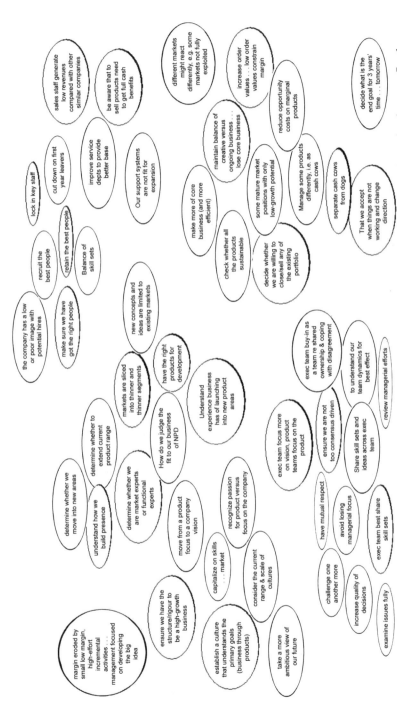

Map 9.1 In 20 minutes the group produced 52 issue statements. Fran moved them into rough topic clusters. In the next stage, topic labels would be attached to the clusters – a useful way of summarizing this first stage.

the working relations and effectiveness of the senior man-
agement team (implying that they are more of a group than a
team); it was encouraging that they were prepared to
acknowledge this so explicitly; there were many issues
about staff (keeping the best, getting the best, locking them
in); and at this stage very little material was included about
specific products or the marketplace.

Issue structuring

The group added more material as they asked questions about and
elaborated the first "dump", and then moved on to explore linkages
across the material. The display on the screen was changed to show
reference numbers against each statement. Using numbers makes
linking easy, as each participant can add a link by typing two
numbers linked by a "+" sign, for example typing 23+46 placed an
arrow from statement 23 to statement 46.

The linked map is shown in Map 9.2. After, not during, the linking,
the statements were moved around the screen to try to make the
picture clearer. As always, the rough clustering undertaken without
attention to causality became changed as the links appeared.
**Linking focuses attention not on topics but on action: what
results might be achieved by doing something, and what
things needed to be done to make other things happen.** This
meant that links were across clusters and themes as much as they
were within them.

After the group felt confident in their *issue structuring,* they found it
easy to suggest some initial ideas about how the large number of
issues could be reduced to a set of priorities. These initial ideas
emerged from considering the new clusters that emerged after links
were made. For example, looking around the screen it seemed
possible that 44, 13, 29, 60, 74 and 68 were likely to be important:
they each seemed to be at the centre of a cluster. **Statements that
seem to be at the centre of many others, with many links in or
out of them, are often good starting candidates for prioritizing issues.** However, sometimes these can simply be "catch-alls",
rather than actionable in a meaningful manner, and so will not be
capable of being prioritized in practice.

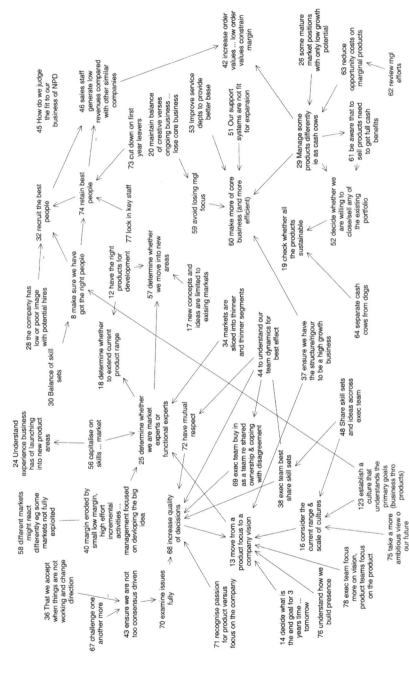

Map 9.2   The group have added more material to their first attempts and added linkages across the material.

Unfortunately, it had taken over 90 minutes to set a good structure to the issues so already the schedule was running slightly late, and developing a consensus about priorities was still required.

Prioritizing strategic issues

To help the group establish how much consensus there was, the *Group Explorer* software was used to allow anonymity in identifying these priorities. The first task was for the facilitator to work with the group to identify no more than about 12 statements that captured clusters of strategic "arenas". The analysis of the map gave the group some clues: some statements were very "busy", in that they had many causes and many consequences. For example, obvious candidates were statements 44, 68, 13, 25 and 29. Other statements were drivers or causes of many consequences (such as statements 26, 37, 40, 56 and 123, each of which connects through to three end points). However, while acknowledging this "rational" approach, the group also wanted to add some other statements that represented arenas they thought were important. The total number of candidates was now 13 different statements.

When considering priorities it is important to pay attention to "busy" statements as possible high priorities, except when they are vague "catch-alls" that are not easily actionable; allow the group to suggest other candidates; and pay attention to the candidate statements that are supported by all participants [Strategy].

The group was asked to identify priorities by allocating "resources" to each statement. Also, group members were asked to allocate some "negative resources", if they were inclined to do so, to items that they did not want to see as priorities; in other words, group members each had a sort of veto power over the establishment of priorities. In effect, each participant was given a restricted number of resources that could be used to implement whatever actions were required to resolve the issue. This allocation was done anonymously, so each of the five participants was invited to be very blunt in expressing their views. The exercise took only 12 minutes with the help of the computer system. The outcome shown on the public screen

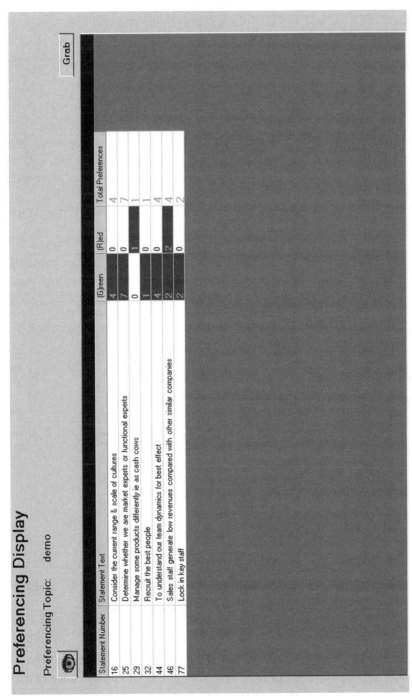

Figure 9.2 The summary public screen showing the results of preferencing.

indicated the total resources devoted to each statement and the degree of veto, and the facilitator's computer showed the degree of consensus (see Figure 9.2). *The process is a replication of the "preferencing" process that is used with the oval mapping technique, where self-adhesive spots are used as the "resources".*[7]

In fact, in this group there was little disagreement and only a couple of vetoes. The priority list is shown below. The preferencing scores are in square brackets, where the "P" indicates that these are the results of a "preferencing" exercise (calling it preferencing, rather than voting, is deliberate). The number indicates the allocated resources, and the letter "G" is for positive resources (which were coloured green) and the "R" for negative resources, the vetos (which were coloured red).

There was a consensus about the importance of the top priority, with all allocating at least one resource to it out of the four they were able to allocate. There was, however, disagreement about dealing with the issue of "sales staff generating low revenues". Discussion revealed, importantly, that this disagreement was the consequence of a disagreement about the assertion rather than about its importance. Again, note that the strategic priorities at this stage of the workshop were largely related to internal issues: culture, team dynamics and getting and keeping the best people:

- Determine whether we are market experts or functional experts [P 7G] 25.

- Consider the current range and scale of cultures [P 4G] 16.

- To understand our team dynamics for best effect [P 4G] 44.

- Lock in key staff [P 2G] 77.

- Recruit the best people [P 1G] 32.

- Manage some products differently, i.e. as cash cows [P 1R] 29.

- Sales staff generate low revenues compared with other similar companies [P 2G 2R] 46.

The priorities at this stage can often be misleading, because they are neither set within the context of agreed goals or the viability of the business model (that is, whether the goals can realistically be delivered). Nevertheless, the exercise provides an initial closure to working with strategic issues – the first milestone. *This stage of the workshop is typically cathartic for participants and was in this case, because they were able to get out in the open the worries, niggles and concerns that would otherwise get in the way of making more analytical progress*. To recognize this progress the group took a break at 11.10 a.m. (40 minutes later than the planned schedule).

Finding the emergent goal system

The group returned from the break to explore why these particular issues had been given a high priority. In other words, why was resolving them so important to the future success of the organization? Answering this question would explain emergent goals that were actually driving the organization. This involved having the group "ladder upwards" from each of these priority issues while remaining cognizant of the full context created by related statements.

At this stage **participants were asked "What is achieved if an effective way were found of addressing the issue?" or "What might happen that is undesirable if the issue were not addressed?"** The answer to the questions about each issue would ladder one level up the causal map. Asking the same question of the answers would continue the laddering upwards towards outcomes that are good or bad in their own right – that is, goals.

Often laddering continues upwards to a series of negative outcomes. Some of these are bad outcomes in their own right, and something needs to be done to make sure they don't happen. If so, these statements may need to remain written as negative goals rather than turned into positive outcomes. Most of the time the negative outcomes can be reversed into positive statements that are aspirational in nature (when doing so, the link will need to be tagged with a negative sign $(-)$ to indicate a switch in type of causality).

Map 9.3 shows an example of how the group started laddering upwards from the prioritized "range and scale of cultures" issue. Thus, the two important and related outcomes of reconsidering cultures were that they felt this would move the organization out of its comfort zone, which would in turn lift the lid on the scale of ambition for the business. Both of these outcomes they considered to be important future goals for the organization. (In Map 9.3 they are shown in a boxed different font in order to identify them as likely goals.) Later in the workshop, lifting the lid on the scale of ambition was taken to be one important goal that would contribute to increasing high growth and turnover potential. (In Map 9.4 the same font is used as for goals, but it is not surrounded by a box, to indicate that this is a *financial* goal for the organization.) For Neil it was important to distinguish financial goals (and the inviolate goals related to shareholder value) from other goals. Similarly, at a later stage high growth potential was linked to the financial goal of fast profit growth.

Just as with the oval mapping technique, but using the networked computer system, the group considered each of the prioritized issues in turn and laddered upwards in each case. Typically there were several different outcomes from addressing each issue. Often the initial outcomes were not goals for the organization; rather, they were the further consequences of these outcomes. As each prioritized issue was discussed, there were fewer new goals presented by the group. This is not untypical, as the goals become increasingly interlinked and gradually lead towards fewer and fewer outcomes at the top of the map.

The general structure of the developing map is shown in Figure 9.3. At this stage of the workshop the group had been concentrating on the top part of Figure 9.3, the surfacing of strategic issues and goals. As this figure shows, the general structure of a strategy map is a linked series of tear-drops. Map 9.4 shows the goal system "tear-drop" drafted at this early stage of the workshop. This draft goal system was established by 1.15 p.m. – in time for a late lunch!

Neil was reasonably buoyant at this stage because *his senior management group was beginning to behave like a team – they appeared to have listened to one another and been constructive in their responses*.

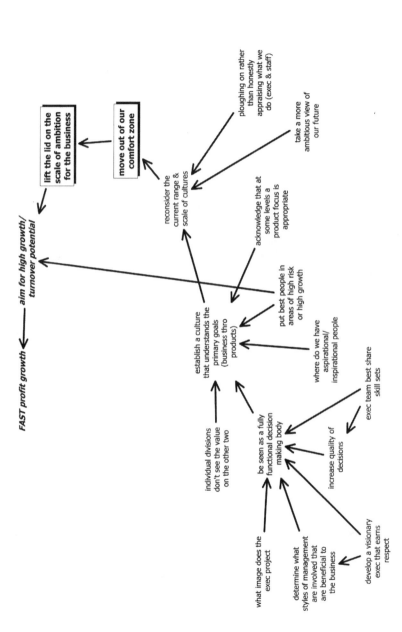

Map 9.3 *Laddering up.* This shows how the group started laddering upwards from the prioritized "range and scale of cultures" issue. (Boxed bold are possible goals and unboxed bold italic are possible financial goals.)

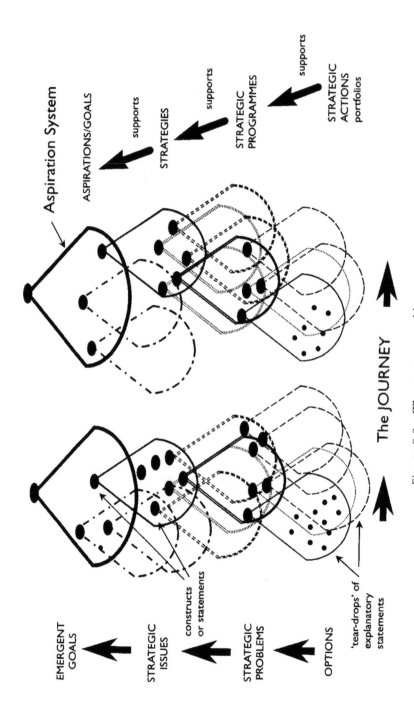

Figure 9.3   The strategy making structure.

Source: C. Eden and F. Ackermann (1998) *Making Strategy: The Journey of Strategic Management*, London: Sage.

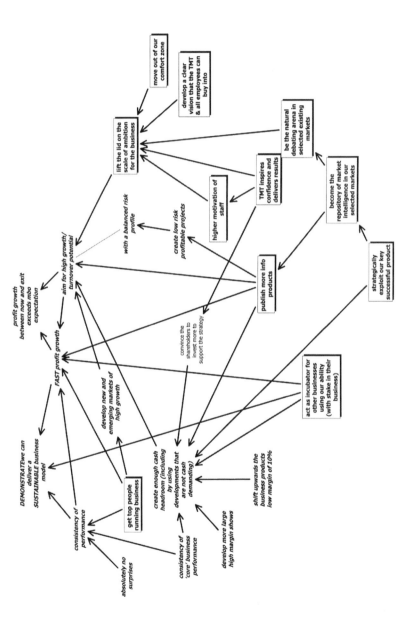

Map 9.4   *The goal system "tear-drop" developing.* This goal system is in draft form at an early stage in the workshop. (Statements without boxes are financial goals, those with boxes other goals.)

Discovering patterns of distinctive competencies
to deliver goals

The most crucial part of a strategy workshop of this type tends to be the work that is undertaken in trying to establish the organization's distinctive competencies. If an organization has nothing distinctive to offer to the marketplace, other organizations can jump in and make equivalent profits. If a competitor is able to do this easily, neither organization is able to make a profit! All organizations must have something distinctive about them in order to survive in the long term.

However, understanding the nature of distinctive competencies is not straightforward. For many years businesses have referred to their "core" competencies, but **core competencies are different from distinctive competencies** [Strategy]. For Neil, what was important was to discover the nature of their distinctive competencies, and subsequently understand how they could be significant in driving the business forward. Only when this question could be answered satisfactorily was it possible to determine core competencies. Core competencies are, naturally, those distinctive competencies that are at the core of future business success – and therefore they are discovered following an analysis of the relationship between distinctive competencies and goals (establishing the "business model").

As noted above, the exercise of exploring competencies and distinctive competencies is often difficult for a group. In public-sector organizations it is not unusual for 15–20 minutes to pass before some material starts to emerge. When helping a group discover their distinctive competencies, it is important for participants to realize that some of the most significant distinctive competencies arise from the existence of a very particular network of competencies. It is often the case that no competence within the network is distinctive, but that *the network itself is distinctive*. As we shall see, this was the case for Neil's organization.

After lunch, the group got together to start this exercise, with Colin leading and Fran in the support role. At this stage, the group was feeling reasonably pleased with themselves – they had mastered the use of the computer technology, ***they felt they had got most of***

Distinctive competencies:

❑ *DISTINCTIVE IN RELATION TO...*
  • *as defined by the goals of your organization*
❑ *difficult to emulate*
❑ *cannot be bought easily*
❑ *very high **cost of entry***
❑ *very **long time to attain***
❑ *a competence is not usually the product, rather it is process:*
  • *ability to **organize** work to deliver value*
❑ *ability to **exploit** competencies*
❑ *potent access to a **wide** variety of markets*

Figure 9.4   Ideas about the type of competencies to consider.
Source: C. Eden and F. Ackermann (1998) *Making Strategy: The Journey of Strategy Management*, London: Sage.

the important issues facing the organization out on the table and understood their impact on each other, each of them expressed the view that they had been able to participate fully in the morning's activities, and they felt that the draft goal system was not a bad starting statement.

To get the group started on the next task, they were **presented with some ideas about the type of competencies to think about** [Strategy]. Figure 9.4 shows the slide used for this purpose. Colin and Fran gave a few examples of each type and also provided examples of some of the difficulties in thinking about competencies. In particular, they alerted the group to the likelihood that they were likely to start by thinking of distinctive *outcomes* rather than competencies. For example, customer loyalty, successful brands and strong reputation are often given as distinctive competencies, when in fact they are the outcomes of underlying competencies. These outcomes must be surfaced, but there is a danger in not digging deeper to discover the competencies that produce these distinctive outcomes.

The group started suggesting distinctive competencies with great confidence – they were beginning to enjoy themselves! Over 30 competencies were surfaced and argued to be distinctive. Many of these were, as usual, distinctive outcomes, but it was nevertheless important that they had been stated and mapped. If they were to prove to be significant in the business model, the group was reminded that they must be "laddered down" to explore the competencies that supported the outcomes.

After discussion, the group was encouraged to focus on those competencies that at least one member of the team argued were definitely distinctive (even if others disagreed). Colin pushed them all very hard during this stage, asking them to argue for (not against) each item on the screen that they had identified as distinctive. This was done without any expectation that an individual would be required to defend his or her own contribution, but rather that the group should, in turn, address each suggested distinctive competence. The final map is shown in Map 9.5: it contains 16 potential distinctive competencies (in boxes) and three other items that are linking explanatory and possible important supporting competencies.

To test the group's view of the relative distinctiveness of each of the 16 items on the map, each participant was invited to rate every item. Using the computer system, they were asked to decide on the least distinctive item and the most distinctive item and rate these at 0 and 10 respectively (thus forming "anchor points"). Every other item was then rated relative to these two "anchor points" on the 0–10 scale. *This process of rating distinctiveness is easy to replicate using flipcharts and self-adhesive dots.* The computer system then calculated the average score and the measure of variability in the assessments made.

The ratings given by the group show that the "ability to build very extensive community products around core brands beyond any other company's focus [R 8,6 1,2]" is the most distinctive competence (with an average rating of 8.6 and a standard deviation[8] of 1.2). The distinctive outcomes of "trusted brands [R 7,8 0,98]" and "events are a hot ticket [R 7,2 1,72]" are highly rated, but there is less consensus about events being a hot ticket.

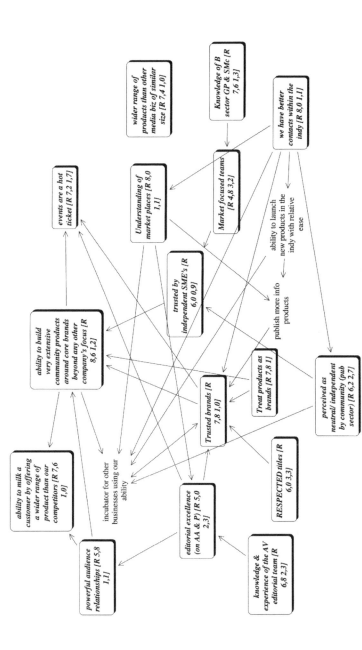

Map 9.5 *Distinctive competencies*. This map emerged from discussion about any potential distinctive competencies (DCs). There are 16 DCs here (in boxes) and three other linking explanations or supporting competencies. Figures in brackets indicate the results of judgements about the degree of distinctiveness (the first number is the rating and the second the degree of variance of view among the team).

There are two feedback loops and both of them are self-sustaining. They are both known as positive feedback loops (where a positive feedback loop is always self-sustaining but can in fact be either a vicious or virtuous circle, depending on whether you want the outcomes or not). Provided that some of the items in these loops support goals (that is, they make up a part of the business model), the loops are likely to be core distinctive competencies because they are self-sustaining. It was important to note that all of the items on the map are linked, with the exception of "have a wider range of products than other media businesses of similar size [R 7,4 1,02]", which was rated highly. *The feedback relationships in the network of competencies were seen to be of great importance by the group*.

Positive feedback loops are very important. Even when a feedback loop is made up of competencies, because they are self-sustaining they may be very important resources for the future of the business [Strategy]. A positive loop means that each of the competencies in the loop feeds all of the others. When the feedback loop is distinctive, this will be even more important because the distinctiveness is self-sustaining.

Given that some of the most distinctive items were outcomes rather than competencies, exploring the network of links to the outcomes would be a first stage in understanding how these outcomes could be managed through levering competencies within the organization. Map 9.6 shows these supporting competencies, or characteristics of the business, that sustain the outcome of "trusted brands".

Very often participants start the process of exploring distinctive competencies by stating the outcome of distinctiveness. Do not be concerned about this phenomenon, but encourage the group to ladder down to what really are distinctive competencies [Strategy]. What is important is gradually to help the group realize that these are outcomes, and encourage them to "drill down" to state the competencies that have delivered these distinctive outcomes.

By now it was time for a break. The exploration of distinctive competencies had taken longer than planned, partly because of the

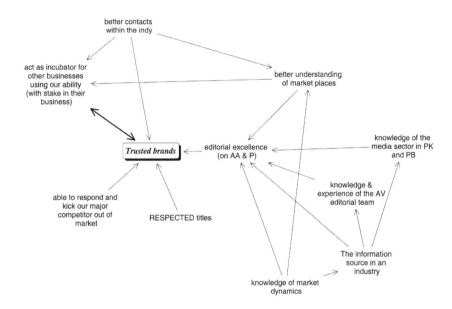

Map 9.6 *Supporting competencies.* Added here are the links to the characteristics of the business that sustain the "trusted brands" outcome.

discussion time. However, **discussion about distinctiveness must be allowed to reach a conclusion because of the absolute importance of distinctive competencies in developing confidence in a sound strategic future for the organization** [Strategy]. It is also worth keeping in mind that often distinctive competencies are of no future use to the organization, even though the managers are very proud of their existence.

The business model

The next stage of the workshop was to test out the role of distinctive competencies (as patterns or single items) in delivering the future goals of the organization.

In the case of Neil's organization, this was easier than is often the case. All of the distinctive competencies supported the goals they had earlier identified. Indeed, the feedback loop became so significant that the distinctive competencies in the loop became

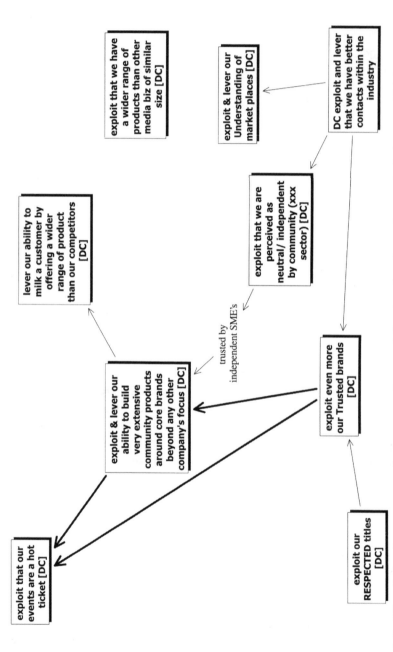

Map 9.7   The distinctive competencies have now been redefined and rephrased as goals (in boxes). Thick arrows indicate that the links are part of a feedback loop.

goals in their own right. Map 9.7 shows that many of the distinctive competencies became redefined as goals and the wording of most of them was changed so that they were re-expressed as goals. In many other cases the wording was changed so that they were expressed as strategies.

As the total map of the links between distinctive competencies and goals emerged, it became clear that one particular pattern was absolutely core to the business future of the organization – this was the core distinctive competence.

Often distinctive competencies (or patterns that are distinctive) become goals. When they do, the wording will need to be changed so that they express aspiration [Strategy]. **Other important distinctive competencies, particularly core distinctive competencies, also need to be reworded so that they are expressed as strategies, usually by inserting the words "exploit and sustain" in front of the existing statement** [Strategy].

Ending the first day

Following the creation of the business model and a strong appreciation of the strategic future that they believed they could create for themselves, the group returned to the strategic issues. The whole issue map was revisited to establish a new set of possible priorities in the light of the new map structure created as a result of the process of laddering up to goals. All of the previous priorities were included. The group then went on to re-establish priorities using the same process as before. However, after priorities had been established, the facilitator required the group to articulate the reasons for the final priorities. This process forces the group to express verbally reasons for the importance of the strategies. In doing so, they will usually use the causality shown on the map, but add the extra wording that brings the strategy alive. Alternatively, the group can add new reasoning that has not been fully explained before, but might be helpful in aiding understanding, in which case the map is elaborated.

The workshop ran on late into the evening (stopping for dinner at 8.00 p.m.). However, when the group stopped for the day they had convinced themselves that they had created a robust business model. The first item on the agenda for Sunday was to convert the business model into a spreadsheet model and test out the quantitative implications of it for the next three years. While the team had dinner, Fran and Colin translated the map of the business model and re-prioritized strategies (now re-evaluated after the business model work) into a narrative *statement of strategic intent for the organization*. In doing so, they literally translated the maps into outline form using a bullet point format and then converted the outlined text into sentences and paragraphs. Their goal was not to create polished language but rather to write out the logic of the business model: goals, core distinctive competencies to deliver the goals, strategic issues that must be resolved to make it happen, and strategies to be delivered in order to exploit and sustain the competencies. Their purpose was to allow the team to **test whether the group was persuaded by the logic of the more traditional narrative statement**, not whether it could at this stage persuade others.

Converting the map of the business model into a narrative statement of strategic intent turned out to be very important for the group. When they reviewed it first thing on Sunday, it reassured them that what they had created worked descriptively as well as analytically.

What Colin and Fran had done was mostly a routine task:

- The first paragraph consisted of a written-out statement of the most superordinate goal as the first, or topic, statement,

    – with those immediately subordinate to it inset as bullet points.

- They picked out any relatively isolated "tear-drops" of goals and expressed those in a similar way, along with a statement that linked the tear-drop upwards to a previous statement (these were the next paragraphs, and each paragraph needed an introductory descriptor for the whole of the tear-drop).

- The next part of the statement of strategic intent stated how distinctive competencies could deliver these goals, by describing the working of feedback loops, with particular emphasis on the role of the core distinctive competencies (this was done to make it absolutely clear how each part of the goal system was supported by distinctive competencies).

- Using the re-prioritized strategies and the map, along with the wording used during the strategy check (above), the final part of the statement of strategic intent described the priority strategies and the reasons for their importance in delivering goals or sustaining distinctive competencies.

Postscript

Neil reported after a couple of years had passed that the strategy was still in place. There was satisfaction in having delivered much of the strategy, but disappointment that other aspects are taking too long. The organization has resolved its cash crisis and is building confidence with its shareholders.

As Neil said: "We have loads of cash in the bank; profits are up on last year and we still have a chance of making budget this year; margins have started to grow on business magazines; and much more.... In short, we are working our way through the strategy actions and the team remain really committed to the program. What the strategy has done is give us all a common language to use and has removed a lot of the 'fire' from argument and debate as we all have to push towards the same set of objectives."

Process guidelines

- Get urgent issues "out on the table" early in the workshop, and make sure there is clear acknowledgement of them.
- The facilitator must watch for scurrilous contributions, and when they arise carefully manage their impact on the group.

- Pay attention to both content management and process management.

- Attempt to build a planned timetable, even though it is rarely possible to stick to it precisely.

- Make sure the explanation about the workshop uses no jargon and makes it clear why each of the tasks is important and how they fit in to the whole programme for the workshop.

- Provide the group with realistic expectations about the objectives and timing of the workshop, and indicate some clear milestones. Make sure participants know what is expected of them.

- Providing a topic label for a cluster of statements is a useful way of summarizing what is in a group of conceptually linked statements.

- Linking focuses attention not so much on what is in a statement but on action: why things are done and what needs to be done to make other things happen.

- Statements that seem to be at the centre of many others, with many links in or out of them, are often good starting candidates for identifying and prioritizing issues.

- In order to identify goals, participants are asked "What is achieved if an effective way is found of addressing the issue?" or "What might happen that is undesirable if the issue is not addressed?"

- Often laddering towards goals continues upwards not to goals, but to a series of negative outcomes, and some of these are "bad outcomes in their own right – we need to make sure they don't happen". If so, these items may need to remain written as negative goals rather than turned into positive outcomes.

The following points are of particular significance for strategy making:

- A statement of strategic aims is powerful when it represents the interaction between all of the goals.

- The power of the emerging goals should be tested by the extent to which they are different from those of competitors (see note 4).

- Ensure that core distinctive competencies are those that are "at the core" of the business model for delivering a successful and realistic strategic future.

- When considering issue priorities, it is important to pay attention to "busy" statements as possible high-priority items, except when they are vague "catch-alls" that are not easily actionable; allow the group to suggest other candidate statements; and pay attention to the candidate statements that appear to be supported by all participants.

- It is useful to present the group with some ideas about the type of competencies to think about before asking them to suggest their own organization's competencies.

- Positive feedback loops are very important; because they are self-sustaining they may be very important resources for the future of the business. Feedback loops made up of competencies may be especially important.

- Often participants start the process of exploring distinctive competencies by stating the outcome of distinctiveness. Do not be concerned about this phenomenon because these do need to be stated, just get the group to ladder down to actual competencies.

- Discussion about distinctiveness must be allowed to be completed because of the absolute importance of distinctive competencies in developing confidence in a sound strategic future for the organization.

- Core competencies are different from distinctive competencies.

- Often distinctive competencies (or patterns that are distinctive) become goals. When they do, the wording will need to be changed so that they express aspiration. Other important distinctive competencies, particularly core distinctive competencies, also need to be reworded so that they are expressed as strategies, usually by inserting the words "exploit and sustain" in front of the existing statement.

Learning points

- Interesting features of the "issue dump" were that it was dominated by internal issues; there were many issues about the working and effectiveness of the senior management team (implying that they are more of a group than a team), although it was encouraging that they were prepared to acknowledge this so explicitly; there were many issues about staff (keeping the best, getting the best, locking them in); and at this stage very little material about specific products or the marketplace was included.

- The senior management group was beginning to behave like a team – they appeared to have listened to one another and been constructive in their responses.

- They felt they had got most of the important issues facing the organization out on the table and understood their impact on each other, each of them expressed the view that they had been able to participate fully in the morning's activities, and they felt that the draft goal system was not a bad starting statement.

- The group saw the feedback network of goals and competencies as of great importance.

- As the total map of the links between distinctive competencies and goals emerged, it became clear that one particular pattern was absolutely core to the business future of the organization – and this was the *core* distinctive competence.

Notes

1 *Group Explorer* is special-purpose software (available through www.phrontis.com) that drives a set of laptop computers permitting each participant to communicate directly with a public screen displaying a *Decision Explorer* map. The facilitator controls the system using a "chauffeur" computer, which also displays information about participation. *Group Explorer* has techniques for a type of "voting" or preferencing, and for weighting of statements.

2 "Groupthink" is a term introduced by Irving Janis to describe the dysfunctional behaviour of a group under particular circumstances. The need for the group to protect its social well-being can mean that it does not surface and address important issues. See I. L. Janis (1972) *Victims of Groupthink*, Boston, MA: Houghton Mifflin.

3 Andersen and Richardson discuss the different roles that a process facilitator must undertake in managing a group; see D. F. Andersen and G. P. Richardson (1997) Scripts for Group Model Building, *System Dynamics Review*, **13**(2), 107–30. Eden discusses the impact of process management on content management and vice versa; see C. Eden (1990) The Unfolding Nature of Group Decision Support, in C. Eden and J. Radford (eds), *Tackling Strategic Problems: The Role of Group Decision Support*, London: Sage, pp. 48–52. Huxham and Cropper extend the debate to include the role of a facilitator in adding substantive content; see C. Huxham and S. Cropper (1994) From Many to One – and Back: An Exploration of Some Components of Facilitation, *Omega*, **22**, 1–11.

4 It is not always easy to make this comparison. Competitors may not have made their goals explicit to themselves, let alone promulgated them to others. Nevertheless, it is usually possible to make a sensible judgement about whether your own goal system is different.

5 The role of a business model, developed by identifying distinctive competencies and relating them to the goal system, is discussed more fully in C. Eden and F. Ackermann (1998) *Making Strategy: The Journey of Strategic Management*, London: Sage, Chapter 6. See also Ackermann, Eden with Brown (2004) *The Practice of Making Strategy*, London: Sage, for a full explanation of the process discussed in this chapter, and for further case studies.

6 An example of a typical two-day workshop is shown in Eden and Ackermann, *op. cit.* p. 393.

7 See Chapter 2 of Eden and Ackermann, *op. cit.*, for further detail on the use of self-adhesive spots for "preferencing".

8 Standard deviation is a statistical measure of the differences of views – the higher the number, the higher the differences.

Part IV

Summary and Conclusions

10

Learning from the Chapters, or How Does This all Fit together and How Can I Make Use of It?

IN THIS CHAPTER WE REVIEW ALL THE CASES WE HAVE presented in a way designed to deepen your understanding of, and ability to use, mapping as an aid to thinking and acting in a complex world. We begin by briefly reviewing the chapters in terms of case highlights. We then analyse the cases to draw out overall themes and observations regarding how to go about mapping and what to expect from it. Finally, we present a set of process guidelines that should serve you well as you go about mapping issues of interest to you.

First, another story! Recently, one of us had a conversation with a friend about this book. Let's call the friend Bob. Bob had participated in a group mapping exercise and was interested in learning more. A "mind dump" about the book seemed to be the best way to give him the big picture. Each chapter was described (including its central story and the kind of mapping involved) in essentially a non-stop oration. Since Bob was a good friend, he listened to the whole show, with an occasional interruption for clarification and detail. At the end, he had an odd look on his face of both excitement and concern that begged asking the inevitable question: "So, what do you think?"

He replied with a story of his own about taking his children to an amusement park. Their mother, let's call her Susan, had come along and okayed all of the rides except for the monster rollercoaster, which of course was the only ride the kids wanted to go on. Bob, in a weak moment and without really thinking about the consequences, said something about not seeing what the big deal was about the rollercoaster. The kids quickly exploited the opening. The eventual compromise was they could go on the ride only if an adult were with them – and that certainly was not going to be Susan! That's how Bob came to ride the rollercoaster.

Bob said the coaster started out slowly and the first hill was exhilarating, but certainly not overwhelming. He thought to himself, "This is good – I can do this!" Then came the next hill, which was a good bit higher and had more twists and turns on the way down. He thought, "That wasn't too bad." Then came the final hill, which was much higher and included all sorts of twists and turns and loops on the way down, and . . . At the end of the ride, Bob said the kids had to help him off.

He commented, "As you were finishing up describing the cases in your book, I couldn't help but think of the rollercoaster ride. You started out real easy and I really thought this is good and will work for me. You then went to the oval mapping [something he had participated in] and I again could understand what was involved. But then you went to the final chapter with all the computer-assisted group mapping, and I thought I just might be over my head!"

We, of course, had an entirely different picture in mind. We imagined conducting an orchestra, where various instruments enter and leave depending on the complexity of the score. A symphony, for example, can begin with a simple, repeated theme and then keep building in an ever more complex manner until the grand finale, which ends in a crescendo of beauty and richness! What is important about the symphony metaphor is that the performance can be as complex or simple as the conductor chooses. Our intention with mapping is to offer the skills and understanding that allow you as a budding conductor – or mapper – to create your own work of art! Bob readily said he could see it that way as well, and thought the metaphor was a useful way of thinking about what we are trying to do in this book.

We think it goes without saying that we much prefer the symphony story to the rollercoaster story. What this chapter is about is helping you take from this book what you need in order to construct really useful maps at whatever level of complexity you wish. We do this by reviewing the basic idea of mapping and the many ways in which it can be applied, and then by presenting detailed process guidelines to help you create your own maps.

A Review of the Cases

We began this journey in Part 1 – Chapters 1 and 2 – with a general introduction to mapping. We discussed the intent, applicability and basic process of mapping. Maps are simply word-and-arrow diagrams that indicate how ideas – and, specifically, actions and outcomes, causes and effects, or influences and results – are linked. Using the music metaphor, think of linking actions and outcomes as the basic melody, which will continue throughout and govern the entire score.

Our first story involved Chuck and Mary's argument over housework (see Table 10.1). The story demonstrates how they were able to use mapping to do two very important things. First, mapping helped them understand their different views of the statement "Mary has to do everything around the house." It quickly became apparent that Chuck and Mary had very different understandings of what needed to be done, when it had to be done and whose responsibility it was. Second, mapping enabled them to break a frustrating and damaging emotional cycle in which they had been caught for a long time. This cycle led from accusation, to defensive reaction, to anger and blame, to withdrawal – and then to the feeling that they both needed to get over it for the present, or something worse might happen. Mapping helped both parties actually *hear* and *see* what the other was saying and helped both develop a plan that would get the housework done in a way that both could support and that would avoid a repeat of the destructive emotional cycle.

How many times have you been in a similar situation? Anyone involved in a long-term relationship has probably experienced issues

Table 10.1 The nature of the problematic situation, its challenges and outcomes

Chapter and title	Brief description of problematic situation	Phenomenon: "pain" from the clients' point of view	Initial statement	Challenge	Secondary challenge	Secondary challenge	Secondary challenge	Products/ deliverables	What changed?
1: What to Do When Thinking Matters	Facing a persistent conflict over housework	Mary sullen, and Chuck is "in trouble, again"	Mary says: "Chuck doesn't help out even when he is at home"	Resolve entrenched conflict	Find a better solution by getting "outside of the box"	Find a way to make life together easier and better for both of them	Help each other "listen" when each is no longer willing to "hear" the other	Mutually agreed solution represented on a map	Chuck does agreed tasks; Mary stops doing Chuck's work for him and feeling exploited as a result
2: Why and How Mapping Works	How to plan a long sailing trip when life is already complicated	Seeking to understand a big dream that would be difficult to make happen	John and Chuck want to spend more time together, which is becoming difficult	This idea will take a lot of time and require careful planning and preparation	Their wives and family must be "on board" or at least supportive	They need money and a boat		John and Chuck realize what they really want is time to reflect, talk and do "soul work"	They might make the trip together, but they also need to explore other options
3: How not to Miss the Boat	A much planned and hoped-for sailing event is threatened	Colin's twin goals of timeliness and quality product seem to be mutually exclusive	No sailing vacation this year!!!	Colin's needs are very different from those of the boat builder	Being a tough negotiator actually has lowered the chances of getting what Colin wants	It is important to get through this without making enemies	Colin must convince third parties to intervene on Colin's behalf	A successful strategy that got Colin what he wanted and made no enemies	Colin got to sail on a quality boat that was delivered on time

4: House of the Rising Fun	Improve quality of life by getting a bigger house and better location	Current flat is too small and that is the reason Fran is unhappy	Fran wants to buy a new flat rather than stay in existing one	What type of accommodation does Fran want and why?	Where does Fran want to live and why?	Fran wants to have more confidence in her decisions, rather than have second thoughts	Make the move with as few disruptions as possible (military campaign)	A deep insight was gained regarding a well-rounded career and private life	Fran is happy about the move and her enhanced social life, while still being able to be productive
5: It's a Bummer to Be JB	Figure out what's really bothering John and how it can be dealt with	John is not happy and it is affecting his family, friends and job	John feels awful: his job is killing his soul	John needs to figure out what is really bothering him	Deal with a lot of anger and frustration that is easily misdirected	John thinks the major decisions are out of his hands and influence	John is a very loyal person, but feels he has to leave in order to get what he wants and needs	A clear plan was developed that let John take more control of his future	John's plan worked, although not exactly as planned in all respects
6: To Merge or not to Merge	Decide whether to merge with another college	To make an informed decision	Determining pros and cons of merging based on what is known	Under-standing all the nuances/issues and how they affect one another	Getting all on board			Insights into issues to be considered and confidence in the outcome	A clear plan that lowered the level of discomfort and instilled confidence in the decision
7: Small College Hoping *not* to Get Smaller!	A dramatic change event is needed to regain stakeholder support and hire a new president	A period of rapid growth, followed by dropping enrolments, has stretched resources to the breaking point and alienated stakeholders	Key stakeholders need to meet and figure out what to do	A quick assessment is needed, along with some rapid changes to stop students, faculty and staff from leaving	A rough outline for change is needed with goals and strategies designed to improve the situation	A job description for the presidential search with supporting information should be developed	Persuade all parties there was indeed hope for success they could work towards	A clear plan for change with goals, strategies and actions that was outlined	The sense of "doom" was alleviated and momentum was built for acting on the plan and searching for a new president to help with the effort

(continued)

Table 10.1 (continued)

Chapter and title	Brief description of problematic situation	Phenomenon: "pain" from the clients' point of view	Initial statement	Challenge	Secondary challenge	Secondary challenge	Secondary challenge	Products/deliverables	What changed?
8: Making the Most of Our Assets	Gain commitment within the firm for a new business strategy	The new product line lacked necessary internal support from already busy departments	The group has to gain commitment, support and cooperation from key departments if the strategy is to succeed	Department heads need to know about the product line in terms of why it is important to them and how they can support it	A clear communication must be developed regarding how this product line will contribute to company success	Department heads need to understand how they can be a part of the process and therefore commit	Cooperation is key for success, but many departments do not practise this strategy	A clear idea of the plan goals was developed, but additional work was needed to achieve necessary depth	An opportunity was taken to surface a wide number of views and interests, which were discussed and selectively integrated into the plan
9: A Question of Turning Around	Develop and commit to a three-year business plan	Will the organization be successful with its present (static) business plan or does it need to change given the cash crisis?	The organization needs to maximize its competencies in a very competitive environment	Key management staff need to develop a larger picture of the business and then commit	A new, more coherent business model needs to be developed and acted on	The idea of competencies is generally known, but not well understood or acted on	The new CEO is largely an unknown and must persuade owners he has what it takes	A well-founded three-year business plan was developed that led to greater success	A firm that levers and supports its key core competencies is more likely to be successful

in which one or the other party thinks that tasks and resources have been allocated unfairly. Or how about those friends who are chronically late to events? Similarly, questions often arise at work over whether everyone on a team is doing their fair share. Next time you have a feeling of "déjà vu all over again", consider using mapping to help sort out what is really going on, clarify any misunderstandings or differences of opinion, and move to a solution that is satisfactory to everyone. Let mapping help you explore the issue in a way that leads to shared understanding and a jointly negotiated action plan. And let mapping help stop everyone from hanging the noose of blame around another party's neck!

The first step in using mapping is to figure out what the question is you want to address, or what the situation is that requires common understanding. Chuck and Mary had to agree jointly on what "doing all the work around here" meant before they stood a chance of negotiating a successful agreement. Maybe you need to help your team members at work understand what needs doing and who should do it so that everyone thinks the work is shared equitably. Or maybe you and your friends need to figure out what being "late" means and why that is a problem for you. Remember that a great deal of success lies in understanding the problem in a manner that allows all parties to work towards a solution – and mapping can be a very useful tool for addressing this challenge.

Chapter 2 discussed how mapping can be used more formally to help people explore issues, actions and goals in a manner that often leads to surprising revelations. The chapter began by showing how mapping uses comparisons and contrasts to help make concepts more *meaning-full*, rather than *meaning-less*. We used the example of John and Chuck's favourite forms of exercise – running and swimming, respectively. We showed that running and swimming are very similar in terms of results and what it takes to do each. But there are also some very important differences, which are so strong that John would rarely choose to swim and Chuck would rarely choose to run.

We then explored a more elaborate personal planning situation, John and Chuck's desire to take a big sailing trip. Recall that they began their mapping exercise by trying to figure out how they could sail from Duluth, Minnesota, to Hilton Head, Carolina, and then discovered in the process that what was really important was to spend time together in contemplation and reflection. They thus established that their real goals could be satisfied in many different ways. They also discovered that their initial intuition – not to discuss this trip first with their wives – was about as mistaken as it could be. The case indicates that we often need to discover what we really want and how to get it – and that we will not, or cannot, know these things in advance. Mapping can be an incredibly valuable aid to the discovery process.

Mapping is particularly useful because for most of us the day-to-day busyness of our lives means we often don't have time to figure out what we really want and how to get it. Mapping helps us explore what we might do, how we might do it and why, by revealing the connections among our thoughts and creating hierarchies of ideas from goals down to strategies, actions, options and assertions. Mapping allows us to explore the connections among them by laddering up and down the map. Linkages are made that allow us to discover what is truly important in the context of problems, issues or opportunities that we are trying to address. We see this discovery process over and over in other cases in the book.

Think about your own situation: You might want to try mapping vacation possibilities with your family or friends.[1] Do you all share the goals of the trip? Or are there desires or needs that are not being answered or other alternatives that should be considered? How about deciding to change jobs or stay where you are? Surely you should be as certain as you can be about your goals when making such a crucial decision!

Part II of the book, Chapters 3–5, illustrated the power of cognitive mapping for helping an individual figure out what is important and how to develop an action plan to obtain what he or she wants. This section also introduced some additional rules and insights that help produce more organized, meaningful and analysable maps. The chapters, in other words, are designed to advance your understanding of the formalities of mapping and to improve your skills, while following the basic mapping rules introduced in Part I.

In Chapter 3, Colin's mapping challenge was to find out what the real problem was that vexed him – namely, that he was going to lose his yearly opportunity to go on an extended sailing trip. After all, he had made plans and invested a lot of money in order to do this very thing! His map quickly showed that he might well be able to force the builder of his new boat to deliver it on time, but the cost would be reduced quality. In addition, he feared he would be alienating many people on whom he would need to depend later for service. So here we have a real dilemma that needed careful sorting out and managing if Colin was to be satisfied and happy. Mapping allowed him to explore options that addressed the dilemma in an "outside of the box" manner.

While not all of us have the desire or means to purchase a sailboat like Colin's, it is surprising how many of us have faced similar circumstances. For example, building a new house, or improving an existing one, has many of these same challenges. Your homebuilder or improver is very much like the yacht builder. He or she sells you a home or agrees to a project that must then be built. But he or she may face many tight timelines and competing needs from other customers who have entered into similar contracts. If weather, building materials, carpenters, permits and so forth do not work out exactly as planned, there are delays. And you may then discover that your move-in or be-finished-by date has passed – with the work still not done. What can you do to avoid such a turn of events or manage the situation when it does happen? As was the case for Colin, we think the time has come to map options. Do you have to settle for an unfinished house, questionable workmanship or even more delays? Are there other options available to you? Mapping can help you clarify these options and evaluate strategies so that you can maximize your satisfaction. To paraphrase Mick Jagger and the Rolling Stones, you might not get all you want, but you just might get what you need.

Fran's challenge, in Chapter 4, was originally to move to a larger apartment, but she soon discovered the real objective was to expand her life options to include more of a social life. She had invested years in accomplishing her work-related goals, but that also meant spending less time pursuing her other important goals. Now that she had reached many of her work goals, she needed to reorganize her life so that she could further develop social relationships beyond the academic domain, where she was already very well connected. So how do you go about changing your life? Fran discovered that having an apartment of sufficient size and in an appropriate location would make it relatively easy to entertain and also visit new friends. Thus she created a situation for herself where it would be easy to change her work–life balance.

And you? Have you some objective to which you aspire but have postponed working on for way too long? The goal might involve figuring out how to graduate from school, or plan a wedding or a trip, or switch jobs, or have children, or retire early, or something else that matters a great deal to you. Mapping can help you sort through your thoughts and understand what actions you might take to achieve your too-long-deferred goals. It might even help you figure out what your real goals are. Mapping can help you reach out and make your dreams real. It can help you figure out how not to miss out on what matters most to you. And conversely, mapping can help you avoid having too many regrets about the things you did not do.

Chapter 5 illustrated how mapping can be used to develop scenarios that allow the mapper to compare and contrast possible futures. John used the maps he developed to discover just how unhappy he was in what most people would think of as a very desirable job situation. By actively exploring his options and goals, he was able to see a way out of a situation that he initially doubted he could make turn out better. John also used his maps to take a serious look at his priorities in terms of job, family and friends. While none of his strategies worked out exactly as planned, he was able to understand how to take control of his life and work towards what he thought was truly important. And in the end, he did get almost all of what he wanted and needed!

How many of us have arrived at a similar juncture in our lives from time to time? In other words, we find ourselves in a bad situation and need help in figuring out how to make it better. Unfortunately, for many of us this story hits all too close to home. We look around one day and the life we are living is not what we wanted or thought it would be. The many roads not travelled may weigh heavily on our soul, to paraphrase Robert Frost. We may feel trapped, defeated and helpless. Some of us decide to tough it out and others simply quit. But are there other options? Are there ways we can take control of our situations and shape our destinies based on what we feel is truly important? The answers to these questions can only come from one person – and that person is you. Mapping is a tool that can help you sort matters out and explore options. The options are yours and the decisions are yours alone to make, but what a tragedy if the choices are not even considered.

Parts I and II were designed to introduce mapping concepts and then illustrate increasingly complex applications in a manner that encourages use and practice. Increasing your mapping skill levels through practice allows you to deal with more complex problems. As with mastering music, each small success opens up ever more challenging opportunities. Mastering simpler mapping activities gives you the opportunity to work on ever more complex problems with expanding increments of mastery.

Part III introduced group mapping, which takes mapping to another level in which groups are engaged in creating maps. The resulting maps embody a jointly negotiated view of the world that furthers commitment and successful decision making. Here we presented you with the full symphony in all its power and complexity. Group members contribute in a concerted way to generate a shared view of a world that they can understand and manage. Chapters 6 and 7 introduced oval mapping in non-computer-assisted circumstances. Chapter 8 showed how cognitive maps developed through interviews can be woven together into a group map whose meaning and content are open to negotiation and further elaboration. Finally, Chapter 9 showcased a meeting supported by fully interactive mapping and decision-making software.

Almost all of us have been in meetings where critical issues that can affect the very future of the organization are discussed, and discussed, and discussed – endlessly, unproductively and without resolution. We believe that such meetings are a tragic waste of time and opportunities and, even more importantly, can lead to cynicism and hopelessness. We have found that group mapping facilitates and supports comprehensive, effective and efficient conversations that actually do lead to timely decisions. The chapters in Part III showed how properly facilitated group mapping can lead to very effective meetings and decisions.

Chapter 6 presented a single crucial issue or question that challenged an organization, in this case a small public college. Fran took you through this first group mapping exercise to illustrate both the overall process of group mapping and the details of how to facilitate it. When properly facilitated, group mapping engages organizations in strategic conversations that rather quickly build understanding, clarify necessary actions, garner commitment to those actions and produce effective decisions. Enhanced organizational success is the typical consequence. For Cardonald College, it was vital that the organization explored just what was involved in merging and what the potentials were for success and failure. Once the decision was made not to merge for the present, the organization could further position itself for effective future action.

Chapter 7 involved a more complex situation, where the "roof" had either fallen or was just about to. Many strategic planners advise that normal strategic planning is not helpful in these circumstances. In other words, when your house is on fire, don't organize a committee meeting, call the fire department! However, in this case, just such a meeting (actually a retreat) was organized with decidedly successful results – in part, because calling a meeting of key stakeholders in effect *was* calling the fire department!

Organizations are exceedingly complex and require support from key stakeholders. Becoming explicitly aware of stakeholders' expectations, goals and thoughts about what needs to be done is the very first step in a turnaround process such as the one facing Hope College. Oval mapping allowed these parties to gather and quickly come to an agreement on desirable goals, strategies and immediate priorities. Because the conversation was pursued in a retreat setting, it also allowed parties who did not know one another, or who had become estranged, to develop trust and a shared commitment to the future. In other words, the retreat setting and oval mapping process provided the occasion, setting and logical platform for discussion, decision and commitment that were inclusive and promoted trust and hope. Other organizations in need of strategic planning should consider similar sorts of retreats that utilize oval mapping.

Chapter 8 illustrated how cognitive mapping and computer-supported oval mapping can be used in tandem to utilize resources efficiently (especially managers' time) and gain commitment to a new direction, in this case to a new product line. Individual cognitive maps were developed much as we saw in Part II. These individual maps were then merged to represent the combined thinking of independent department heads, whose commitment and cooperation were key to the success of the new product line.

As many firms either merge or are merged in a business environment where the common thinking is that survival means always growing, we see many instances where parts of the organization that are used to working independently on their growth prospects need to find effective ways of working together. Some management literature refers to the separation of units as "stove piping". So how do you get commitment and cooperation across the "stove pipes" when that is needed? Mapping can help people recognize common interests and the value of cooperative effort.

Our last case, presented in Chapter 9, demonstrated what we might call "state-of-the-art" mapping, where oval mapping is both supported by a wireless network and also supports the application of some of the most current thinking in strategic management. In this chapter, we introduced fully computer-assisted mapping and priority-setting techniques. We also showed how mapping was used to explore an organization's "core" and "distinctive competencies", the exploration of which many management theorists think is key to organizational success. Our own experience is that while there is much discussion regarding competencies, little has been done to help organizations identify and utilize these resources. We believe that mapping is an ideal tool for helping managers both discover and support these critical components of their organization's long-term success. We also think that the use of computerized assistance results in an even more efficient use of the scarcest executive resources – time and attention.

In terms of the symphony metaphor, we would consider Chapter 9 the "grand finale", where, guided by the conductor, the entire might of the orchestra contributes to a powerful success in which complexity and individual contributions are managed in such a way that the whole is far greater than the sum of its parts. Group mapping, enhanced by computer support and followed by decision making and action planning, shows the power and speed of mapping in even the most complex, time-pressured situations. Simply put, mapping employs a straightforward rationale, which, through practice and computer support, can help with the most complex and daunting challenges that face us as individuals, groups or organizations. You may choose to work with the basic musical score and a few instruments, or with practice move on to the full score and complete orchestra. Each approach has real value and can help you, your group or your organization make sense of your world and move effectively to accomplish your goals.

Inputs and characteristics of the cases

Here we discuss various inputs and characteristics of mapping exercises generally, and of the cases specifically. Table 10.2 provides a summary.

Client objectives

Mapping is an exercise that takes time and mental effort. As we remarked in Chapter 1, often mapping is not needed – for example, when the issue at hand is fairly straightforward and the action required is obvious. But in all of the cases presented in this book, the client (who sometimes was one of us!) was using mapping because the issue was important and the answer was not obvious, while the benefits of success were substantial and the costs of failure were generally high. Mapping, in other words, was used when it was worth it. Mapping thus should be considered whenever the issues involved will directly and dramatically affect the client.

Facilitation

Facilitators are generally used for two reasons in mapping exercises. First, sometimes people need some help so that they can focus on the content of the map, without having to worry so much about the process of developing it. We first saw facilitation used in Chapter 5, in which John was readily able to address major issues with some gentle nudging and help from Chuck. Second, groups often require some help with the process of mapping so that they can focus on the content of the map. All the group mapping exercises in Part III made use of facilitation.

Participants

Mapping involves from one to potentially hundreds of participants. For example, Chuck and Mary were a two-person group when they mapped their argument, and John and Chuck were a two-person group when they mapped their potential sailing adventure. All of the cognitive mapping exercises in Part II involved no more than two people. In contrast, the oval mapping cases in Part III involved from five to sixteen participants, with some additional facilitation or technical help. In general, groups of five to ten work best, as everyone has an approximately equal chance of contributing fully. Larger groups typically require additional facilitation and often must be subdivided into small groups of five to ten. However, John and Chuck once conducted a mapping exercise (with four additional facilitators) involving 140 people. And Colin and Fran have involved 175 people on several occasions without extra facilitators, but with computer support.

Resources

With the exception of computers and software (to be discussed shortly), the resources needed for mapping are almost ridiculously inexpensive and easily obtained. Most offices have these materials on hand, which makes mapping on the spur of the moment always a possibility. We tend to keep markers, Post-it notes, pencils, flipchart paper, masking tape and coloured dots in a nearby soft-sided carrying case for easy access when needed. Our experience is that issues that call for mapping often crop up with little notice, and we try to be prepared.

Duration

All of the mapping activities we have presented in the book took less than two days to accomplish, and the cognitive mapping exercises took no more than a few hours. However, we have been involved in

Table 10.2 Inputs and characteristics of the cases

Chapter and Title	Brief description of problematic situation	Client objectives	Facilitation	Participants	Resources	Duration	Facilities
1: What to Do When Thinking Matters	Facing a persistent conflict over housework	To deal with a never-ending sense of "déjà vu all over again"	None	Two: Mary and Chuck	Markers; Post-its; flipchart paper	Two hours	Dining-room table
2: Why and How Mapping Works	How to plan a long sailing trip when life is already complicated	Figure out how to be happy at work and home	None	Two: John and Chuck	Markers; Post-its; flipchart paper	Two hours	Large table
3: How Not to Miss the Boat	A much planned and hoped-for sailing event is threatened	Get to go sailing in my new (quality) boat	None	One: Colin	Markers; Post-its; flipchart paper	Two hours with additional time for contemplation	Desktop in office
4: House of the Rising Fun	Improve quality of life	Figure out whether to move and why	None	One: Fran	Computer with *Decision Explorer*	Two hours with lots of time for contemplation	Desktop in office
5: It's a Bummer to Be JB	Despite apparent success, John is not happy about the future	Deal with sense of unhappiness and helplessness	Facilitative interview with some joint participation	Two: John is interviewed by Chuck, who provides feedback	Writing pad; pencils; eraser	Two hours	Office table
6: To Merge or not to Merge	Decide whether to merge with another college	Reach a decision; gain board "buy-in"	Four facilitators; with three of them trainees	Sixteen: governing board plus senior management group	Ovals; pens; sticky putty; masking tape; laptop computer software for capturing material	Half a day	Large room divided in two by a folding wall

7: Small College Hoping *not* to Get Smaller!	A dramatic change event to regain stakeholder support and hire a new president	Strategic assessment to demonstrate change and commitment to a new, better approach	Dual facilitators taking turns in front of group while the other managed content on the computer	Fifteen, representing a broad array of on- and off-campus stakeholders	Markers; Post-its; flipchart paper; masking tape; voting dots; digital camera; laptop computer	1.5 days	Hotel away from college to ensure attention by participants
8: Making the Most of Our Assets	Gain commitment within the firm for a new business strategy	Develop the necessary understanding and commitment to support the new product line	One facilitator who developed cognitive maps through interviews and then conducted an oval mapping process	Six: Department heads from key areas related to the new product line	Ovals; pens; sticky putty; masking tape; laptop computer; paper and pencils	Six hours of interviewing and two three-hour group meetings	Conference room off site
9: A Question of Turning Around	Develop and commit to a three-year business plan	Develop a sound three-year plan for the firm based on what it does best	Two facilitators exchanging roles facilitating up front and managing content with the computer in the back	Five: Senior management who were also owners of the firm	Networked laptop computer for each participant linked to a server that projected the map	Two days	Off-site hotel to ensure commitment to meeting

mapping exercises that have gone on intermittently for many days, or involved long-distance travel by participants and facilitators, or have taken months to wrap up. Imagine working with a multi-national organization with tens of thousands of employees in a dozen countries and you can see why this can take time! However, there was nothing involved in these long-term efforts in terms of the mapping process that was not also addressed in the cases we have presented.[2] Planning, preparation and follow-up are always crucial. As a rough estimate, in the beginning you will find that for every hour of group mapping time, you may spend an additional three hours on preparation and follow-up. This ratio will drop dramatically as you become more familiar with the process.

Facilities

Mapping can be done almost anywhere, from a kitchen table to a conference room to using an entire conference centre. The mapping exercises in this book took place in a dining room, office or conference room. The determining factor in choosing where to map is that you should have enough space so that your participants can actively engage in the map-building experience. With group mapping good wall space is key, along with enough room to allow participants to view the map, walk around and socialize, and carry on a discussion of what the map reveals. Adequate restroom facilities are also a must! As we are often working with busy executives, we usually try to schedule group meetings at some distance from the work site. This helps protect the participants from the day-to-day incursions of their work.

Mapping types and processes

Mapping types and processes can vary a good deal from case to case. In this section we discuss some of the more important distinctions between mapping types and processes. Table 10.3 summarizes the discussion.

Individual or group maps

You will recall that there are basically two categories of mapping. The first is cognitive mapping for individuals, in which the individual is trying to make sense of his or her world, typically in

Table 10.3   Mapping types and processes

Chapter and title	Brief description of problematic situation	Individual or group map	Nature of links	Categories used	Analyses used	Computer assisted
1: What to Do When Thinking Matters	Facing a persistent conflict over housework	Group map	Informal: identifying rough associations between differing views	Actions and implicit goals and negative goals	Verbal discussion and negotiation	No
2: Why and How Mapping Works	How to plan a long sailing trip when life is already complicated	Group	Formal: with some identi-fication of clusters, goals and actions	Issues, actions and goals	Verbal discussion with a focus on "laddering" up and down a hierarchy of concepts	No
3: How not to Miss the Boat	A much planned and hoped-for sailing event is threatened	Individual	Formal and causal	Issues, actions strategies and goals		No
4: House of the Rising Fun	Improve quality of life	Individual	Formal and causal	Issues, actions and goals		Yes
5: It's a Bummer to Be JB	Despite apparent success, JB is not happy about the future	Individual	Three cognitive maps with formal causal links	Options, actions, goals and negative goals	Verbal discussion with comparison and contrast of potential futures and actions	No
6: To Merge or not to Merge	Decide whether to merge with another college	Two group maps, integrated later	Formal and causal: developing a hierarchy with a small number of outcomes at the top	Issues, goals, potential key issues and context	Verbal discussion assisted by use of "sticky dots": identifying "busyness" and top of hierarchy	No, during group workshop. However, used following workshop to integrate two sets of material

(continued)

Table 10.3 *(continued)*

Chapter and title	Brief description of problematic situation	Individual or group map	Nature of links	Categories used	Analyses used	Computer assisted
7: Small College Hoping *not* to Get Smaller!	A dramatic change event to regain stakeholder support and hire a new president	Group map	Formal and causal: developing a hierarchy with a small number of outcomes at the top	Goals, strategies and immediate and long-term actions developed	Verbal discussion with comparison and contrast of potential futures and actions against present conditions	No
8: Making the Most of Our Assets	Gain commitment within the firm for a new business strategy	Individual cognitive maps combined into a group map	Formal and causal: developing a hierarchy with a small number of outcomes at the top	Issues, actions, strategies and goals	Cognitive maps developed from interviews, which were then combined and utilized as the basis for group discussion	Yes, after initial cognitive maps were developed by hand and then entered into the computer for the workshop
9: A Question of Turning Around	Turn around the company over the next three years	Group map using both *Decision Explorer* and *Group Explorer* software	Formal and causal: developing a hierarchy with a small number of outcomes at the top	Issues, actions, strategies, distinctive competencies and core distinctive competencies	Group oval mapping utilizing computer support rather than ovals on walls	Yes

order to identify effective actions. Group or oval maps represent efforts by groups to arrive at shared understanding and commitment – again, typically in order to take effective action. Part II of the book was devoted exclusively to cognitive maps, while Part III was devoted to group maps. In addition, some of our early basic mapping examples in Part I were group maps.

The nature of links

There are certain general rules for making links that should be followed in order to help mappers make sense of their maps, to help others make sense of their maps, to make analysis of the maps easier, and generally to increase the efficiency of the process. For example, developing a hierarchy in which goals are towards the "top" of the map, with issues or strategies below them and options or actions below them, supported by assertions, helps people understand the logic of the map. Orienting a map in this way is analogous to north always being "up" on highway maps.

We tend to classify maps in terms of whether or not they are constructed using the formalities of mapping outlined in our process guidelines. Maps that follow the formalities are formal maps, while those that do not are informal maps. For example, our first map of Chuck and Mary's argument was an informal map; all the other maps in the book followed the formalities of mapping. We have found in particular that oval mapping and large group maps are easier to build and communicate if they adhere to the formal conventions of mapping.

Categories used

We have identified assertions, actions, options, issues, strategies, goals and negative goals as general categories. These categories lend themselves to the basic hierarchical organization of ideas discussed above. It is not necessary for a map to include all these categories. However, it is helpful to classify statements in order to understand where they might fit in the hierarchy. This allows us to explore what we intend to do (action or strategy) in terms of why we would do it (goal). Life is short, and while not everything has to serve a goal, it is helpful to recognize when we are not acting in our interests. All of the maps in the book from John and Chuck's sailing trip in Chapter 2 on make use of all or most of the categories noted above.

Analyses used

Resource B offers an in-depth discussion of types of analyses that may be performed on maps. Clearly, discussion and dialogue are the most important ways of making use of these types of analyses; in other words, only through discussion and dialogue can you figure out what the analyses might be telling you. Computer support is often needed when performing analyses of maps containing very large numbers of statements and links. We use *Decision Explorer* software to help analyse large maps, as it contains a suite of analytical tools. However, these analytical tools can only help inform discussion and dialogue, which is how people come to agreement on how to interpret what they see. We know of no substitute for inclusive, comprehensive discussion informed by a map.

Computer assistance

It might seem from some of our cases that the use of computers is required, especially in terms of moving to some of the advanced group applications we have discussed, but nothing could be further from the truth. While computers using *Decision Explorer* software do help us quickly develop and analyse content, they are chiefly utilized so that we can more quickly and efficiently gather and organize data. None of the cases presented was dependent on computer support, although *Decision Explorer* could have been used in all of them.

Let's take a moment to summarize. We hope you are persuaded that our journey has been more like a symphony than a rollercoaster ride. Mapping is based on some simple concepts and rules. The complexity of the mapping you choose depends on the complexity of the problem facing you and your own skill and comfort level with mapping. Just because you cannot envision yourself leading a large oval mapping process at this point does not mean that you cannot produce an individual cognitive map or a smaller oval map! As we said at the beginning of the chapter, practice is the key to moving on to advanced mapping.

The contributions mapping made in the cases

At this point, we hope you understand how our symphony "works", but we still need to address why we believe that mapping is such an important tool for helping us all deal with the challenges we face. Table 10.4 is a compilation of the contributions that we think mapping made to addressing the problems presented in the cases.

There are four major categories of contributions and fifteen sub-categories. Simply put, we use mapping because it organizes and develops content; helps facilitate the emergence, or revelation, of new content; helps users come to informed and shared decisions; and finally helps individuals and groups deal with their emotions, which could very well be mapping's most important contribution. The four categories and fifteen sub-categories are not necessarily mutually exclusive.

Mapping organizes content

We have emphasized throughout the chapters that mapping helps develop and organize ideas and actions. When you and others write down or post on a board your ideas and then begin to ladder up and down the hierarchy of ideas, you find that you begin to see the logic and strength of everyone's thinking. This inspires confidence and allows you all to communicate more articulately. You see the complexity of participants' thinking, but also appreciate how it is organized and can be communicated effectively. An important sub-category of organizing content is *exploring options*, something that happened in all of the cases. Another sub-category is *reducing complexity*, with which mapping helped in about half the cases. Finally, mapping helped with *developing strategy*, which happened in almost all of the cases.

Mapping reveals content

Another theme you see throughout the chapters is the discovery of additional information, insights, goals and linkages that subsequently guide people's thinking and actions. Mapping encourages emergent thinking through adding content and exploring linkages. As you and others develop your own maps, you will also begin to "see" new options and points of view. Strategies begin to surface along with the necessary actions to support them. Most importantly, you begin to explore your goals and how and why you might want to take action in the first place. Mapping helps reveal emergent content in at least five ways, namely through *developing ideas* (in all but two of the cases), *exploring other points of view* (in a majority of the cases), *identifying real issues and goals* (in all but one of the cases), *exploring*

Table 10.4 Contributions that mapping made to the cases

Chapter and title	Organizes content				Reveals emergent content				Helps improve decision making
	Explores options	Reduces complexity	Develops strategy	Develops ideas	Explores other points of view	Identifies real issues/goals	Develops common ground	Helps develop outside-of-the-box solutions	
1: What to Do When Thinking Matters	×	×			×	×	×	×	×
2: Why and How Mapping Works	×	×		×		×			×
3: How not to Miss the Boat	×	×	×	×	×	×		×	×
4: House of the Rising Fun	×		×	×		×			×
5: It's a Bummer to Be JB	×		×	×		×			×
6: To Merge or not to Merge	×	×		×	×		×		×
7: Small College Hoping *not* to Get Smaller!	×		×	×	×	×	×		×
8: Making the Most of Our Assets	×		×		×	×	×		×
9: A Question of Turning Around	×	×	×	×	×	×	×	×	×

Chapter and title	Deals with conflict	Helps manage the emotional domain				
		Helps cope with distress or anger	Diagnoses emotional dynamics	Reduces anxiety	Promotes trust	Develops commitment (ownership)
1: What to Do When Thinking Matters	×	×	×	×	×	×
2: Why and How Mapping Works				×		×
3: How not to Miss the Boat	×	×	×	×	×	
4: House of the Rising Fun		×	×	×		×
5: It's a Bummer to Be JB	×	×	×	×		×
6: To Merge or not to Merge		×		×	×	×
7: Small College Hoping *not* to Get Smaller!	×		×	×	×	×
8: Making the Most of Our Assets	×			×	×	×
9: A Question of Turning Around				×	×	×

outside-of-the-box solutions (in three of the cases) and *developing common ground* (in all of the group mapping cases).

Mapping helps improve decision making

Have you ever noticed that the mood changes in a meeting when the time comes to make a decision? We have all been in meetings where everything seems to have gone well up to the point of decision and then it all falls apart. Mapping helps you through these rough times by being there as a readily available resource and reference, showing what a decision might mean in terms of goals, strategies and actions. When people question assumptions, the map may clarify what they are. When logic is challenged, the map may help. When people want to know how goals and strategies are linked, the map may show how they are. The map does not make the decisions. Rather, it provides a record that preserves complexity, yet organizes and categorizes that complexity in such a way that people can understand and manage it. And if more mapping needs to be done, the map is there as a base on which to build.

In situations where mapping has been used, the moment of decision for many groups is actually a non-event, as the rationale and way forward are clear from the map. The "merge or not to merge" case illustrates this, since the map revealed the answer to the question that prompted the mapping. In such cases, the ability of mapping to organize ideas, reveal emergent content and develop common ground and commitment made the decision a foregone conclusion. Mapping assisted with decision making in all of the cases.

The emotional domain

Our discussion to this point has focused largely on what mapping is and how it can be used. It is also important, however, to emphasize the affective aspects of the mapping process. After all, we are not beings of pure logic and our relationships, decisions and commitment are more often than not heavily influenced by our emotions.

We have discovered that mapping has some very significant positive impacts on emotions. First, it can be utilized to *manage conflict*, as was seen in several of the chapters but was particularly evident in Chuck and Mary's argument in Chapter 1. Second, mapping can be used to *help cope with distress or anger*, a role it played in Chuck and Mary's case and in all of the cognitive mapping cases. Third, mapping can help with *diagnosing emotional dynamics*. Again, mapping helped do this in Chuck and Mary's case. Mapping also helped Colin understand why he was so upset about his boat-building problems, helped Fran understand that she really wanted a better social life, and helped John understand just how unhappy he was and what he could do about it. Mapping also helped the participants in the Hope College case understand the sources of some of the conflict, distrust, fear and disappointment they felt, and also revealed paths to a much happier future.

Fourth, mapping can help *reduce anxiety*, which turns out to have been an important contribution to all of the cases. Fifth, mapping can help promote trust, which was a factor in a majority of the cases. By trust we mean that the individuals involved in the mapping exercise had higher confidence that others would follow through on their promises and that decisions made with the assistance of mapping would be more likely to be carried to fruition. Finally, mapping can help *develop commitment*, or ownership, of the goals and the strategies and actions leading to them.

The emotional domain has powerful short-term and long-term effects on individuals and organizations. Because of its contributions to understanding and managing emotions, mapping likewise can have powerful effects on the individuals and organizations that use it. The cases in this book indicate that mapping made significant positive contributions through revealing, embracing and helping guide the emotional aspects inherent in each situation.

We hope that this quick summary and review of the cases is useful and inspires you to become adept at mapping. As we have noted several times throughout the book, we think that mapping is what you should do when thinking matters. The final section in this chapter provides detailed guidelines for how to go about mapping, either for individuals or groups.

Process Guidelines for Constructing Cognitive and Oval Maps

As you progressed through Chapters 1–9 you saw us identifying process guidelines that would help you in your own mapping endeavours. In this section we pull the process guidelines together, categorize them and present them as a "one-stop" summary of how to go about mapping. In addition, we have incorporated a series of "mapping formalisms" (MF) designed to help you develop and analyse maps according to a consistent set of rules.[3] The mapping formalisms are also presented in Table 10.5. Resource E contains a complete set of the process guidelines from Chapters 1–9.

The process guidelines focus primarily on oval mapping in a group setting, although obviously many of them apply to cognitive mapping as well. The mapping formalisms apply to oval mapping, cognitive mapping and interviewing. In the last section we present specific guidelines for use when mapping via interviews.

Recognizing when a situation can be mapped – and is worth mapping

Since mapping takes time and effort, it should be clear that not every issue or challenge is worth mapping. In addition, some situations require immediate action and there is no time for mapping. For example, as noted, when your house is on fire you call the fire department. You don't get out a writing pad and pencil! But there also are plenty of situations when thinking matters, and mapping can help you or those you are working with get the thinking straight. The issue at hand simply must be important enough that it appears to justify the (relatively) little time and effort it takes to map what is going on, what might be done about it and why.

We recommend three things you can do to help you recognize a mapping opportunity:

1   Digest the stories we have presented and imagine how you might do something similar. Experience – even vicarious experience – is the best guide to knowing when mapping might help.

Table 10.5   Some specific mapping formalities

The following topics are covered in this table:
- Getting the wording of statements right.
- Getting the direction of the arrow (causality) right.
  - Being clear about options and outcomes, means and ends etc.
  - Dealing with generic statements appropriately.
  - Dealing with assertions and facts.
  - Dealing with feedback loops (see Resource B).
- Goals, negative goals and constraints.
- Doing mapping in interviews.

Wording statements
- Make statements action-oriented by including a verb – without doing violence to what was said where possible.
- Aim for 6–8 words as this will ensure that each statement is discrete and yet descriptive.
- If there is ambiguity about a statement, consider identifying "who", "what", "where" and "when" in the statement (although this may make the statement too long).
- Exclude words such as "should", "ought", "need" etc., in order to make statements more option-like rather than imperative.
  - E.g. "we ought to hire more sales people" becomes "hire more sales people".
- Avoid using "in order to", "due to", "may lead to", "as a result of", "through", "caused by" etc., as these imply two statements linked together by an arrow.
- When a statement includes several considerations, as for example "postpone writing mapping book, several articles and book chapters, and other books", it is important to decide whether the statement should become several statements.
  - Ask whether:
    - The considerations have different consequences.
    - They each have the same importance.
    - They each might involve different types of actions/explanations in order to create the outcome.
  - Thus, in the example:
    - Writing an article may be more important than books or chapters, in which case the statement should be separated into two parts.
    - Postponing the mapping book may have different consequences because it involves other colleagues, in which case it should be separated.
    - Writing other books may require large chunks of time, whereas others can be done using small intervals, in which case it should be a separate statement.
  - Therefore, watch the use of "and" as this might suggest two options rather than one.
    - E.g. split "increase and improve services" into "increase services" and "improve services", as these might lead to different outcomes and have different explanations.

Using contrasting poles
- The *meaning* of a statement is often best discovered by listening for the contrast.
  - For example, the meaning of "warm rather than hot weather" is different from "warm rather than cold weather"; "buy 2 computers rather than 6 computers" is different from "buy 2 computers rather than hire more staff" etc.

(continued)

Table 10.5   *(continued)*

– Difficulties arise when each contrast is an option in its own right, and there might be several options. When the contrast illustrates meaning by suggesting a possible alternative outcome, circumstance etc. (often contrasting past with now, past with future, now with future), then use the contrast as a part of the statement; when the contrast is a clear option, then make it a separate statement (sometimes linked without an arrowhead to other options).
  • e.g. "status quo" rather than "leave the school", rather than "stay but renegotiate terms" – might best be treated as separate options.

Getting linking right: Direction of the arrow (causality)
See Figure 10.1 for basic map structure.

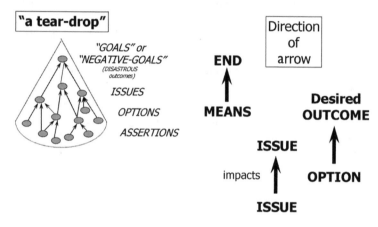

Figure 10.1   Developing "causal maps"

• The direction of an arrow should indicate the direction of causality and influence: means to ends, options/actions to outcomes.
• One person's means can be another person's ends.
  – For example, A→B might be what one person thinks, while another person may think B→A is correct.
  – For example, "turning things around means we have to win every battle in the next 5 years" may be coded with "winning every battle" as the desired outcome from "turning things around", or "winning every battle" is required in order to "turn things around", depending on the desired ends of the interviewee.
• But bear in mind that some "objective" truths might be subject to debate.
  – For example, "putting more policemen on the beat will reduce crime" may be an objective truth to one person; another person might argue that the objective truth is that more crime leads to more policemen on the beat.
• Sometimes A→B can be treated as so consensual that it need not be debated, e.g. "obvious" arithmetical relationships.
  – For example, more sales cause more sales revenue.
• Means to ends are most difficult to judge when considering a hierarchy of criteria; that is, values and goals.

(continued)

Table 10.5 (continued)

- For example, is "be unhappy and upset much of the time" more disastrous than "crawl into my shell and give up"? That is, does "be unhappy" lead to "into shell" or vice versa? This can only be judged by the person being mapped, or at least this choice must be open to consideration.
- It sometimes helps to work with a hierarchy of goals, such as "objectives" lead to "goals", which lead to "ideals or values". So objectives are shorter-term and more easily measurable; whereas goals are expression of desirable longer-term outcomes; whereas ideals or values are unlikely ever to be attained but guide purposeful behaviour.*
- Avoid mapping time sequences which are not causal relationships (as this will produce flow diagrams or process maps that are not amenable to the same sort of analysis or meaning as causal maps).

Getting linking right: Avoiding duplicate and double-headed arrows
- Ensure that the map does not contain duplication of links.
  - For example, where the map shows A→B→C→D along with A→C and C→D and A→D, ensure that the latter three links show different causal chains (through additional material).
- Avoid double-headed arrows, as these are implicit feedback loops suggesting either:
  - muddled thinking that can be resolved by determining means and ends;
  - a legitimate feedback loop consisting of additional statements that might provide more intervention options (see Resource B).

Dealing with generic statements
- It is best to ensure that all members of a category are subordinate to the statement expressing the generic category.
  - For example, "buy more saucepans" should in most circumstances lead to "buy more kitchen equipment" – that is, the specific leads to the generic.
- When a sub-category has different consequences from those of other members of the category, it will need its own out arrow to other consequences (along with the link to the generic).
- Sometimes the generic statement may not be necessary because there are no specific consequences that follow from it; rather, they all follow from specific sub-category statements.

Dealing with assertions/facts
- We presume that when someone makes an assertion they have a reason to do so, and that it is intended to suggest that an implied action is required.
  - Thus, if someone states that "Glasgow has a population of over 500 000 people" then we ask why this assertion is being made – what is its meaning in action terms? For example, they might know that it was 600 000 last year and so the statement "obviously" implies that the "Council will be short of taxes next year" which is also is stated as a "fact" with implied consequences.
- Thus, assertions tend to be at the "bottom" of a map, with consequences following from them.

Goals, negative goals and constraints
- Goals are desired outcomes that are "good in their own right" (so much so that they are hardly seen as optional by the proposer).
- Negative goals are undesired outcomes that are bad in their own right.
  - For example, "become bitter".

(continued)

Table 10.5   (*continued*)

- Constraints are often stated as if they were goals, but will be subordinate and have consequences that constrain actions, goals, issues etc.
  - For example, "attaining minimum levels of shareholder return" may act as a constraint on management behaviour, rather than acting as a goal (even though shareholders would wish to see it expressed as a goal).

Mapping in interviews
- Capture the richness – don't worry about the map looking a little "messy".
- Given that maps are used to work on complex issues, producing a tidy map straightaway is unlikely.
- Capture statements first – it is easier to recall the links later.
- Use natural breaks in the conversation to:
  - Feed back material to reassure the interviewee she or he is being listened to.
  - Update the map with material not yet captured (but in the brain!).
  - Test understanding.
- Build in time for review to:
  - Link material currently isolated.
  - Check whether sufficient laddering up and down has been carried out.
  - Feed back emergent characteristics, e.g. goals, negative goals, busy points, clusters, etc. (see Figure 10.1).
- Recognize that for some people maps will be broad but relatively shallow, whereas for others they will be narrow and deep.

---

*Based on the Ackoff and Emery typology in R. Ackoff and F. Emery (1972) *On Purposeful Systems*, Chichester: John Wiley; see also the discussion on "values" in C. Eden, S. Jones and D. Sims (1979) *Thinking in Organizations*, London: Macmillan.

2   Mapping may be particularly useful in situations where you feel frustrated or helpless (Chapters 1, 3, 5) or don't really know what to do (Chapters 6, 7, 8, 9). Simply knowing that there is a tool for situations like these may prompt you to map. Some concrete preparations may facilitate this cueing process. Assemble the necessary materials for mapping and store them in a readily available location (Chapters 2, 9). Think of doing so as analogous to purchasing and installing a fire extinguisher in your home. Once you have a fire extinguisher, you are far more likely to use it when a fire breaks out!

3   Finally, we have found that once people see what mapping can do for them, they use it frequently to handle new challenges. We also recommend that you actively seek out partners or clients and let them know about this valuable resource and your ability to help (Chapter 1, 5, 8).

Preparing for mapping

Good preparation can make for a productive and satisfying experience; poor preparation can lead to an unproductive one:

1 Create a workspace in which participants can readily observe and participate. The space can vary from a bare tabletop to a room with plenty of flat wall space (Chapters 2, 6). Participants must be able to engage with the mapping process if they are to develop ownership of the map's contents and implications for action.

2 Carefully plan the list of participants to ensure that key stakeholders are part of the process (Chapters 6, 7, 8, 9).

3 Be sure to have enough mapping supplies on hand (Chapter 6, 7) (See Table 10.6).

4 Decide on the purpose of the mapping event and craft a question or statement to begin the mapping session (Chapters 6, 7, 8, 9). Make a list of "urgent" issues you already know need to be discussed to help ensure that content related to the issues gets on the map [mapping formalism, MF].

5 Hold the event at a time and place away from the distractions of day-to-day business (Chapters 4, 6, 7, 9). Be sure to schedule enough time so that participants can converse, interact and reflect (Chapters 6, 7, 8).

6 Arrive early enough for the mapping session to deal with the inevitable unforeseen glitches, including making sure that the room is adequately prepared (Chapter 6, 9).

7 Introduce yourself and the other participants, keeping your remarks short and targeted on the task at hand. Include some supportive remarks from your client (Chapter 8, 9).

8 If your participants have not mapped before, take some time to explain the process (Chapters 4, 8). Review the "ground rules" for the process:

   • If you don't like an idea that someone else has placed on the map, don't remove it. Instead, add your own statement that presents a different view or shows why you disagree.

Table 10.6   Checklist of mapping supplies that might be needed

Notebook containing process guidelines section of this chapter		200 ovals or Post-it notes
Agenda		Masking tape and/or self-adhesive putty
List of participants		Several packs of coloured stick-on "dots" (for straw polling or voting)
Name tags or placards		Scissors
____ flipchart pads		Stapler
____ note pads: one for each participant		Necessary background materials
____ pencils: one for each participant		Digital camera
____ black water-soluble markers: one for each participant		Refreshments
____ additional water-soluble markers in a variety of colours to identify goals, strategies, actions or other categories of concepts		Clock or watch
Soft "gum" pencil erasers		

- Keep your statements to around 6–8 words and write big enough so that the statements are legible.

- Each statement should begin with a verb or action.

9   Generally, we try to keep the introduction to mapping to a minimum, so that individuals or groups can get on with the process and learn by doing. However, it is important to provide enough of an introduction for unnecessary confusion to be avoided. Particularly when using mapping to interview someone,

we try to keep the introduction to a minimum, so that we are able to capture the interviewee's own initial thoughts (Chapter 3, 5, 9).

Beginning the map

The initial stage of mapping – especially in a group setting – can be a somewhat stressful time, since you may find yourself quickly in the midst of a cascade of thoughts and argumentation that may not appear to be related. This is when the "dam" of interests and frustrations may open and they all come flooding out. You need to be ready for this flood and for the temporary appearance of chaos. Your objective at this point is to make sure you capture all of this creativity so that you can sort it out and work with it later in the process. To that end, there are some process guidelines and mapping formalisms that are particularly useful:

1 Start with brainstorming:

- Begin by asking participants to brainstorm individually as many ideas as they can in answer to a specific starting question or about a particular issue. You might consider asking participants to write down quickly as many ideas as they can on a piece of notepaper, or you might ask them to write their ideas on separate oval cards or Post-it notes, one idea per card or note. Be sure to get "urgent" issues out early on the map and ensure there is clear acknowledgement of them (Chapter 9, MF).

- Make a point of asking participants not to censure themselves and to avoid spending a lot of time crafting their words or thoughts (Chapters 2, 4, 6).

2 Wording statements:

- Ask participants to fashion 6–8-word action statements beginning with a verb (Chapters 3, 4, MF). Take some time to help those who are not sure what to do (Chapter 6).

- Discourage the use of words such as "should", "ought", "need" etc., as these do not encourage thinking in terms of options (MF). For example, suggest saying "hire more sales personnel" rather than "we need more sales people".

- If participants are having trouble articulating what their thoughts are, use "who, what, where, when" questions to help them articulate their ideas. This is particularly helpful when dealing with statements of assertion or fact. We presume that when someone asserts something, there is probably at least an implicit intention to do something about it. Asking "What might be done about it?" can often tease out the "intent" of the statement (MF).

- Avoid using "in order to", "due to", "may lead to", "and" etc., as their use indicates more than one idea. Each idea should be written separately and then connected to the other idea appropriately with an arrow (MF).

- Individuals may interpret the same statement entirely differently. When this happens, consider editing the statement to clarify its meaning, or else adding the differing interpretations to the map (MF).

- Introduce the idea that concepts always have at least one contrast. In other words, when you write concept or statement A, there is always an implied opposite pole. This idea of "A" *rather than* "something else" is represented by the shorthand convention of an ellipsis (...); thus "A ... B" is a means of capturing the alternative aspect of statement A (Chapters 4, 6, MF).

3 Once participants have developed their statements, ask them to transfer each statement to an "oval", using a coloured marker, and to begin posting them on the wall (Chapter 6).

4 Number the ovals as they are posted to facilitate easy recall and linking (Chapters 3, 6).

5 Finally, ask participants to group similar statements together in clusters, but remember that it is more important at this point to get all of the ideas up than to build a tidy map (Chapter 6).

Establishing a hierarchy of concepts

Establishing a hierarchy of concepts is an important part of the process of a group map or cognitive map. Causal maps move from assertions and actions to overarching strategies and on to goals or negative goals (see Figure 10.1 in Table 10.5 and Figure 2.1). A well-structured map should clearly reveal this hierarchy. Given the essential simplicity of the mapping process, this structure is typically not hard to develop (Chapters 1, 2, 3, MF).

1   If the map is a cognitive map, begin by listing the main options that the interviewee thinks he or she has. List them in small print in the upper-left-hand corner of the paper, or spread them across the paper. Build a map around each option by laddering down from main options (or strategic issues) to possible actions and assertions. Then ladder up to possible goals (Chapters 2, 3).

2   If the map is a group map, before posting any ovals consider drawing a dashed line horizontally across the mapping surface with a marking pen, about one-third of the way down from the top. The line can be used to separate goal-, negative goal- and mission-related ovals above the line from strategy- and action-related ovals below the line (Chapter 7). Usually you will begin by asking for strategy- and action-related ovals, in response to a question such as "What do you think we should do?" (Chapter 7).

3   If the map is a group map, after ovals have been clustered read out to the group all of the contributions in the cluster. Position the ovals so that the most abstract or general outcomes or issues (that is, the broad motherhood-and-apple-pie items) are at the top of the cluster, and the more detailed options and assertions are near the bottom (Chapter 6). Where there appear to be two statements on an oval, it is a good idea to separate them by making two ovals so that they can be explored fully (Chapter 6).

4   Begin to develop the chains of argumentation within each cluster. This process is called linking and is part of formalizing, and ultimately finalizing, laddering up or down from one statement to another.

Developing categories of clusters of ideas

Cluster labels provide a useful way of summarizing what is in a group of conceptually linked statements (Chapters 6, 9). It is therefore important to take a moment to organize issues so that the group recognizes the individual categories and is aware of what they contain.

1 Make sure that there is lots of room between clusters (Chapter 6). This can be started while the group is taking a break after the brainstorming and initial clustering process, or can be done with the group as a whole (Chapters 6, 9).

2 In order to ensure that participants are familiar with the ideas in the map, take some time to "tour" the map by discussing the "intent" of each cluster. Look for a statement within the cluster that represents the overall subject or theme of the cluster. This statement will be the cluster's label and should be at the "top" of the cluster; that is, at the end of the chains of arrows that link ideas in the cluster. If a line has been drawn across the mapping surface to separate issues and strategies below the line from goals and negative goals above the line, this label should be placed just below the line. If no existing statement adequately captures the theme, develop this statement with the group and identify it as the cluster heading (Chapter 7).

3 As you discuss a cluster, make sure that all of the statements within it are truly subordinate to the cluster heading. Move ones that are not subordinate to a more appropriate cluster or perhaps develop a "sub-cluster" (MF).

4 If the cluster seems very large, explore whether there are two or more clusters or sub-clusters involved. Create as many clusters and sub-clusters as make sense (Chapter 6).

5 The next step is to look for identical statements. Clarify whether these statements are identical by discussing them with the group. If the group agrees, remove the redundant item (Chapters 6, 7).

6 Once you have finished identifying the first category or cluster, move on to succeeding groups until the participants are familiar with the entire map (Chapter 7).

Identifying goals, strategies, actions and assertions

Each statement on the map should identify an action, since all should be worded in an action-oriented way. But much of the power in a map comes from showing how bundles of actions add up to strategies, and how strategies can lead to the achievement of goals or purposes. As you move up the map from assertions and actions to strategies and goals, the statements should move from being narrowly specific and concrete to becoming more inclusive, general and abstract. Each statement results from, or is an outcome of, what is linked to it in a causal way. Towards the "top" of the map – that is, towards the end of the chains of arrows – you should find or create general statements that represent goals, negative goals and purpose or statements of mission (Chapter 2).

1   Goals are outcomes that are "good in their own right". Generally they are not immediately obtainable, but progress towards them can be measured. The individual, group or organization "owns" or "claims" the goal as one it wants to pursue (Chapter 2, MF).

2   To find out what the real goals are, ask "Why would we want to do that?" or "What would be the consequences, or results, of doing that?" Those consequences that are good in their own right are likely to be goals (Chapters 2, 9, MF). By pushing on consequences (ends) of doing what might be done, you can find out what the real purpose is of doing the thing (Chapter 2).

3   Try to identify obvious goals and strategies and clearly mark them as such with an agreed colour of marker (Chapters 4, 9).

4   Remember there often is a hierarchy of goals determined by causal relationships. Participants often begin by thinking that all goals should be linked, which is not necessarily true. Encourage participants to think about subordinate and superordinate goals.

5   Also remember that laddering towards goals may reveal negative goals, statements that identify "bad outcomes in their own right that we must make sure do not happen". In general, negative goals are a natural consequence of pursuing a desirable goal, and therefore must be managed as part of the process of goal achievement. Sometimes negative goals can be recast in more positive terms by focusing on the opposite pole (the rather than...) (Chapters 2, 5, 9, MF).

6   Goals are usually immediately apparent after they emerge from brainstorming, clustering and laddering and linking efforts. In a business context, these "emergent goals" should be tested to see how advantageous they are, particularly because they may be different from those of competitors (Chapter 9).

7   One type of powerful emergent goal is one that represents the interaction between most or all of the goals. This superordinate goal is quite useful, as it summarizes the essence of what the organization wants to pursue – its strategic aims (Chapter 9). However, be cautious about the "need" some participants may have to link everything. The links should be examined carefully to make sure they are substantive.

8   Strategies are typically identified by cluster headings at the head of a bundle of actions believed to be necessary to achieve one or more of the goals (Chapters 2, 7). The actions that comprise a strategy are typically part of a larger cluster with the same name that initially identifies a strategic issue. In other words, the strategic issue is a bundle of possible actions from which comes the set of actions actually chosen – the strategy. The process of selecting actions, and adding any additional ones that are needed, converts a strategic issue to a strategy.

9   Actions are often underpinned by assertions, which are statements of fact, value or condition that are either taken as given or may be made the subject of research (Chapter 2).

Linking statements

Once all statements are categorized and some hierarchy is developed through laddering, it is time to start linking, if that process has not already begun. Linking is a way of formalizing, and ultimately finalizing, the process of laddering up and down the map. It is also typically a creative process, because it results in additional content being added as gaps in logic become apparent. And linking is a meaning-making process, because it establishes and clarifies the context – and therefore the meaning – surrounding specific statements (Chapters 2, 3, 4, 6, 8). Linking focuses attention not so much on a statement itself, but on what other actions surround it – in order to clarify how and why things might be done (Chapter 9). As one moves up and down chains of arrows from a statement, more and more of the context – or big picture – becomes apparent.

1   Before beginning the linking process, it is helpful to let participants know that mapping the first cluster will take a lot

of time. Subsequent clusters will take less time as people know more about the process of linking (Chapter 6).

2   Select a cluster and, with the consent of the group, begin drawing links (arrows) between statements. Recall that the direction of an arrow should indicate causality and influence: causes to effects, means to ends, or actions to outcomes (MF). In order to ladder and link down a chain of arrows, ask "How would we do that? What would it take to do that?" Conversely, to ladder and link up a chain of arrows, ask "What would happen if we did this? What would result from doing this? Why are we doing this? (Chapters 2, 3, 4, 5, 8, 9).

3   Remember to use both positive and negative links when needed. Negative links indicate that doing something will make something else less likely to happen, or result in less of something else. Negative links can help identify some of the trade-offs or dilemmas that should be considered (Chapters 4, 5).

4   It is often best to draw in links with a pencil first, as mistakes or changes in thinking can be erased as needed. One disadvantage of pencilling in links is that they may be hard for a group to read from a distance (Chapter 7).

5   There may be a difference of opinion about which way an arrow should go. When this happens, encourage discussion to help clarify the basis for the differing views. Agreement should be sought, but not forced. It may be that the arrow goes both ways, but two-headed arrows should be avoided, since they usually mean that some concepts and links are missing (MF).

6   Be careful to link statements only when you can establish a direct causal or influence relationship. If you believe that two statements are somehow connected, but cannot quite make the argument about how they are connected, some additional statements and links probably need to be added (Chapter 4, MF).

7   One way to begin the linking process is to select a central statement in a cluster of statements and then begin laddering up and down, adding statements when necessary to further clarify and provide detail to the map. Typically, you should begin by laddering down by asking "How would you do that?" or "What would it take to do that?" You then ladder up to outcomes, and

ultimately to goals and purposes, by asking "What would we get out of doing that?" or "Why would we do that?" (Chapters 5, 8). However, you should move in whatever direction the participants want to move (Chapter 5).

8 Avoid mapping temporal sequences, rather than causal relationships, as these will produce flow diagrams or business process maps that are not amenable to the same sorts of meaning creation and analysis that causal maps are (MF).

9 When one cluster has been mapped, including adequate detail and links to goals, move on to another. Ladder down and up in the new cluster, adding necessary detail and connecting to statements and goals from the previous cluster. Finish by creating additional goals that emerge and explore additional linkages among goals and the statements in the first cluster. Continue in this manner until all clusters are mapped (Chapter 8).

10 Cycling between generating new material and reflecting on existing material is helpful in generating even more material (Chapter 4).

11 Avoid duplicate statements. If you discover a duplicate statement, discuss with the group whether it truly is a duplicate and, if they think it is, remove it and draw or retain the links to the one you keep. This is a common occurrence as maps become more developed (Chapter 6, MF).

12 You must ensure the map does not contain duplicate links. These may occur when you begin adding detail to a map. For example, you might first have linked statement A to statement B. However, with some additional discussion, you decide that A should go first to D, then to E, then to B. Be sure to erase the original linkage – A to B – if there is no direct causal link between the two (MF).

13 As noted above, when attempting to determine means and end, some participants may wish to use a double-headed arrow. When this happens, it is possible that there are some missing statements and links. Another possibility is that you have discovered a legitimate feedback loop that may well be also describing a distinctive competence (Chapter 9, MF).

14 When linking, avoid getting worried about finalizing endpoints. Rather, go with the flow of the conversation, knowing that you will attend to these details during the finishing stage of mapping. If you are using a computer, you can always develop separate views of the map that highlight different end points (Chapter 4).

Finishing the map

Finishing a map is a combination of tidying it up, testing out the connections and making any desirable commitments to action. This process of finishing up is where everything can become very "real" for participants, if it hasn't been before.

1   Tidying up a map means in part making sure that all statements are linked, and that there is a flow from options or actions to issues or strategies, and on to goals or negative goals. Begin this process by looking for "orphans" – unconnected statements – and linking them to other statements (Chapter 4).

2   Then begin testing the causal thinking in the map by following the links. One way to test links is to see if they and the statements they connect tell a plausible "story" about linked causes and effects. A fully developed map should offer many stories based on causal linkages. These stories should support or give life to strategies that might be pursued to achieve desirable goals (Chapter 2).

3   Explore the goal area of your map to ensure that each of the goals is supported by at least one strategy (Chapters 2, 7).

4   It is often helpful to review a cognitive map with a friend or an outside party to see if it makes sense to them (Chapter 4).

Analysing the map

Analysis can be accomplished by careful review of the map, or alternatively through the sophisticated analyses that are possible with computer support (see Resource B). It is important to keep in mind that a cognitive or oval map is meant to represent, respectively, a person's or a group's thinking. It is therefore important to have the individual or group examine the map frequently to see what it is saying and check that it accurately reflects the individual's or group's thinking (Chapters 2, 3).

1 Look for "busy concepts" with many arrows leading to or from them. Busy concepts often represent "potent" options or actions that support many strategies. These options or actions are likely to be particularly valuable, and may also reveal a possible distinctive competence (Chapters 2, 5, 8, 9).

2 Once goals have been identified, it is important to re-examine the possible strategies for achieving them to see if there are additional ways to pursue the goals (Chapter 2). Remember that some goals are more important than others and this means that the strategies supporting those goals are also more important (Chapter 2).

3 Ladder down from the goals to determine whether statement(s) immediately supporting them are also goals, albeit subordinate goals (Chapter 8).

4 Think carefully about the contrasting pole of statements, the "rather than" aspect, symbolized by an ellipsis (...). Try to understand statements from varying points of view, and particularly from the point of view of those with whom you disagree.

5 Examine negative links and negative goals to surface dilemmas and trade-offs that can affect decisions (Chapters 4, 5).

Using a map to inform decision making

A map usually presents a variety of choices. Indeed, typically a map will present more possible strategies and actions than are possible to undertake all at once. Analysing the map can help inform choices about which strategies and actions to pursue, who should pursue them, when and how. The following guidelines may help people make wise choices:

1 Have participants attach priorities to goals, strategies and actions. These priorities will reveal what participants think is most important. One way to elicit preferences is to provide participants with a fixed number of coloured dots, which they

can place next to preferred statements. Different coloured dots can be used for different categories of statements (e.g. goals, strategies or actions) (Chapters 6, 7). Similarly, it may be helpful to have participants identify their least preferred goals, strategies or actions. You can do this by supplying participants with a certain number of a specific colour of dot to be placed on their least favourite statements. Let participants know they can choose to place all of their dots on one statement or category to express especially strong support or opposition. Make sure that the explanation about how to indicate priorities is very clear to avoid mistakes or misunderstandings (Chapter 6).

2 Once straw polling or voting is completed, review and discuss the results with participants to ensure that the outcome does indeed reflect the group's preferences.

3 Chosen actions should be assigned as tasks. It is often helpful to write the name of the person in charge of completing a task on the statement with an agreed date of completion (Chapter 6).

4 When the task-assignment process is completed, review the whole mapping exercise with participants. The review should highlight progress and provide a sense of achievement and closure (Chapter 6).

Following up on a mapping exercise

Mapping is a new experience for many that is both stimulating and simultaneously so different that it is hard to incorporate into their day-to-day practice. This means that follow-up is often necessary to reinforce any important learning that occurred or commitments that have been made.

1 Provide a tangible product, such as a report consisting of a brief description of the event, maps and other appropriate materials, so that participants have a record of what happened (Chapter 6). Follow-up should occur as quickly as possible after the event, and ideally within five working days, so as to maintain understanding, enthusiasm and commitment (Chapters 7, 8).

2 Be sure to provide an explanation of next steps together with details of agreed actions and persons responsible.

3   Maps that provide an overview of agreed goals and strategies are particularly useful in helping participants see the whole and the parts (Chapters 6, 7).

Facilitating mapping exercises

Mapping exercises often work better when they are facilitated. Facilitation is a real art, and practice is a necessary part of developing one's artfulness as a facilitator. The following process guidelines may help:

1   Groups have more confidence in a confident facilitator who is also open and willing to make mid-course adjustments. The facilitator must have enough confidence to be able to intervene in conversations or actions that do not contribute to, or actually undermine, the process (Chapter 9).

2   Pay attention to both content and process. Typically it helps to build an agenda or timetable, even though it is rarely possible to stick to it precisely. Having an agenda or timetable is especially important when there is a deadline for ending the meeting. Participants will tend to discipline their work accordingly (Chapter 9).

3   It is important to make sure people have enough time to start building relationships with one another and to establish the beginnings of a sense of common understanding, concern and trust. If the group is new or will be working together for a long time, taking time early on to develop an effective group will pay off later (Chapter 7).

4   Be sure that participants have some idea of what will occur during the process, particularly if mapping will be a new experience for them (Chapter 8). Letting people know what will happen is especially important during the initial steps of brainstorming and posting ideas, since the number and variety of statements may overload some participants with unexpected quantities of information. Make sure that process descriptions and explanations contain little or no jargon. Clarify how each of the tasks is important and how it fits into the whole agenda for the workshop (Chapters 7, 8, 9).

5 When beginning a group map, it is often helpful to have the facilitator place the first ovals on the mapping surface, while also checking with the group regarding the placement of the ovals. As participants gain in their understanding of the process, they can be encouraged to place their ovals themselves. Facilitators and participants will engage with the material in the maps through adding, modifying or subtracting statements, links and category labels (Chapters 7, 8).

6 Continually monitor the group to ensure that everyone is involved and participating. Be attentive to participants' inputs and make any reasonable changes that are suggested, as doing so will increase the group's engagement with and ownership and development of the map (Chapter 8).

7 Use natural breaks in the process to catch up and tidy up (Chapter 8). You may be able to use these opportunities to review and evaluate the content of the map with any available participants by challenging them to explain or defend what is in the map. Encouraging participants to tell a story about what the map is saying seems to work well.

8 If different groups are working concurrently in different places, make a point of visiting the other groups, if you can, to see how they are doing. You might also enter into discussions in appropriate ways to help participants improve their mapping skills (Chapter 8).

9 When asking participants to do something difficult, it is helpful to give examples of, or ideas about, what you are asking them to do. For example, when asking participants to think about distinctive competencies – which can be a challenging concept for many – it helps to give examples (Chapter 9).

10 Being sure about distinctive competencies is a crucial part of developing confidence in a sound strategic future for an organization. So discussion about distinctive competencies must be allowed to proceed until it reaches a logical and natural conclusion (Chapter 9).

11 Often participants start the process of exploring distinctive competencies by articulating what in fact are outcomes of distinctiveness. Do not be concerned about this phenomenon,

because the desired outcomes do need to be stated. Just get the group to ladder down to actual competencies (Chapter 9).

Mapping in an interview format

A good interview usually depends on good rapport between the interviewer and the interviewee. The following guidelines may help build this rapport and lead to a useful map:

1   An interview often begins with a general conversation to get acquainted and to explain the purpose of the interview. The interview proper typically starts with the interviewer asking a prepared question (Chapter 8).

2   Interviewees often reply to this question with a list of issues they wish to discuss. It is important to capture these issues and the interviewer should list them on the side of the mapping surface without trying to link them. Once the issues are listed, begin mapping with an issue of the interviewee's choice. Write that statement in an open space on the mapping surface and begin exploring it by laddering up and down (Chapter 8).

3   As the interviewee's ideas may come quickly, capture as much of the conversation as you can, focusing primarily on the statements, not the links between them. It is easier to recall links than statements (MF). Also, don't worry if the map looks "messy", as it can be tidied up later. In fact, messiness should be expected (MF).

4   As the map of each issue is completed, have the interviewee choose another and map that one. As the map becomes more elaborate, try to explore links between issues. Also, ladder up to explore emergent goals (Chapter 8, MF).

5   Continually test your and the interviewee's understanding of the map by asking the interviewee whether it correctly represents his or her thinking. Ask about links and encourage the interviewee to participate actively in making links (Chapter 8, MF).

6   Use natural breaks in the conversation to feed back material for review and comment and to reassure the interviewee that he or she is being listened to. These breaks are also a chance to enter into the

map statements or links that are still in the interviewer's memory but have not yet been included, before they are lost (MF).

7 One big difference between maps is the relative depth and/or breadth of the map. Some are broad and shallow, while some are narrow and deep (MF). It is important to make sure you have mined the interviewee's thinking appropriately.

8 Another difference is that interview maps can surface strong emotions on the part of an interviewee. The map has to somehow capture and represent these emotions, as they often underpin the interviewee's willingness to commit to action. Sometimes the interviewer needs to stop mapping and just let the interviewee talk so that the strong emotions may be clarified (Chapter 5).

9 Emotions are also often complicated and may involve many issues that must be untangled some before they can be made sense of in a map. It may be necessary to have interviewees discuss their emotions without mapping them in order to help them organize their thinking enough that it can be mapped. Taking some time to talk first may help produce useful ideas for action (Chapter 5).

10 Remember that if the interviewee wants another person to do something, he or she will have to figure out what will motivate action by that person (Chapter 5).

11 Build in time between interviews to allow the interview to run beyond the formal time limit, since that may be quite useful. Having additional time will also allow you to tidy up the map while your memory is still fresh (Chapter 8).

Summary and Conclusions

In this chapter we have reviewed all the cases presented in the book. We also offered a set of process guidelines and mapping formalisms designed to help you create your own maps. The purpose of reviewing the cases was to help you make sense of them and to build up your appreciation of how mapping works and how it can help you. The cases focus on a variety of different kinds of situations (Table 10.1). They varied in terms of the client's objectives, facilitation required, number of participants, resources required, duration and physical facilities needed (Table 10.2). The cases also varied according to whether the maps were created by individuals or groups, had informal or formal links between concepts, and whether they used differing categories of statements, analyses or computers (Table 10.3). Finally, mapping made differing kinds of contributions to the resolution of the cases. It varied in the extent to which it was used to organize content, reveal emergent content, improve decision making and manage emotions (Table 10.4).

We offered process guidelines that should serve you well as you go about mapping issues of interest to you. We presented guidance on how to recognize when mapping can help and how to prepare for mapping. We then guided you through the process of beginning the map; establishing a hierarchy of concepts; developing categories of clusters of ideas; identifying goals, strategies, actions and assertions; linking statements; finishing the map; and analysing the map. We also discussed using the map to inform decision making and how to follow up on a mapping exercise. Finally, we offered guidance on how to facilitate a mapping exercise and how to map in an interview setting. We hope the review and process guidelines will give you what you need to become a successful mapper!

Notes

1 Mapping is particularly helpful when there is a risk that everyone might agree to going on holiday to a place where no one wishes to go. This is often known as the "Abilene paradox", where agreement on a goal that *no one wants* is the problem. The story that gave its name to the paradox was developed by Jerry B. Harvey and can be found in his 1996 book, *The Abilene Paradox and Other Meditations on Management*, Chichester: John Wiley and Sons.
2 Several vignettes describing work that has been of a more long-term nature can be found in C. Eden and F. Ackermann (1998) *Making Strategy*, London: Sage.
3 The formalisms are from Eden and Ackermann, *op. cit.*

11

Benefits, Limitations and the Future of Mapping

IN THIS CHAPTER WE OUTLINE THE MANY BENEFITS OF mapping, along with several of its more important limitations. We also discuss its future. The benefits of mapping are tied to how it assists with thinking-related processes. The limitations have to do with problems with the mapping metaphor, the need to learn the process and the challenges in linking mapping to action.

Benefits of Mapping

You will recall that in Chapter 2 we showed that mapping works because it builds on the way human beings make sense of their world. Mapping also helps us become self-conscious about our thinking process and logic. As we noted, educational psychologist R. Samson argues that there are eight *fundamental* thinking processes. These are representing in context, describing attitudes, comparing, categorizing, part–whole relationships, sequencing, cause-and-effect reasoning, and relational reasoning (or reasoning by analogy).[1] Mapping helps with each of these processes – and helps us be self-conscious about using them. By doing so, it helps us as individuals or in groups effectively construct, elaborate and change our system of interconnected concepts so that we can figure out what we want, how to get it and why. That is why we think that, in general, mapping should be the tool of choice when thinking matters.

Mapping is a tool that can enhance your own or your group's ability to think because it builds on and strengthens the fundamentals of thinking. It does so in a variety of ways. Mapping helps as well with the following *thinking-related* processes:[2]

- Thinking about thinking.

- Problem solving and systems thinking.

- Constructing and organizing abstractions.

- Storing information outside the body.

- Learning in groups.

- Creativity.

- Deriving meaning from experience.

- Changing response patterns.

In addition, mapping is easy to learn, which means that it is easy to use it to enhance thinking. Let us consider each of these thinking-related processes in turn.

Thinking about thinking

Chuck and Mary's map in Chapter 1 helped them understand what previously they had not. It helped them both understand *why* Mary was feeling so angry (because she thought Chuck was not doing enough around the house) and *why* Chuck thought he was being treated so unfairly (since he thought he was helping). The map also helped them understand what they could both do to make the situation better.

One big advantage of mapping is that it provides a graphic way of displaying your reasoning process. In other words, mapping lets you (and any audience you have) *see* what you are thinking. The ability to visualize what a person is saying is captured by the statement "I see what you're saying." In fact, that is exactly what Chuck said to Mary and what Mary said to Chuck. That mutual understanding resulted in reduced anger and resentment, which enabled them to reaffirm their love and affection for one another and to commit to some changes in the way each behaved towards the other.

The process of constructing a map thus allows you to reflect on your own thinking, or that of someone else. Mapping helps you become conscious of your reasoning and to understand clearly what another person is thinking. In turn, that consciousness and understanding can help you reaffirm what you think or else change your mind. Shared understanding and mutual agreement also become possible.

Problem solving and systems thinking

Humans are by nature problem solvers. We have to be, since we are forever being confronted with challenges of all sorts. Chuck and Mary had to find a way to transcend a constant source of tension in their marriage. Colin (Chapter 3) had to get a boat delivered on time and to a high standard of quality. Fran (Chapter 4) had to figure out where to live. John (Chapter 5) had to work out how to have a more satisfying job. Cardonald College (Chapter 6), Hope College (Chapter 7), Francis's group (Chapter 8), and Neil's company (Chapter 9) all had to determine how to address their strategic challenges. In each of these cases, mapping was a tool for figuring out exactly what the problem was and how it could be solved. The resulting maps didn't provide a rigid blueprint for action, but they did help point the way towards satisfactory solutions.

The maps these individuals and groups created helped them:

- develop and articulate the connections between and among their values, purposes, goals, issues, options and underlying premises;
- develop viable strategies that would help them achieve their respective purposes and goals;
- understand sequences, alternative branches, choice points and pathways on the routes to achieving their purposes;
- find problems that were both *solvable* and *worth solving*.

In short, their mapping efforts helped them figure out what they should do, how to do it and why.

Maps assist with problem solving by allowing people to understand how ideas fit together as a whole – into a *system*. They allow people to see the connections between wholes and parts, the forest and the trees. That is what systems thinking is all about: seeing how the world and its parts are interconnected, often in indirect and non-linear ways.[3] Once Chuck and Mary, Colin, Fran, John and the participants in the oval mapping exercises could see the big picture (the whole), as well as the details (the parts), they were able to make wiser choices about what to do and why. To use a painting metaphor, they were able to repaint the picture of their situations so that it more accurately reflected what they wanted. They were able to change what was figure and what was ground, as well as the relationships between the two.

Constructing and organizing abstractions

Any attempt to organize information is inherently conceptual. For example, in the paragraph above we spoke of the idea of a "system", which is an abstraction denoting the inter-relatedness of elements that make up a whole, as well as the idea that the whole is greater than the sum of its parts. We also referred to a whole and its parts and to the forest and the trees. In each case we were using abstractions (and in the case of the forest and the trees, a metaphor) to help clarify the relationship between one thing and another. We did this because fundamentally the meaning of anything is understood – *defined* – only in relation to other things. Think of how words are defined in a dictionary. Each word (an abstraction) is defined in terms of its relationship to other words (also abstractions). At the most basic level, we do not know what anything means until we know at least one thing it is like (a comparison) and one thing it is not like (a contrast). For example, the maps we are describing in this book are *like* road maps in that they show the links of parts to wholes, but are *unlike* road maps in that they show how ideas are related, not places.

Thus maps and mapping are useful because they help reveal the "pattern of connects" that define the world.[4] Mapping provides the tool and technique (know-how) to construct and analyse connections among concepts, so that knowledge can be created (know-what) and evaluated (know-why). In turn, the world can be understood and influenced. Maps and mapping assist with constructing and analysing data by:

- summarizing information;

- organizing and revealing patterns in data;

- making sense of data and patterns;

- evaluating data and patterns.

Most of the time we take for granted the power of maps and mapping to help construct and organize abstractions. If we are lost we may be grateful for a good map, but we rarely reflect on what an incredible invention maps are. Nevertheless, they rank right up there with some of the most important products of the human mind. Consider what the historian of cartography Arthur H. Robinson has to say:

> The act of mapping was as profound as the invention of a number system...The combination of the reduction of reality and the construction of an analogical space is an attainment in abstract thinking of a very high order indeed, for it enables one to discover structures that would remain unknown if not mapped.[5]

Storing information outside the body

Maps are records of an individual's or group's thinking. They are artifacts that represent external memory; that is, memory held outside the body. That is why we have referred to them as a "transitional object" or "facilitative device". Maps provide a visible bridge from one way of thinking in transition to another. They allow individuals and groups to display their thinking as it proceeds, and holistically when it is completed. Maps can be recalled and interpreted by you and by others. And they can be manipulated. People can come back to their maps at a later time and take their thinking further; they can also change their minds.

Having a tangible record is very useful for a variety of reasons. Most importantly, humans can handle only seven plus or minus two pieces of information in their consciousness at one time,[6] while maps can contain tens or even hundreds of times that amount of information. For example, consider the amount of information being used in the maps illustrated in Chapters 6–9. In addition, "external memory" – a record stored outside the body in hard copy or electronically – is often necessary for sharing, manipulating or preserving information.

Finally, externalizing information in a sense depersonalizes it and allows it to be viewed more objectively.

John referred to his maps periodically to remind himself what he decided his overall job strategy had to be. His was a fairly long-term strategy that took over two years to implement. (One might ask why anyone would stay in a job they didn't like for that long, but John had his reasons.) In the day-to-day busyness of his life, John occasionally lost sight of his long-term objectives. The urgent, or at least the immediate, often drove out attention to what was of long-term importance. So John needed the maps to remember what his long-term objectives and strategies were. Similarly, Neil and his management team used all of the maps as a constant reference in their delivery of their strategy.

Learning in groups

Individuals' maps shared with others, and maps constructed by a group, provide the benefit of *reciprocal learning*, which typically has significant advantages over individual learning. As Arthur Costa notes:

> *Humans learn best in groups. Intelligence gets shaped through interactions with others – justifying reasons, resolving differences, actively listening to another person's point of view, achieving consensus, and receiving feedback.*[7]

John learned more about what he might do by sharing the construction of his maps with Chuck. Chuck and Mary were able to understand each other better and make commitments to change their behaviour as a result of their joint mapping exercise. Francis's group, the college groups and Neil's management team all learned how they individually and collectively viewed their respective situations, including what they might do about them. In each case, the meaning and implications of the maps were more completely understood as a consequence of having *negotiated* what the meaning was. Out of negotiated meaning came a heightened *commitment* to specific actions.

Shared mapping produces a special benefit for enhancing reciprocal learning, because mapping allows individuals and groups to display their thinking *holistically*. Understanding is thus more complete.

Beyond that, while it may be easy for a dominant individual or group to dismiss a single idea or a few statements, it is harder for them to dismiss an interconnected set of ideas. Each individual's thinking is therefore more likely to be taken seriously, with attendant increases in understanding, learning and commitment.

Creativity

At least four things are typically *created* as part of a mapping process:

- Knowledge.
- A tangible representation of that knowledge (a map).
- Understanding.
- New solutions to challenging issues.

The mapping process produces tangible and typically useful knowledge. This is really one of the significant benefits of mapping – namely, participants must play an active role in the creation and modification of knowledge. As participants form and reform knowledge, they *inform* the map. Information is created and changed as the map unfolds.

A tangible representation of that knowledge is created. Understanding is fostered as an individual maps his or her thinking, or as a group constructs its own maps. And often novel and useful solutions – a kind of product – are created. These outputs must be seen as creative because one or more of the following is typically new: the knowledge, the map, the understanding, or the solution or product. We have never been involved in a mapping process where at least one of these outputs was not new.

Mapping enhances creativity because mappers quite often find – as they articulate their thinking and construct and evaluate arguments – that they are constantly on the edge of discovery. At its most stimulating, a kind of *flow* can ensue as mappers push their thinking, seek to comprehend all the connections, and lose themselves in the excitement of producing knowledge and learning.[8]

Colin and Fran, for example, decided to use the mapping process because they couldn't see any other way forward. Through mapping Colin discovered a creative solution to his problem of getting his new boat delivered on time in such a way that a lot of reworking wouldn't be required. Fran started out thinking that all she wanted was a new apartment and found out that what she really wanted was a better social life. In other words, mapping helped her create a new goal for herself. Both Colin and Fran became absorbed in their maps and let them evoke and channel their thoughts in a transitional way towards a more satisfying future.

Deriving meaning from experience

Mapping is a way of making sense of the world. It helps organize or pattern data of various sorts (e.g. assertions, actions, observations) so that it becomes information. In other words, mapping takes data and informs it through creating connections and patterns that become information. The meaning of a situation and what might be done about it are found in the relationship among concepts. Meaning, in other words, comes from comparing and contrasting relationships and patterns among concepts. Meaning also comes from the action orientation: what to do, how to do it and why it should be done. Working with the connections and patterns of data – the information – can produce insights that may ultimately lead to a kind of wisdom. This wisdom can then be used to change behaviour. In sum, mapping can help reveal the "news" embedded in similarities and differences among concepts, which can result in understanding (meaning), insight and ultimately wise choices.[9]

The wisdom for Chuck and Mary lay partly in deciding to create a map in the first place. Doing so helped them to do several things, but perhaps most importantly it provided a tangible affirmation of their relationship. After all, they wouldn't have created a map if they didn't care about each other and their relationship. The insights their mapping exercise produced helped them develop a joint understanding of what they both did to put pressure on their relationship, as well as figure out what they could do to reduce the pressure. It also allowed them to make promises to each other about how they would change their behaviour, and it gave them a framework for evaluating the changes in the future. It is easy to argue that a simple conversation would have achieved the same result, but typically it doesn't, because the very act of writing things down and linking the statements of one person with those of another is a non-linear process where concentration is not just on the last statement made. Finally, their map provided a record to which they might return for future sense making and problem solving. Chuck and Mary thus made a wise choice to use mapping in the first place; and in the end – in addition to the insights produced – the wisdom lay in the process itself.

Oscar Wilde says, "Experience is the name everyone gives to their mistakes."[10] In each of the cases in this book the mappers also learned from experience, so that they could get out of or avoid situations that were troublesome. The mappers had not necessarily made mistakes prior to mapping their situations, but if they had stayed in the problematic situation and not acted on the insights the maps produced, they most certainly would have made a mistake.

Changing response patterns

In each of the cases in this book, the mappers responded to their situations differently as a result of their mapping exercise. The mapping exercise produced relevant information and insights, which allowed the participants to make wiser choices. And these choices were different from what the actors were likely to have done without the insights that mapping produced. In each case, the mappers were stuck in a response pattern that was not doing them any good, but they didn't really know what or how to do anything that was any different. Mapping helped them get unstuck. Beyond that, mapping pointed them in the right direction.

Mapping helped the mappers do something different and better by first getting them to take a "time-out" from what they were doing. They then had to suspend judgement while they generated an array of alternatives. They had to explore each of these alternatives in some detail, including what it would take to act on the alternative and why they might choose to do so. Empathy with one's deepest desires or purposes was encouraged, along with the restraint of any impulsiveness to act on the first thing that came along. In other words, mappers were encouraged to suspend judgement, to consider being flexible about their responses to their situations, and to pursue responses that attended to their real interests. Finally, the mappers were moved to act – differently than they had in the past, and differently from what they would have otherwise done.

We often think of *power* as the ability to get someone to do what they would not have done otherwise.[11] Mapping was thus a source of power in each of the cases: it tapped the power of the participants' thinking so that they could act in their own best interests. Mapping helped give the mappers the power to be their own best friends. Mapping helped them empower *themselves* to change their own thinking and behaviour – to do what they would not otherwise do – and thus to change their situations.

Mapping also helped each participant be more optimistic. Optimism is about seeing difficulties as temporary, rather than permanent; specific, rather than pervasive; and as the result of circumstances, rather than personal failure or inadequacy.[12] Mapping helped the mappers be in charge of their lives and move forward, rather than become depressed and apathetic.

Mapping is easy to learn

The final benefit of mapping is simply that it is easy to learn and use. It really is remarkable how such a powerful tool can be grasped so quickly. The basics of constructing an individual map can be put to use easily in less than an hour. Learning the more formal basics of constructing a group map can take a little longer, but not much.

The power of the mapping quickly becomes apparent. The mental models of inter-relationships emerge before your eyes. Linear and non-linear relationships can be accommodated. You can see how the process can be applied to situations involving differing levels of complexity and depth. You also quickly become aware of your own thinking processes and are able to reflect on them as a result. The tool then becomes all the more powerful as you internalize the process and apply it on a regular basis.

Limitations of Mapping

As should be apparent, we are strong advocates of mapping as a tool, but we also recognize that it does have some limitations. For instance, while it is easy to learn, it still must *be* learned. You and your colleagues have to take the time to learn the principles, practise mapping, and then practise and learn some more until all of you become experts. While this doesn't take a huge amount of time, it still does take time.

And of course, people must be willing to be *reasonable* – meaning both logical and sensible – and many people would rather, as a matter of choice, act only on their emotions. Of course, emotions and thinking are not disconnected – the statements in most of the maps discussed in this book show lots of emotion. What mapping does is help people sort out and clarify their emotions so that they can be channelled and managed in such a way that they get more of what they really want, and less of what they don't want.

There are significant limitations that result from the use of the mapping metaphor. The simplest way to summarize these limitations is to note that "the map is not the territory".[13] The map may not be an accurate representation of the situation being mapped, and mappers must be on their guard against assuming that it might be. Checking your perceptions with those of others and with the "facts" of the situation is always advisable.

In a related vein, thinking changes and so do situations. Mapping that leads to action is likely to prompt the need for re-mapping as circumstances – the territory – change. People need to realize that maps are not fixed once and for all, but really are "transitional objects" between here and there, where here and there are changing much of the time. So while mapping can be incredibly helpful, it is no panacea and must be used often and wisely when thinking matters.

In addition, some people cannot work with visualizations of thinking, or even with pictures. They prefer discussion and linear text. Pushing mapping onto people who don't have any enthusiasm for maps can be a hopeless task. Nevertheless, we should also observe that on many occasions we have found that those who start with a negative view of maps do gradually develop an enthusiasm as they discover that a picture can help in understanding, negotiation and the development of consensus. The ends justify the means!

It is also important to realize that there are important trade-offs in mapping between simplicity, generality and accuracy. You can have any two of these, but not all three. You can have a simple, general map, but it won't be very accurate. You can have a simple, accurate map, but its small scale won't allow it to be very general. And you can have a general, accurate map, but it won't be simple. So you must choose which advantages you want and which failure you are willing to tolerate.[14]

For mapping to be really useful, it must be linked to action. Thinking alone is unlikely to change a situation. It takes committed actors to make something happen. So it is important to be willing to act on the basis of the map, or the time spent mapping may well be wasted. The importance of action is also why we are so firm about having statements on a map phrased in action terms – that is, as propositions for action written as options. Indeed, we would assert that the ultimate point of causal maps is to create an informed and wise action plan.

The Future of Mapping

We think that the future of mapping is very bright. It clearly helps people think about what they want, how to do it and why. And it is quick and simple to use. In a management context, it can give its practitioners a powerful tool and a competitive edge. We fully expect that in the not-too-distant future mapping will be a tool that virtually all managers will be expected to use, or at least be familiar with. We also expect that within a generation virtually all primary, secondary, undergraduate and graduate students will know about mapping.

The development of mapping software will speed the use and appreciation of mapping. *Decision Explorer* is our software of choice, but others are available as well, and even most word-processing software has drawing features that support the construction of maps. Resource D provides guidance on where to find software that can assist with mapping.

The need for clear and logical thinking is not going to go away, it will only increase. Globalization, interconnectedness, competition, the increasing speed of change and the need for effective integration of parts into workable wholes all demand clear and logical thinking.

When faced with such demands, mapping should be among the first tools of choice.

Summary and Conclusions

We have argued that mapping has a number of significant benefits. Specifically, it can assist with a crucial set of thinking-related processes, including thinking about thinking, problem solving and systems thinking, constructing and organizing abstractions, storing information outside the body, learning in groups, creativity, deriving meaning from experience, and changing response patterns. Beyond that, mapping is very easy to learn and to use.

On the other hand, mapping does have several limitations. "Good mapping" must be learned, although it can be learned relatively quickly. It is also important never to confuse the map with the territory being mapped, since doing so may lead to serious mistakes. This is particularly true when knowledge and situations are changing, because maps can easily become out of date and re-mapping may be required. There are also trade-offs between the simplicity, accuracy and generality of any map; namely, you can have any two, but not all three. Finally, mapping must be linked with action to be really useful.

When compared with the benefits of mapping, however, the limitations seem rather minor to us, or at least easily manageable. That is part of the reason why we think the future of mapping is extremely bright. As we noted, the need for clear and logical thinking is not going to go away, it will only increase as the complexity of the world and the speed of change increase. Mapping provides a powerful tool for managing complexity in an effective and timely way so that people can figure out what to do, how to do it and why. Mapping should be among the very first tools of choice *whenever thinking matters in order to create the future you want.*

Notes

1 R. Samson's work is cited in D. J. Hyerle (1996) *Visual Tools for Constructing Knowledge*, Alexandria, VA: Association for Supervision and Curriculum Development, pp. 105–6.

2   The categories are from A. L. Costa's prologue to D. J. Hyerle, *op. cit.*, pp. v–xiv.

3   For more on systems thinking, see P. Senge (1990) *The Fifth Discipline*, New York, NY: Currency; and B. Oshry (1996) *Seeing Systems, Unlocking the Mysteries of Organizational Life*, San Francisco, CA: Berrett-Koehler.

4   "Pattern of connects" is from G. Bateson (1979) *Mind and Nature, A Necessary Unity*, New York, NY: E. P. Dutton.

5   A. H. Robinson (1982) *Early Thematic Mapping in the History of Cartography*, Chicago, IL: University of Chicago Press, p. 1.

6   The classic article describing the rather severe limits on conscious human information processing capacity is G. A. Miller (1956) The Magical Number Seven Plus or Minus Two: Some Limits on Our Capacity for Processing Information, *The Psychological Bulletin*, 63, 81–97.

7   A. Costa in Hyerle, *op. cit.*, p. xi.

8   The concept of flow refers to the kind of "optimal experience" that comes from getting lost in a meaningful, challenging and stimulating task. See M. Csikszentmihalyi (1991) *Flow: The Psychology of Optimal Experience*, New York, NY: HarperCollins.

9   News refers to new information. Seeing the comparisons, contrasts and patterns of interconnections that mapping provides almost always presents new information that can create new understandings, understanding, insight and informed actions. For more on the process by which information can be transferred from individuals, to groups and to organizations, see M. Crossan, H. Lane and R. White (1999) An Organizational Learning Framework: From Intuition to Institution, *Academy of Management Review*, 24(3), 522–37.

10   Oscar Wilde (1892) *Lady Windermere's Fan*, Act III.

11   For example, in a widely cited book on power, Pfeffer defines power "as the potential ability to influence behavior, to change the course of events, to overcome resistance, and to get people to do things that they would not otherwise do". J. Pfeffer (1992) *Managing with Power, Politics and Influence in Organizations*, Boston, MA: Harvard Business School Press, p. 30.

12   These insights about optimism come from M. Seligman (1991) *Learned Optimism*, New York, NY: Alfred Knopf.

13   The idea that "the map is not the territory" comes from the work of Alfred Korzybski, as discussed in C. Hampden-Turner (1981), *Maps of the Mind*, New York, NY: Macmillan, p. 140.

14   For more on the trade-offs between simplicity, generality and accuracy, see K. Weick, Introduction: Cartographic Myths in Organizations, in A. S. Huff (ed) (1990) *Mapping Strategic Thought*, Chichester: Wiley, pp. 1–10.

Resource A

Glossary of Terms
not Defined in the Text

Assumptive worlds – the way in which an understanding of a situation is developed using a series of underlying, often unconscious, assumptions or premises.

Candidate goals – possible goals to be considered for adoption.

Cathartic – bringing repressed ideas and feelings to consciousness.

Causal – a relationship indicating a cause and its effect.

Chain of argumentation – a coherent series of reasons linking a set of statements.

Cognition – the act of knowing, perception, awareness; the mental act or process of acquiring knowledge.

Constructs – short phrases or ideas that contribute to someone's understanding of a situation.

Disaggregation – breaking the whole into its constituent units or parts.

Emergent – gradually coming into view or being.

Facilitative device – an artefact that helps a group achieve an outcome; it does for groups what transitional objects do for individuals.

Feedback loops – return of part of the output to the input in a manner that is self-sustaining or self-controlling.

Inferential – a conclusion arrived at by considering the available evidence.

Logical – structured through reasoning.

Orphans – statements with no links in or out to other statements.

Qualitative business model – a business model developed and explored through text and causal relationships rather than through numbers.

Reciprocal learning – learning through interaction with others.

Ritual structure – a patterned and purposeful way for a group to figure out what to do, how to do it and why.

Sequential – arranged as a continuous progression.

Strategic plan – an organized, coherent scheme of action that incorporates *purposes* (aims), *goals* (outcomes that are good in their own right), *strategies* (a set of interconnected actions designed to achieve the goals), *actions* (discrete deeds, behaviours, or movements), and *assertions* (statements of belief or fact). Strategies address *strategic issues* (highly consequential interconnected sets of possible *options* for action) and *negative goals* (outcomes that are at the same level of abstraction as a goal, but undesirable). Strategic plans are typically, but not always, written, rather than presented in graphic word-and-arrow form.

Temporal – relating to time.

Transitional object – a device that helps someone move from one way of thinking, doing or being to another.

World-taken-for-granted – knowledge that is used as if its veracity is obvious.

Resource B

Analysing Causal Maps

Structural Properties through the
Two-dimensional Character of a Map

When a map is relatively complex (typically more than 40–50 nodes and 70+ links), redrawing it in an easy-to-read graphical representation will give rise to a pattern or "shape", or a series of patterns depending on the layout. These patterns help reveal emerging characteristics simply by the way in which the structure of the map forces a "best" way of laying it out in two dimensions. For example, the need to locate linked nodes close to one another, the need to keep the number of crossing links to a minimum and adopting a hierarchical layout (for example, all arrows going up the page) will determine a particular layout for the map. This visual structure can be seen in many of the examples shown in this book. Typically maps have been deliberately set out in a hierarchical form with the "heads" at the top of the map (see Figure B.1), as this tends to show the clusters of options well ("tails") and draw attention to their flow upwards to goals. In addition, the node(s) that appears in the centre of a map is usually significantly central to the way the problem or issue being depicted is seen by the person being mapped.

Figure B.1 shows an imperfect two-dimensional layout of a small map. The figure demonstrates how the layout illustrates the likely centrality of one statement to the structuring of the problem/issue, along with the positioning of tails and heads.

The analysis methods discussed below are, in effect, more formal ways of detecting the best ways of representing and displaying the map.

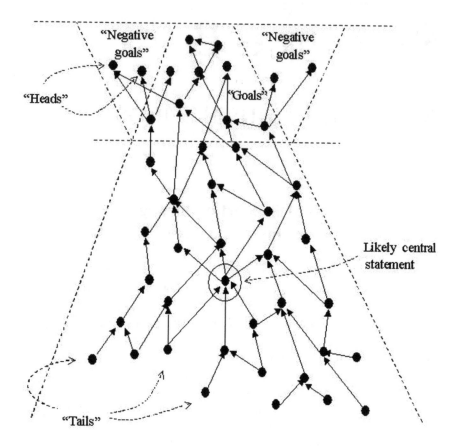

Figure B.1   A problem/issue map – two-dimensional character.

The Complexity of a Map

Determining the relative complexity of a map can be helpful because it acts as an appropriate preface to "chunking" analyses (means of working on specific clusters or chunks of the map) that are aimed at determining the "nub of the issue" (the key elements/nodes).

There are a couple of simple analyses of maps that indicate their central features (which is often referred to as a directed graph). The first of these explores the total number of nodes and the total number of links; the second is concerned with the "centrality" of particular statements.

The extent of the map

The first analysis is based on the premise that the *more nodes* (or statements) in a map, the more complex is the map and so the more complex is the issue. The method of eliciting the statements captured on the map is crucial in determining the validity of such a measure. For structured interviews the number of statements will be affected significantly by the structuring provided by the interview itself; whether the structure or lack of structure is in the form of poor interviewing skills; or whether the interviewer has a tight agenda of structured questions, all of which provide little opportunity for depth and richness. Use of multiple-choice or closed questions as well as an explicit expectation that the interviewee should be consistent can have a profound effect on the openness of the interviewee. Interviews designed around pre-prepared agendas will push the number of statements elicited towards an interviewer-determined level. This level will be a function of the number of questions asked and the time given for each answer. Our experience indicates that the number of statements elicited during an interview depends on the length of the interview, the skills of the interviewer and the degree of openness regarding the areas/issues discussed. Poor interviewing skills such as evaluative non-verbal signals and the interviewer taking too much airtime will vitally affect the size and shape of a map. Thus analyses that depend on the number of nodes should be treated with great care.

It is not surprising that the degree of openness in an interview depends on the extent to which the interview is itself a rewarding experience for the interviewee. Interviews can be a cathartic experience that encourages the interviewee on the one hand to be more open and on the other hand to develop their own thinking about the topic (see Chapters 3, 4 and 5 for illustrations of this). The suggestion that we do not know what we think until we hear what we say[1] is particularly significant in relation to the construction of maps.

The complexity of the map as a network

In order to take some account of these concerns about the reliability of using the absolute number of nodes as a measure of the complexity of the map, an alternative analysis of map complexity is to determine the *ratio of links to statements*. Thus a higher ratio indicates a densely connected map and a higher level of complexity. The robustness of this analysis depends on the coding skills of the mapper. Inexperienced mappers tend to generate a map with a smaller number of nodes than those identified by an experienced mapper and in addition they generate more links.

For example, more links result from coding A causes B, B causes C, C causes D (4 nodes, 3 links) with elaborated links adding A causes C, B causes D, and A causes D (4 nodes and 6 links). Each of the last three links is true as a summary of more detailed paths, but does not represent a different causality to the indirect linkage. However, the ratio of links to nodes has increased from 0.75 to 1.25, suggesting an apparent, but incorrect, increase in complexity. We would expect ratios of 1.15 to 1.25 for maps elicited from interviews following the form of mapping introduced in this book.[2]

Idealized thinking?

Other simple analyses of complexity derive from consideration of the ratio of the number of "heads" and the number of "tails" to the total number of nodes. So-called idealized thinking about a topic tends to generate maps with a small number of "heads" (ideally a single end/goal/outcome/objective/value – a "pyramid" map). The map depicts someone able to think about situations within the context of a simple hierarchical value system where each value implies another that ultimately implies a single superordinate value.

A person might be judged to be cognitively simple and well organized in relation to the topic if his or her map takes the form of an "idealized" pyramid structure. In this case, the person will probably be dealing with a relatively tractable issue. Conversely, a map with a relatively large number of "heads" indicates recognition of, and a concern for, meeting multiple and possibly conflicting objectives; such a person could be seen as tackling a complex problem (as is seen in Chapter 5). In this case, issue/problem structuring will play a significant role.

The content of the nodes that are heads is also of some significance in this type of analysis, particularly when the same content appears as a tail for one person and a head for another. For example, our work with public policy makers has shown some of them viewing "mandates" as legitimizing goals (heads), whereas others in the same organization see them as constraints (tails). It is important to be clear about which of these is most helpful in using the map to decide ways forward.

Interpreting the analysis of the ratio of the number of "tails" to the total number of nodes is more problematic. The number of tails gives some indication of the range of possible options for acting to alleviate the issue. In general, the ratio of tails to total nodes provides an initial indication of the relative "flatness" (see also below for an analysis of shape) of the map structure – a structure is relatively flat where causal arguments are not well elaborated and use short chains of argument.

Exploring the Emergent Properties of a Map: Finding "the Nub"

If a map is complex, there is a need to use appropriate methods of analysis of the emerging structural properties of the map, and then to employ those emerging properties as a basis for finding the "nub of the issue".

A map has two structural properties: the property of hierarchy and the more general property of linkage. Each of these provides opportunities for the analysis of structure. The analyses, discussed below, are easier to conduct with the help of a computer and associated software (for example *Decision Explorer*[3]), although all of them can be determined manually or through visual inspection of the map. However, in these instances the validity may be uncertain as it is hard to be as accurate.

This section presents six types of analyses, which when taken together provide a compendium of emergent properties, each of which gives an insight into ways of managing the issue or problem depicted in the map. The analyses are:

- "Islands" of themes: clusters – without accounting for hierarchy.
- Networks of problems: clusters – accounting for hierarchy.
- Finding "potent" options.
- Virtuous circles, vicious circles and controlling circles.
- Central statements as the "nub of the issue".
- Simplifying the issue through emergent properties.

"Islands" of themes: clusters – without accounting for hierarchy

At one extreme a map can comprise several clusters of nodes and links that are all disconnected from one another: "islands" of material. In this circumstance the detection of each "island" as a separate map allows an exploration of the content of each island to identify themes that describe each cluster. At this extreme, the map may contain no links at all between nodes – each node forms an island in a fragmented map. Towards the other extreme, a map may be highly interconnected (most likely when the ratio of links to nodes is high). In this case it is difficult to "break apart" the map into relatively separable but connected clusters: the map is one "island". However, more typically a map is not in the form of islands or a single "unbreakable" cluster, but rather connected clusters of nodes. In this case the identification of clusters that break the map into a system of inter-related themes becomes worthwhile.[4] However, the identification of themes depends on seeking out tight interconnections between nodes, and usually pays no attention to the nature of the link.

Thus one important analysis of emerging features relates to the detection of clusters, where a cluster may be more or less separable from other parts of the map. This process helps with managing the complexity of a large map along with giving insights into the emerging themes. One form of analysis follows the principles of something called "simple linkage clustering"[5] by looking at each node and its immediate context of nodes to determine a similarity rating. Clusters are formed gradually by putting relatively similar nodes into the same cluster until a defined level of dissimilarity has been reached. The intention is to attempt the formation of clusters where the nodes in each cluster are tightly linked to one another (similar) and the number of links (or bridges) with other clusters is minimized. In some senses this analysis identifies the "robust" parts of the map – those parts that are relatively insensitive to small changes in the structure of the map.

Each cluster so formed and the inter-relationships between clusters form summary characteristics of the overall map. Clearly, this type of analysis provides a further insight into complexity, where the proposition suggests that a map that can be broken apart into relatively unconnected smaller maps represents lower complexity than one that is difficult to break apart. In other words, cluster analysis can suggest whether or not (or to what extent) the world has been simplified by a form of categorization.

Although this analysis is easily done using the facilities available in *Decision Explorer*, it is possible to see clusters by visual inspection, and in many of the cases in this book examples of visually determined clusters are given.

The purpose of analysing for clusters is to identify the *system of problems* that make up the "issue" being addressed. Thus each cluster, when summarized through a descriptor, represents a relatively separable part of the issue – a "problem" that *may* be addressed independently of addressing other parts or problems.

Networks of problems: clusters – accounting for hierarchy

Alternatively, clusters may be formed by consideration of the hierarchical structure of the map. Simon says, "Complexity frequently takes the form of hierarchy and...hierarchic systems have some common properties that are independent of the specific content...hierarchy...is one of the central structural schemes that the architect of complexity uses."[6] Each node is supported by a "tree" of other nodes that have implications for the original node of interest. Thus, in general, each node can be inspected for its own hierarchical cluster. However, in order to detect these emerging features of the map, it is more helpful to consider a subset of nodes of particular interest and their hierarchical relationship to one another and to other nodes not members of the subset rather than the entire map. In this way, selected hierarchical clusters may be formed and the thematic content explored in relation to other hierarchically linked, hierarchical clusters. Often hierarchical clusters determined by using the subset "goals" are helpful because they show the range of nodes that "hit" each goal and so form possible options for action to address the goal. Each hierarchical cluster is similar in form to another: it will have a superordinate "head" that represents the "goal" for the particular cluster, and "tails" that represent the most detailed options for addressing that goal.

In contrast to the first type of cluster analysis, hierarchical clustering permits any node (excluding those in the chosen subset) to appear in more than one cluster. This is a very useful addition to the analysis because, as we shall see below, it suggests options that are most likely to attack the maximum number of goals determined by the subset of nodes used as the basis for the analysis – they are therefore "potent" options. Therefore, if the map has been coded properly, the top part of the map ("heads") will depict the "goal system" and the bottom part the detailed potential action points or options (Figure B.2 shows this conceptualization). In attempting to solve problems depicted by a map, the task is gradually to provide the support that enables the network of "problems" to be translated into portfolios of actions as options are validated as actions.

An additional, helpful and exploratory form of this analysis is often conducted using "core, or central, statements" (as they are defined below) and "heads" as the subset of seed nodes. This means that analysis is focused on those statements that are central in linkage terms and those nodes that are, by definition, at the top of a hierarchy. This ensures that all nodes in the map are considered within the analysis, and considered with respect to goals and to central/core statements. The analysis then traces down the tree from each member of the subset and continually pulls nodes into a cluster until another member of the subset is met or the trace reaches a "tail". In this way the hierarchical relationship between each hierarchical cluster is noted.

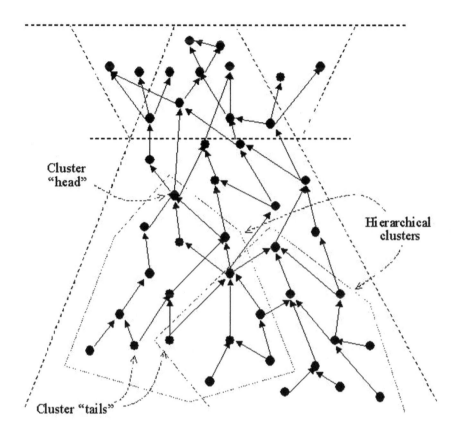

Figure B.2   Hierarchical clusters.

Obviously, the meaning of an analysis for hierarchical clusters is dependent on the selection of the subset. With care in the choice of content-based seed nodes, interpreting the analysis is likely to be easier when the starting subset can be formed with reference to the content of nodes, where the content indicates different topics.

Hierarchical clusters are another view of "chunks" of the map. Here each chunk is not mutually exclusive of other chunks, but is representative of that part of the map that relates to any particular goal within the goal system or to "central" nodes that are descriptive of different content aspects of the problem or issue. Thus once again, the analysis suggests that the issue or problem is made up of a system of inter-related sub-problems.

Finding "potent" options

The appearance of nodes in a number of hierarchical clusters creates a further emergent characteristic of the map or issue. A node that appears in several clusters is "potent", because it has ramifications for a large number of hierarchical topics, central statements or goals, depending on the basis for choosing the subset of seed nodes.

Figure B.3 shows how an analysis of two possible hierarchical clusters reveals three potent options – tails that are within both clusters.

For problem solving, an important "chunk" of the map, resulting from this analysis of hierarchical clusters, is that of determining "potent options" for achieving the "goal system".

Significantly, the analysis can also reveal the extent of dilemmas that are a common consequence of the recognition of multiple ramifications or goals. Each potent node may have both positive and negative consequences, indicating the recognition of a dilemma.

Virtuous circles, vicious circles and controlling circles

Within any context of the analysis of maps, the existence or not of feedback loops will be of interest for two reasons. First, the existence of a loop may be a coding accident that needs to be corrected. Second, and of greater interest, loops imply the possible existence of dynamic considerations – that is, the map indicates the potential for growth, decline or feedback control.

Unintended incorrect coding with respect to loops tends to be common with maps of the sort presented in this book because of the problematic nature of determining what is a cause and what an effect. Figure B.4 demonstrates how two different and plausible beliefs about the relationship between "expanding the range of courses" and "business experience" result in either a feedback loop or a hierarchy depending on your point of view. For the mapper it is very important to establish which point of view is correct in the particular instance being considered.

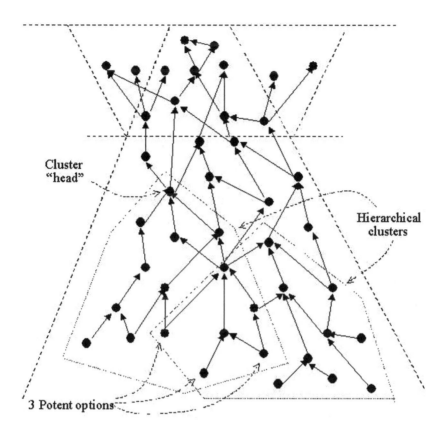

Figure B.3   "Potent options" based on two hierarchical clusters.

The existence of loops will have a significant impact on the results of all the above analyses by leading to completely erroneous results. In most of the analyses, every concept on the loop will be accorded the same analytical status. This means that analysis for the existence of loops should usually be undertaken before conducting any other analysis. In this way, the coding can be checked and corrected if necessary before any other analysis is conducted.

The formality of coding demands that "options" lead to "outcomes", "means" lead to "ends" and the head of an arrow shows the *more* desired outcome or goal. Without such formality, any of the analyses described here is meaningless; this is particularly the case for an analysis to discover loops. Without consistent formal "rules" of the sort we have introduced through this book, loops will be found that are not really vicious circles, virtuous circles or controlling circles.

When analysis results in the existence of "true" loops, there will be a concern to establish the nature of feedback. When the loop contains an odd number of negative links, the loop is depicting self-control. That is, any perturbation in the state of the nodes in the loop will result in stabilizing dynamics to bring the activity into control. Alternatively, an even number of negative links or all positive links suggests regenerative or degenerative dynamics, where a perturbation results in exponential growth or decline. In many studies loops relate to a small number of nodes and it is possible that the implications of the loop are well known to the individual whose issue is depicted. However, where maps contain the views of a number of people, both the identification and exploration of the loops can be of significant interest, as in these cases the loops are not recognized by any one person and can often be counter-intuitive.

Figure B.4 shows a loop recoded as a hierarchy. This recoding depends on the point of view of the person being mapped.

Interventions that may be considered are:

- Positive feedback loop:

    - Virtuous circle: reinforce one or more of the nodes by exploring influences on each node in turn.

    - Vicious circle: "rub out" one of the arrows by a change in policy or by changing the nature of one of the beliefs (make the loop into a controlling loop [negative] by changing the direction of causation, or destroying the causation); find a number of influences on nodes that can shift the direction of behaviour so that a vicious circle becomes a virtuous circle.

- Negative feedback loop – if the degree of control is undesirable:

    - If possible, break the loop by a change in policy: change the direction of causation so that the loop behaves as a virtuous circle.

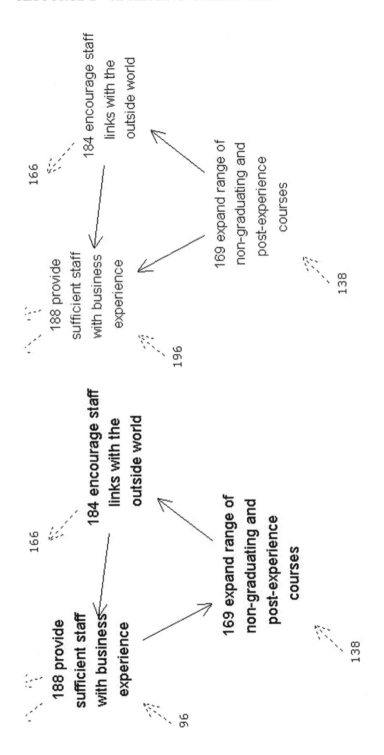

Figure B.4 A feedback loop recoded as a hierarchy (depending on the interpretation of the link between 169 and 188).

● Major strategic change:

  – Occurs when the structure of the situation is changed: e.g.
    new loops become dominant; the "central" core of the map
    shifts by the deletion of some beliefs (that become insignif-
    icant) and others move to prominence; the desired outcomes
    (goals – those variables with no arrows out of them) change.

Central statements as the "nub of the issue"

The simplest analysis available for seeking out the "nub of the issue"
is generally known as a "domain analysis" because it calculates the
total number of in arrows and out arrows from each node; that is, its
immediate domain. Those nodes whose immediate domain are most
complex are taken to be those most central. The analysis indicates
the richness of meaning of each particular statement. For the
purposes of detecting the structural characteristics of issues, these
analyses can be a "first draft" of the "nub of the issue".

Attending only to the immediate domain of a node, the analysis
completely ignores the wider context of the node. It is possible to
extend the analysis of the structural significance or centrality of
single statements within the map by exploring the impact of adding
successive layers of domain to the domain count. Intuitively, it
seems sensible to give each successive layer of statements a
diminishing weight – a distance decay function. For example, each
node directly linked to a central node may be given a weight of 1.
Nodes in the next layer out are given a weight of 1/2. The next layer
is given a weight of 1/3, and so on. Where a node with a high domain
score is linked directly to another with a high domain, the two will
bolster one another's domain score. Thus, for example, if three
nodes with equal local domain scores form a row, usually the middle
node will score most highly given this form of analysis, indicating
greater centrality. This is an important distinction between the
output from a simple domain analysis and a weighted extended
domain analysis.

A domain analysis that considers more than the immediate context
will reveal "bridging nodes". If the cross-linkage did not exist, the
centrality of other local nodes would drop significantly. Thus, within

the context of the issue structure, they are worthy of further exploration in any problem-solving attempts.

Whereas the simple domain analysis is easy to undertake visually or manually, the second requires the use of computer software such as *Decision Explorer*.

Figure B.5 shows an example of the difference in the analysis results.

Simplifying the issue through emergent properties

Simplification, or complexity reduction rather than the management of complexity, is always a dangerous process. It will often lose the subtlety that characterizes the issue. Nevertheless, a highly complex map can be debilitating.[7] The appropriate management of complexity is an important aspect of the added value from mapping detail and subtlety and yet providing summaries that can encompass simplification without losing what is significant. The detection of systemic, emergent properties is an effective way of ensuring that richness is retained and less necessary detail lost, and thus that the "nub of the issue" is identified.

When no prior analysis has been conducted and each node has the same status as all others, the map can be simplified by excluding those causal paths that are simple elaboration. If nodes have one causal link in and one causal link out, the path can be collapsed from two links into a single link by, in effect, merging the node with its tail or head node. Thus, an argument that has been mapped as A→B→C can be reduced to A→C with loss of detail only. Similarly, nodes with a single link to other parts of the map can be deleted to strip the map of detail. The process must not be incremental (where each stage assumes no prior stages), as this is likely to lead to the deletion of the whole map; the starting state of the map must be retained and each deletion determined in the light of this initial state. When computer software is used this process can be undertaken with greater assurance that the subtlety of detail contained in argument strings is not lost. The software allows nodes to be merged easily, with attention to content and yet automatically retaining structure. Without this careful merging

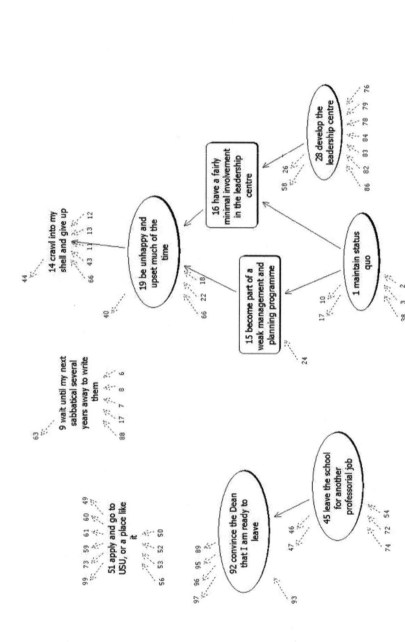

Figure B.5   Domain analysis of the map from Chapter 5. Statements in ovals score high in both analyses, those in rectangles score high in a weighted domain analysis, those with no border score high on an immediate domain analysis.

process, which is difficult to undertake manually, it is likely that the "bridging nodes" discussed above will be lost.

The effect of this process of stripping out detail is to "collapse" the map to include only those nodes with a domain score of three or more. This retains those nodes that sit at branch points and deletes those that are simply a part of extended elaboration.

Conclusions

This resource note[8] has introduced a variety of methods for exploring maps. They were all developed within the context of using maps to help individuals[9] and teamwork on complex issues or strategy development.[10]

The analyses provide *indications* of features of the map and enable emerging features to be detected. It is absolutely crucial to see analysis within the context of a clear theoretical framework and so a map coding procedure, as well as an analytical purpose, without which the interpretation of the analysis will be problematic.

An overview is an important aspect of providing complexity reduction and a focus on the most important aspects of the problem or issue. The ability to "collapse" a map by focusing only on those emerging characteristics discussed above is in its own right a powerful analysis. Thus, the sum of core statements, heads, loop nodes and potent options provides an important overview, or summary, of the map by showing the linkage between its "important" elements. However, the cluster analyses reveal the structural properties of interconnections between the themes detected from an analysis of the content of each cluster. Notably, the cluster analysis that does not root itself in a starting subset, and produces clusters with no overlapping nodes, provides the most "naturalistic" overview of the structure of the map.

Notes

1 A view expressed by K. Weick (1979) *The Social Psychology of Organizing*, Reading, MA: Addison-Wesley.

2   This expected ratio does not seem to vary to an extent that could
     significantly identify differences in cognitive complexity. There are
     likely to be many other more plausible reasons for this relatively
     constant ratio, such as the nature of verbal argument in interview
     conditions.

3   See www.banxia.com to purchase a version of the software.

4   Simon's arguments about the property of near decomposability have
     relevance here. In many complex, hierarchical systems, intra-
     component linkages are stronger than inter-component linkages and
     the discovery of where the weakest linkages lie within the system is
     one basis for the analysis of complexity. See H. A. Simon (1981) *The
     Sciences of the Artificial*, 2nd edn, Cambridge, MA: MIT Press.

5   For more detail on simple linkage clustering, see J. C. Gower and
     G. J. S. Ross (1969) Minimum Spanning Trees and Single Linkage
     Cluster Analysis, *Applied Statistics*, **18**, 56–64; and N. Jardine and R.
     Sibson (1971) *Mathematical Taxonomy*, New York, NY: Wiley.

6   From H. A. Simon (1962) The Architecture of Complexity,
     Proceedings of the American Philosophical Society, **106**, 467–82.

7   For an interesting discussion of the tension between the need to deal
     with complexity and simplifying to manage the stressful impact of too
     much complexity, see C. Eden, S. Jones, D. Sims and T. Smithin
     (1981) The Intersubjectivity of Issues and Issues of Intersubjectivity,
     Journal of Management Studies, **18**, 37–47.

8   This resource note is adapted from C. Eden (2004) Analyzing
     Cognitive Maps to Help Structure Issues or Problems, *European
     Journal of Operational Research*, forthcoming.

9   Initially from the work reported in C. Eden, S. Jones and D. Sims
     (1979) *Thinking in Organisations*, London: Macmillan.

10   See C. Eden and F. Ackermann (1998) *Making Strategy: The Journey
     of Strategic Management*, London: Sage.

Resource C

A Brief and Selective History of Causal Mapping for Facilitating Thinking and Other Commonly Used Mapping Techniques

IN THIS RESOURCE NOTE WE CONSIDER SOME OF THE HISTORY of where mapping came from and why it seems to help humans think. We focus primarily on causal mapping, but also show how it is related to other kinds of commonly used mapping techniques. In the concluding part, we discuss the mapping metaphor to indicate how causal mapping differs from geographical mapping.

For as long as human beings have been on the planet, we have been interested in how we think. For many psychologists, consciousness and thinking are regarded as crucial features of humanity. We are curious about the world. We want to understand others and ourselves. We want to make plans for ourselves and to control as much of the future as we can, which also means that we want to make predictions about what others might think and do.

Knowing how others think is usually helpful in understanding how they might behave and interact with others. So understanding thinking is also related to the nature of social interaction. The understanding of what "behaviour" is must be expanded to include the act of speaking and expressing a point of view designed to change how others think and act. Thinking and listening to others' views are important parts of how people "change their mind", and so are important parts of how they learn and develop, how they engage in social interactions and negotiations, and how their emotions may be influenced by their thinking and acting. (Although psychologists prefer, for convenience, to separate thinking from emotion, the two are obviously closely intertwined.)

If we are to understand more about how to help with thinking, we must pay attention to the work of *cognitive* psychologists, since cognitive psychology is the discipline that concentrates on making assertions about the nature of thinking. These assertions are based on research experiments and on bodies of persuasive argument presented by theorists. Some psychologists take a view of thinking that focuses on how the brain works – its physiology. Others are more concerned with the principles of "making sense" of what goes on around us. In either case, most psychologists agree that there is something akin to maps or networks, sometimes known as a "schema", of constructs that enables us to think. Whether there is or not matters less than whether accepting that, or acting as if, there is seems to help us construct a picture of what another person or ourselves think about specific issues that need resolution.

In this book we build on the idea, or principle, that humans make use of maps or networks of constructs to understand our world, make predictions about it and, to the extent we can, control it. Toulmin[1] is generally taken to be the first, in 1946, to refer to cognitive mapping – mapping of thinking. The maps were not like those we have been using in this book, but at least the idea of a map of thinking was launched. In 1955, a psychologist called George Kelly[2] took the idea further by taking an interest in how cognitive psychology might help him do his job of counselling students better. He argued that we are each a "scientist", continually experimenting in our life to try to build "theories" to explain the way the world works. He considered us as problem solvers who were driven by the need to better manage and control our lives. So he saw us as continually striving to make sense of – to understand – what was going on around us so that we could act effectively to change it.

If Kelly was to help his students, he believed he needed to know more about how this process of *sense making* took place. His view was that to do so he should not be interested in words and phrases used as if they were definitionally absolute, but should see how they were used to distinguish one experience or object from another in relation to the need to act in a problematic world. The language "tools" we use to help us make sense and think things through he called *constructs*, because they were the things we used to construct our understanding of our situations. Thus his theory was known as Personal Construct Theory, or PCT for short. As we can see, PCT involves a relativistic view where constructs are used to identify likenesses and differences – similarities and contrasts. This view of the way we think is important, because it also reflects an important statement that guides the processes we have introduced in this book: that "if men [sic] define situations as real, they are real in their consequences".[3] This is why we are so interested in this book in getting out a picture or map of "the reality" as it is interpreted by each of the participants in a group situation.

Kelly was a theoretician, but he was also a practitioner, so he wanted a tool to help him in his practice. His tool needed to be as faithful as possible to his theory. What he developed was a form of cognitive mapping called the "Repertory Grid". Because he argued that we made sense of our world through contrasts and similarities, he argued that we could discover something about how each of us thinks by asking a person to consider three objects/situations/people (a triad) and then to compare and contrast them. By asking us how we saw two of the triad as similar and yet different from the third, we would articulate a "construct" – one aspect of our thinking about how we make sense of this type of object or situation or person. He was mostly interested in understanding how we related to people, so his repertory grids were developed by comparing triads from a "repertoire" of people. Each triad used would elicit one construct that would have two "poles" or dimensions of analysis – the similarity and the difference. Each triad would elicit at least one construct and eventually a grid would be formed with people (called "elements") as one axis and the "constructs" as the other. Asking the respondent to enter a cross or check mark in each grid square, where a check mark indicated that the person would be seen as being described by the construct, could then complete the grid. The grid was the map.

Many years later, the repertory grid would be used for market research and the study of architecture, as well as in a wide range of psychotherapy situations.[4] Thus, for example, customers for perfume would be given three perfumes and asked to describe how two were similar and yet different from the third. The process enabled researchers to understand much more about the way customers evaluated perfume than any previous questionnaire had.

Of course, it was not long before researchers spotted that a grid could be analysed mathematically to help identify which perfumes were similar and which were very well differentiated in the marketplace. By asking for a number on a scale to indicate the *degree* to which a construct described the object/person/situation, the mathematical analyses could become more sophisticated.

Nevertheless, although Kelly's repertory grid was true enough to his theory, in practice it only revealed very small maps (grids were usually about 12×12), whereas most problems involve thinking about more aspects of the situation. Grids could have been bigger, but they would be very laborious to create and complete.

Following the approach Kelly had set out, a researcher called David Hinkle[5] developed the "Implication Grid". This grid has a person's constructs along both axes and so completing it was closer to what we have described as maps in this book. The grid, when completed, showed the *implication of one construct for another*, which is the equivalent of an arrow on one of our maps. This approach became the template for many other approaches used in the study of managerial and organizational cognition by management researchers. Some employed a technique known as a "card sort" where participants (or usually research subjects) were invited to sort a series of cards on which were written objects or situations of interest to the researcher. The sort could be used to produce a pile of similar statements or, using some additional manipulations, a picture or set of relationships between items. Each participant was given the same items to map, so that comparisons could be made easily and statistics could be used to indicate similarities in participants' thinking.

The Development of Causal Mapping

A further step was taken in 1976, when Bob Axelrod edited a book called *Structure of Decision*.[6] This used *causal mapping* to analyse documents. He, and many of his colleagues, were political scientists. They were interested in the thinking of politicians as it was expressed through what they and others wrote about situations. However, the book also contained some interesting maps about other problems, such as the Chicago transit system.[7] These maps had statements and arrows that represented causality.

At the same time, a team in the UK consisting of Colin Eden, Sue Jones and David Sims had been studying real policy makers in regional government and had linked Kelly's theories with an approach to mapping[8] that was far less tedious than repertory grids.[9] By spending considerable time with policy makers, they sought to map out their thinking by listening to them as they tried to make decisions. The researchers could not use grids, because the policy makers would not have participated if they had been forced to do all the work of dealing with triads and completing the grid. Also, they felt strongly that grids lost the individual richness of the policy maker's thinking. This research launched the development of the type of causal maps used in this book.

As work on cognition in organizations progressed, Michel Bougon and Karl Weick became involved in a study of the Utrecht Jazz Orchestra[10] and other researchers considered the cognitive aspects of competition.[11] The field grew and an interest group in Managerial and Organizational Cognition was formed at the American Academy of Management, bringing together those with an interest in thinking in organizations. The group was so successful that it became an official Division within the Academy.[12]

Ann Huff edited a book in 1990[13] whose goal was to present many of the different approaches to mapping that US researchers (for the most part) were taking. Interestingly, in order to manage the overwhelming amount of data that might be collected using mapping, maps became smaller and in effect summaries of a point of view rather than representing the richness of thinking. The distance between thinking and the map gradually became greater.[14] More recently Huff edited another book[15] that put together a more international perspective on current approaches to mapping in strategic management.

Not surprisingly, during the 1990s three of the authors of this book published two books that made extensive use of mapping as a part of strategic management. Colin Eden and Fran Ackermann in *Making Strategy*[16] discuss mapping and provide guidance on how to use it in the context of developing an organization's strategies. It targets senior managers in organizations, consultants to them, and students on strategy courses in universities, not the more general audience of managers that this book seeks to reach. Similarly, John Bryson in *Strategic Planning for Public and Nonprofit Organizations*[17] targets senior managers in public and non-profit organizations, consultants to them, and students on strategy courses. Some examples of mapping are presented in the book and there is an appendix by all four authors of this book on how to do oval mapping.

Logic Models, Forward Mapping and Backward Mapping

Logic models are maps of cause–effect relations that have been used primarily for purposes of evaluation.[18] They are typically designed to chart the desired or expected relationships between inputs, processes and outputs and outcomes of programmes, and then to assess whether the desired or expected actually happened. If the desired results have not been achieved, the models can be used to help think through what changes might need to be made. The maps are usually not very detailed or action-oriented. Causal mapping of the kind presented in this book can be used to develop very detailed and action-oriented logic models.

Two types of logic modelling have been particularly useful for the purposes of implementation planning. These are "forward mapping" and "backward mapping" and were popularized by Richard Elmore.[19] Forward mapping begins with a clear statement of a policy maker's intent and proceeds through a sequence of increasingly more specific steps to define what is expected of implementers at each step. At the bottom of the process, or the end of the proposed causal chain, a statement is made with as much precision as possible about what a satisfactory outcome would be, measured in terms of the original statement of intent. The assumption, of course, is that policy makers control enough of the process to produce the desired results.

Backward mapping starts not with policy makers but with problematic situations. The first step is to develop a clear statement of some problematic behaviour "on the street" that merits a policy intervention. Next, planners formulate an objective consisting of possible organizational actions at the lowest or street level that would result in changed behaviour or a minimized problem. Then they work "backwards" up a chain of command or set of possible causal relationships to see if there is anything that can be done to provide the resources, rules or whatever that would have a desirable effect on the problematic situation. The advantage of backward mapping is that it does not assume that policy makers are in charge or that their intentions should be the measure of success. Instead, the focus is on who or what can actually make a difference in a problematic situation, and what that difference might be. Again, causal mapping of the kind presented in this book can be used for purposes of both forward mapping and backward mapping.

Systems Thinking and Mapping

"Systems thinking", particularly as expressed by Peter Senge in his successful management book *The Fifth Discipline*,[20] illustrates the power of a particular kind of causal map that is concerned only with modelling feedback relationships. These models present a "feedback view of the world" in which the world is seen not as linear, but as a set of interacting loops. Senge uses archetype feedback models to illustrate particular situations and behaviours, but he does not show how to build a feedback model. It takes extensive expertise to build a good model, and while a feedback model is a kind of logic model, it does not indicate how to develop a theory of action for changing it.

There is a large community of simulation modellers who are interested in quantifying feedback behaviour through the construction of system dynamics models.[21] Many of these modellers use forms of word-and-arrow diagrams that are similar to causal maps and are called "influence diagrams". These aim to depict the causal links between variables that will continuously change in value as time unfolds (as the variables do in the loops presented by Senge). Indeed, the causal mapping presented in this book is often used as the starting point for building influence diagrams and subsequently more formal flow diagrams that are formatted for use in quantitative computer simulation models.[22]

Related to system thinking proponents is the less well-known work of Eliyahu Goldratt and his "theory of constraints".[23] Goldratt developed his own theory of how to understand a system and its functions and dysfunctions. He also offers a certain amount of advice on how to intervene in a system to produce different results. As with Senge's work, there is advice on how to construct a logic model based on the theory, but Goldratt also does not show how to develop a theory of action for changing it.

During the 1990s Robert Kaplan and David Norton successfully introduced and championed the Balanced Scorecard (BSC) as a way of performance measurement and management in organizations.[24] The idea is that organizations should have a "balanced" set of strategic objectives that includes financial, customer, internal and learning objectives. They argue that there should be systematic causal linkages across levels and functions in an organization in order to achieve good performance against the whole set of objectives. Their approach to mapping is based on offering "templates" of typical connections. The causal mapping introduced in this book has been of use in developing balanced scorecards. This book is also aimed at providing the kind of detailed guidance that people would need if they tried to implement a balanced scorecard or other performance management approach. Causal mapping can be used to create the theories of action and logic models needed to implement an effective performance management system.

The causal mapping presented in this book is about understanding and displaying influence structures rather than temporal relationships, so this summary of mapping techniques should point out the possible confusion that might exist for some readers when they also consider the variety of project management, quality improvement and work design maps, such as Program Evaluation and Review Technique (PERT) charts, Critical Path Method (CPM) charts, process flows and work flows of various sorts. These latter maps are particular kinds of causal maps that emphasize temporal ordering in a way that the causal maps in this book do not.

Mind Mapping and Brainstorming

The discussion above focuses on mapping that is derived from psychology theory and theories of management, strategy, planning and evaluation. However, within the general field of mapping, probably the most successful proponent of a type of mapping that does not explore causality, but rather association and linkage, is Tony Buzan, in association with the British Broadcasting Corporation.[25] His technique of "mind mapping" is introduced in a series of books and is now a widely used technique – to the point that it is taught in elementary schools, high schools, colleges and universities, and in an array of continuing education courses. Mind mapping is essentially visually based "circular outlining". In other words, ideas are developed around and linked to a central concept. Mind mapping is a useful technique, but if you start with the wrong central concept you usually have to begin all over again. Causal mapping allows for polycentric maps in which you can add new "centres" whenever you like without having to re-map everything. Mind maps also do not lend themselves easily to the creation of strategy maps or logic models, or to analyses other than visual inspection.

Alongside the mind-mapping approach there are a number of writers on creativity – Edward de Bono and Roger von Oech,[26] for example – who have developed good tools and techniques for coming up with new ideas through processes generally known as brainstorming. Because the ideas are deliberately "off the wall" they do not connect with, or elaborate, the participants' existing "construct systems" or maps and so often do not get implemented. Also, brainstorming is not intended to show how new ideas can be linked together to think through strategies. Instead, it demonstrates how some important raw materials for mapping can be created.

The Mapping Metaphor

This book has been built on the idea that mapping is an important way in which we humans make sense of our world and try to change it. Mapping focuses people on the concepts and links they use to make sense of their world. It helps them become more self-conscious about their thinking, and especially their logic. Causal maps, in other words, are very much like street maps or highway maps. They help people locate themselves in space – in this case, conceptual space – and figure out what the pathways are from here to there and how to traverse them.[27]

Let us pursue the mapping metaphor further, as a way of helping the reader understand more clearly what causal mapping does and does not do.[28] We do this by comparing and contrasting – what else! – causal mapping with creating and using street maps or highway maps.

Street maps, highway maps, topographic maps, airline route maps and so on are *surrogates* for space. They are *analogues* of the territory being mapped. In general, a really good map is one in which the analogy is very close. The map, in other words, is a truthful *representation* of reality.

Good maps – whether spatial or conceptual – are valuable because they help people literally and figuratively understand where they have come from, where they are now and where they might wish to be. Locating oneself involves naming and placing, both of which are acts of classification. Mapping consists of naming, placing and classifying entities in real or conceptual space.[29] For example, action-oriented maps name, place and classify goals, negative goals, strategies, actions and assumptions or assertions. Importantly, the *spatial relatedness* of names, places and classifications embodied in maps taps into a quality of thinking that the human mind may require for understanding *anything*; since, as Karl Weick argues, the smallest unit of meaning involves three things: two elements and their relationship.[30] Because what maps do is relate elements – and therefore make meaning – mapping metaphors are extremely common.

There are a variety of additional comparisons between "ordinary" maps and causal maps:

- They are always drawn from a certain perspective. Edson, an expert on medieval spatial maps, argues, "The hand of the map maker is guided by a mind located in a certain time and space and sharing inevitably the prejudices of his or her surroundings."[31] In our time, diarist Anaïs Nin said, "We do not see the world the way *it* is; we see it the way *we* are."

- Both spatial and conceptual maps are subject to interpretation.

- Each is intended to provide an overview of context (the forest, figure or frame) as well as attention to the details (the trees, ground or cues). Each kind of map, in other words, embodies differentiation and integration, difference and similarity.

- Each allows connections to be seen that are linear or non-linear, thematic or non-thematic.

- Each facilitates the recognition of patterns.

- Each assists with navigation, whether physical or conceptual.

- Each allows for visualization, imaging and exploration of the unknown.

- Each allows for understanding of many kinds: intra- or inter-personal, objective or subjective, disciplinary or inter-disciplinary.

- Each involves a search for explanation, and those explanations can vary in their generality, accuracy and simplicity. Often these explanations are embodied in the "story" the map can tell. Karl Weick notes the close connection between a good story and a good causal map when he says, "[A] good story, like a workable cause map, shows patterns that may already exist in the puzzles an actor faces, or patterns that could be created anew in the interest of more order and sense in the future."[32]

There are also a number of ways in which the metaphor does not necessarily hold.[33] First, when mapping physical space, the map clearly is not the territory. In contrast, when mapping conceptual space, the distinction between map and territory is not as clear. Second, causal maps can vary in how "metaphorical" they are. They can be *real* starting points that soon become *fictions* as people's experience and conceptual frameworks change, whereas spatial maps typically – though not necessarily – stay "real". Third, causal maps may not need to be "accurate". They simply need to provide a reasonable basis for action and learning. In contrast, one typically counts on the continuing accuracy of a street map.

So the comparisons between spatial mapping and causal mapping are very strong, but there are some important differences. In either case, mapping represents a tremendous human ability and achievement.

The construction of an analogical space represents abstract thinking at its best. Mapping helps people figure out where they were, where they are and where they want to be, as well as how to get there. And it helps people discover, document and make use of what otherwise would be unknown.[34] At their best – and in perhaps the grandest praise of mapping we have seen – Gerard Mercator's biographer, Nicholas Crane, asserts, "Maps codify the miracle of existence."[35]

Computer Software for Mapping

The software called *Decision Explorer* is the resource used during many of the cases reported in this book. *Decision Explorer* is a resource for causal mapping. It was the brainchild of Colin Eden, although prompted by discussions with Matt Bonham,[36] and has been developed over the years by Colin Eden and Fran Ackermann as a support for causal mapping. It is powerful, flexible, Windows-based software. The *Decision Explorer* software will accommodate maps of up to 100 concepts and includes the most widely used analysis routines. The software is available through http://www.banxia.com.

Notes

1 S. E. Toulmin (1958) *The Uses of Argument*, Cambridge: Cambridge University Press.

2 G. A. Kelly (1955) *The Psychology of Personal Constructs*, New York, NY: Norton.

3 W. I. Thomas and D. S. Thomas (1928) *The Child in America: Behavior Problems and Programs*, New York, NY: Knopf.

4 For uses of grids for market research, see C. Eden and S. Jones (1984) Using Repertory Grids for Problem Construction, *Journal of the Operational Research Society*, **35**, 779–90.

5 D. N. Hinkle (1965) *The Change in Personal Constructs from the Viewpoint of a Theory of Implications*, PhD thesis, Columbus, OH: Ohio State University.

6 R. Axelrod (1976) *Structure of Decision*, Princeton, NJ: University of Princeton Press.

7   For example, F. S. Roberts (1976) Strategy for the Energy Crisis: The Case of Commuter Transportation Policy, in R. Axelrod *op. cit.*

8   This work was published as C. Eden, S. Jones and D. Sims (1979) *Thinking in Organisations*, London: Macmillan.

9   See Sylvia Brown's analysis of comparative methods in organizational research, S. Brown (1992) Cognitive Mapping and Repertory Grids for Qualitative Survey Research: Some Comparative Observations, *Journal of Management Studies*, **29**, 287–308.

10 M. Bougon, K. Weick and D. Binkhorst (1977) Cognition in Organizations: Analysis of the Utrecht Jazz Orchestra, *Administrative Science Quarterly*, **22**, 609–32.

11 For example, see P. Johnson, K. Daniels and R. Asch (1998) Mental Models of Competition, in C. Eden and J. C. Spender (eds), *Managerial and Organizational Cognition*, London: Sage, pp. 130–46.

12 See the Academy website, www.pace.aom.edu.

13 A. S. Huff (ed.) (1990) *Mapping Strategic Thought*, New York, NY: Wiley.

14 Eden discussed this issue as part of a special issue of the *Journal of Management Studies*: C. Eden (1992) On the Nature of Cognitive Maps, *Journal of Management Studies*, **29**, 261–5.

15 A. Huff and M. Jenkins (eds) (2001) *Mapping Strategy*, London: Wiley.

16 C. Eden and F. Ackermann (1998) *Making Strategy: The Journey of Strategic Management*, London: Sage. Also F. Ackermann and C. Eden with I. Brown (2004) *The Practice of Making Strategy*, London: Sage.

17 J. M. Bryson (1995) *Strategic Planning for Public and Nonprofit Organizations*, San Francisco, CA: Jossey-Bass.

18 A. Millar, R. Simeone and J. T. Carnevale (2001) Logic Models: A Systems Tool for Performance Management, *Evaluation and Program Planning*, **24**, 73–81. H. T. Chen (1990) *Theory Driven Evaluation*, London: Sage.

19 R. F. Elmore (1982) Backward Mapping: Implementation Research and Policy Decisions, in W. Williams, (ed.), *Studying Implementation*, Chatham, NJ: Chatham House.

20 P. Senge (1992) *The Fifth Discipline*, New York, NY: Doubleday.

21 See www.systemdynamics.org.

22 This approach to system dynamics modelling is often referred to as qualitative system dynamics; see E. Wolstenholme (1985) A Methodology for Qualitative System Dynamics, *Proceedings of the 1985 System Dynamics Conference, Nathan Forrester, Keystone, Colorado*, 1049–58. When the computer simulation modelling involves an interview process as the starting point for modelling, as with litigation modelling (see T. Williams, F. Ackermann and C. Eden (2003) Structuring a Delay and Disruption Claim: An Application of Cause-Mapping and System Dynamics, *European*

Journal of Operational Research, **148**(1), 192–204), causal mapping may be an integral part of the process (see C. Eden (1994) Cognitive Mapping and Problem Structuring for System Dynamics Model Building, *System Dynamics Review*, **10**, 257–76).

23   E. M. Goldratt (1992) *An Introduction to the Theory of Constraints: The Production Approach*, New Haven, CT: Avraham Y. Goldratt Institute.

24   The influence of the balanced scorecard largely came through the writing of Kaplan and Norton: R. Kaplan and D. Norton (1996) *The Balanced Scorecard*, Boston, MA: Harvard Business School Press. However, Niven introduces a more practical perspective on developing scorecards: see P. Niven (2002) *Balanced Scorecard Step-by-Step*, Chichester: Wiley. The general approach used to be known more formally as Multi-Criteria Decision Analysis.

25   T. Buzan and B. Buzan (2003) *The Mind Map Book: Radiant Thinking, the Major Evolution in Human Thought*, London: BBC Books.

26   E de Bono (1970) *Lateral Thinking*, London: HarperCollins; E. de Bono (1982) *De Bono's Thinking Course*, London, BBC; R. von Dech (1982) *A Whack on the Side of the Head*, Menlo Park, CA: Creative Think; R. von Dech (2002) *Expect the Unexpected or You Won't Find It*, San Francisco, CA: Berrett-Koehler.

27   In more formal terms, a map is "a visual representation; that establishes a landscape, or domain; names the most important entities that exist within that domain; and simultaneously places them within two or more relationships. More complex maps facilitate images of being 'within' the domain, encourage mentally moving among entities . . . and suggest options for movements and change" (Huff and Jenkins *op. cit.*).

28   We explore in greater depth the limitations of mapping in Chapter 11.

29   G. Bateson (1979) *Mind and Nature: A Necessary Unity*, Toronto: Bantam Books, p. 30.

30   K. E. Weick (1995) *Sensemaking in Organizations*, Thousand Oaks, CA: Sage, p. 135.

31   E. Edson (1977) *Mapping Time and Space: How Medieval Mapmakers Viewed Their World*, London: British Library, p. x.

32   Weick, *op. cit.*, p. 61.

33   K. E. Weick (1990) Cartographic Myths in Organizations, in A. S. Huff (ed.), *Mapping Strategic Thought*, Chichester: Wiley, pp. 1–9.

34   A. H. Robinson (1982) *Early Thematic Mapping in the History of Cartography*, Chicago, IL: University of Chicago Press.

35   N. Crane (2002) *Mercator*, London: Phoenix, p. xii.

36   Matt Bonham was instrumental in constructing some early mapping software running on mainframe computers. His software was used in some of the political science mapping reported in Bob Axelrod's book (Axelrod, *op. cit.*).

Resource D

Additional Resources

As WE HAVE COMMENTED THROUGHOUT THE BOOK, THE utilization of mapping techniques has really come to fruition over the past few years. Mapping approaches are now commonly utilized in creative projects (mind mapping), promotion, brainstorming, project management, cartography and presentation software, to name a few. Even wordprocessing software such as *Word* and *Corel* includes the ability to produce maps! In order to reduce confusion, we will briefly discuss the few programs we have found to be helpful for creating, diagnosing and presenting cause maps. First is software with some analytical capability and second is common software that can be utilized for presentation.

We would also like to suggest additional reading and opportunities to enhance your mapping skills.

Analytical Software

The first program, of course, is the one discussed extensively in the book, *Decision Explorer®* produced by Banxia Software® (http://www.banxia.com). This was developed expressly for causal mapping, with in-depth analytical and presentation capabilities. Indeed, the authors of this book have contributed significantly to the development of the software over the years, incorporating new analytical routines and presentation possibilities as they were developed. Without doubt, *Decision Explorer* is our preferred software for these challenges. Look to Resource B for a partial listing of analytical options available in *Decision Explorer*.

Dr Jeffery Conklin is considered the leader in the development and marketing of *QuestMap*® by Corporate Memory Systems in the late 1980s. Based on early hypertext technologies, he developed the IBIS (issue-based information structure) software approach. *QuestMap*®, with a further evolution, *Compendium*® by the Compendium Institute (http://www.compendiuminstitute.org), are probably the closest competition to *Decision Explorer*. This software offers easy map construction using a series of developed icons to prompt discussion, such as ?, +, − and an "idea light bulb". Each statement is "tagged" by the software to allow for searching and grouping. *Compendium* is written in Java, which supports a GUI interface. The software is marketed as a dialogue mapping instrument that captures, records and presents group conversation.

A final program that requires mention is *Inspiration*® by Inspiration Software (http://www.inspiration.com). This is largely a visual thinking tool that supports brainstorming, organizing ideas and group thinking. While this program offers little in the way of the kind of analysis supported by *Decision Explorer*, its large user base (a reported ten million) certainly supports our claim that thinking and communicating with maps has come of age. *Inspiration* has been marketed heavily in the educational environment. The program is capable of including text and graphics in its maps. Each statement (object) is tagged so that complex maps can be reduced to outline form and then to wordprocessing environments.

Presentation Software

Microsoft Word® and *Corel*® (*WordPerfect*) wordprocessing programs are almost ubiquitous products in today's computer environments. Both offer some drawing capability that can be used to construct maps. While this can be a tedious process, it does allow most computer users to transfer their maps to this environment for publication and presentation.

Microsoft and Corel both offer additional software (*Powerpoint*® and *Corel Draw*®) that allows even more sophisticated drawings to be more easily created and presented. While none of this software allows for analysis and indeed it has no ability to deal very effectively with concepts, almost every classroom, meeting place, hotel and retreat has it already loaded on their system. This allows for relatively easy portability and presentation.

Additional Reading

Case applications demonstrating the approach to causal mapping used in this book:

J. Bryson and C. Finn (1995) Creating the Future Together: Developing and Using Shared Strategy Maps, in A. Halachmi and G. Bouckaert, *The Enduring Challenges in Public Management*, San Francisco, CA, Jossey-Bass.

C. Eden and F. Ackermann (1998) *Making Strategy: The Journey of Strategic Management*, London: Sage.

F. Ackermann and C. Eden (2001) SODA – Journey Making and Mapping in Practice, in J. Rosenhead and J. Mingers, *Rational Analysis in a Problematic World Revisited*, London: John Wiley.

F. Ackermann, C. Eden and I. Brown (2004) *The Practice of Making Strategy*. London: Sage.

J. Bryson (2004) *Strategic Planning for Public and Nonprofit Organizations*, 3rd edn, San Francisco, CA: Jossey-Bass.

Readings providing more detail on how to analyse maps:

C. Eden (2004) Analyzing Cognitive Maps to Help Structure Issues or Problems, *European Journal of Operational Research*, forthcoming.

C. Eden, F. Ackermann and S. Cropper (1992) The Analysis of Cause Maps, *Journal of Management Studies*, **29**, 309–24.

C. Eden and F. Ackermann (1998) Analysing and Comparing Idiographic Causal Maps, in C. Eden and J.-C. Spender, *Managerial and Organizational Cognition*, London: Sage.

Readings offering additional insights into the use of mapping for purposes of strategy change in a variety of settings:

J. Bryson, F. Ackermann, C. Eden and C. Finn (1996) Critical Incidents and Emergent Issues in the Management of Large Scale Change Effects, In D. Kettl and H. Brinton, *The State of Public Management*, Baltimore, MD: Johns Hopkins Press.

F. Ackermann, C. Eden and T. Williams (1997) Modeling for Litigation: Mixing Qualitative and Quantitative Approaches, *Interfaces* **27**, 48–65.

V. Belton, F. Ackermann and I. Shepherd (1997) Integrated Support from Problem Structuring through to Alternative Evaluation Using COPE and V.I.S.A. *Journal of Multi-Criteria Decision Analysis*, **6**, 115–30.

F. Ackermann and C. Eden (2003) Stakeholders Matter: Techniques for Their Identification and Management, *Proceedings of the Academy of Management Conference*, Seattle, WA.

F. Ackermann and C. Eden (2004) Using Causal Mapping: Individual and Group; Traditional and New, in M. Pidd, Systems Modelling: Theory and Practice, Chichester: John Wiley.

J. Bryson (2004) What to Do When Stakeholders Matter: A Guide to Stakeholder Identification and Analysis Techniques, *Public Management Review*, **6**(1), 21–53.

Training Opportunities

Banxia Software® (http://www.banxia.com) offers workshops on *Decision Explorer* and other software.

Think Visibly (http://www.visible-thinking.com) offers workshops and an on-line introduction to its approach.

Resource E

Listing of Process Guidelines

T HE FOLLOWING IS A LIST OF PROCESS GUIDELINES FROM ALL of the chapters. The guidelines are organized according to the same categories as are used in Chapter 10.

Recognizing When a Situation Can Be Mapped – and Is Worth Mapping

Digest the stories we have presented and imagine how you might do something similar (Chapter 10).

Mapping may be particularly useful in situations where you feel frustrated or helpless (Chapter 10) or don't really know what to do (Chapter 10).

Some concrete preparations may facilitate this cueing process. Namely, assemble the necessary materials for mapping and store them in a readily available location (Chapter 10).

We also recommend that you actively seek out partners or clients and let them know about this valuable resource and your ability to help (Chapter 10).

Preparing for Mapping

Have a reason for mapping, assemble the necessary materials and find a place to map (Chapter 2).

Table E.1 is a checklist of mapping supplies that might be needed (Chapter 10).

Table E.1   Checklist of mapping supplies

Notebook containing process guidelines section of this chapter	200 ovals or Post-it notes
Agenda	Masking tape and/or self-adhesive putty
List of participants	Several packs of coloured stick-on "dots" (for straw polling or voting)
Name tags or placards	
– flipchart pads	
– note pads: one for each participant	Scissors
– pencils: one for each participant	Stapler
– black water-soluble markers: one for each participant	Necessary background materials
	Digital camera
– additional water-soluble markers in a variety of colours to identify goals, strategies, actions or other categories of concepts	Refreshments
	Clock or watch
Soft "gum" pencil erasers	

Beginning the Map

Start with an introduction from the client (Chapter 6).

Explain to the entire group the process to be followed and the meeting's objectives (Chapter 6).

Note that the capturing and structuring process helps build a shared understanding (Chapter 6).

Review the "ground rules" (Chapter 6).

- If there is something that you don't agree with written up and posted on the wall, don't remove it. Add your own statement that presents a different view or shows why you disagree.

- Keep "oval" statements to around 6–8 words.

- Once you have written two or three ovals, get up and place them on the wall.

Start mapping with what people can imagine themselves doing, or with issues they think they face (that is, where they feel some "pain"), rather than with a statement of goals (Chapter 2).

Begin with the issue that is of concern (Chapter 4).

Keep each statement to no more than eight words (Chapter 3).

"Dump" as many ideas as you can and make a point of not censoring yourself (Chapter 3).

Statements, as options or actions, have an active verb in them (Chapter 2).

Ensure that the statements are worded in an action-oriented mode (Chapter 8).

Some statements represent different aspects of the problem; these differences can be identified using coloured pens (Chapter 3).

Capture the alternative aspect of a statement – the "rather than" (Chapter 4).

The shorthand convention for "rather than" is an ellipsis (...), which saves time and space (Chapter 3).

Number every concept based on the order in which it was generated (Chapter 3).

Write down circumstances that act as constraints (Chapter 3).

It is more important to get down an individual's stream of consciousness about the situation than to build a tidy map (Chapter 3).

Enter thoughts into the computer as they occur (Chapter 4).

Avoid spending too much time considering the position or wording of thoughts (Chapter 4).

Capturing detailed options and linking them to the generic options helps flesh out the idea (Chapter 4).

Cycling between generating new material and reflecting on existing material is helpful in generating even more material (Chapter 4).

Typically, the interviewer should start by prompting the interviewee to ladder down into the "hows" of the first option (Chapter 5).

After laddering down, then ladder up to outcomes and ultimately to the purposes of the option – the "whys" (Chapter 5).

Sometimes it is best to ladder up to consequences first before laddering down to what it would take to pursue an option (Chapter 5).

Get group members to write up everything they can think of in relation to the issue; this way there is a greater "wealth" of material with which to work and less chance of something being missed (Chapter 6).

Encourage the group to start writing on ovals with a coloured felt-tipped pen and post the ovals on the wall (Chapter 6).

Help those who aren't sure what to do (Chapter 6).

Number each of the ovals using a coloured felt-tipped pen (Chapter 6).

Write the last number used on the edge of the flipchart paper to keep track of numbering (Chapter 6).

Be sure that two statements that look the same actually mean the same, regardless of whether they use the same words (Chapter 8).

Avoid duplicating chains of argument (Chapter 8).

Get urgent issues "out on the table" early in the workshop, and make sure there is clear acknowledgement of them. (Chapter 8).

Establishing a Hierarchy of Concepts

If an interview is being conducted, begin by listing the big options that the interviewee thinks he or she has. List them in small print in the upper-left-hand corner of the paper, or spread them across the paper (Chapter 5).

Build a map around each option (Chapter 5).

In a group setting, position the ovals so that superordinate outcomes or issues (that is, broad motherhood-and-apple-pie items) are at the top of the cluster, and the more detailed options and assertions are at the bottom (Chapter 6).

Start by reading out to the group all of the contributions in the cluster (Chapter 6).

Develop the chains of argument within the cluster (Chapter 6).

When there seem to be two ideas on an oval, it is a good idea to separate them by making two ovals so that each idea can be explored fully (Chapter 6).

Request that new contributions be written on an oval so that they can be included in clusters (Chapter 6).

Continue the process of laddering both up and down the chains of argument, continuously asking the group about options and constraints as well consequences (Chapter 6).

Build up the hierarchy by putting potential goals at the top with key issues supporting them, and options, assertions and context supporting the issues (Chapter 6).

Draw in all the links between these different contributions (Chapter 6).

Make sure that cross-cluster links are captured, as they help reveal how the decision areas are interconnected and how decisions in one area have an effect on another area. (Chapter 6).

Review the material in the cluster for a final check (Chapter 6).

Reassure the group that usually the first cluster takes quite a long time (Chapter 6).

Consider drawing a dashed line horizontally across the mapping surface with a marking pen, about one-third of the way down from the top. The line can be used to separate goal- and mission-related ovals above the line from strategy- and action-related ovals below the line (Chapter 7).

Additional structure can be added to the clusters by pencilling in links in the form of arrows representing causal links. The advantage of using a pencil is that links can be erased easily if need be; the disadvantage is that pencilled links are not as easy for the group to read (Chapter 7).

Cluster labels provide a useful way of summarizing what is in a group of conceptually linked statements (Chapter 9).

Developing Categories of Clusters of Ideas

Make sure there is lots of room between clusters (Chapter 6). This can be accomplished while the group is taking a break after the brainstorming and initial clustering process, or can be done with the group as a whole (Chapters 6, 9).

Start by reading out to the group all of the contributions in the cluster (Chapter 6).

If the cluster seems very large, explore whether there are two or more clusters or sub-clusters involved. Create as many clusters and sub-clusters as makes sense (Chapter 6).

Position the ovals so that superordinate outcomes or issues (that is, broad motherhood-and-apple-pie items) are at the top of the cluster, and the more detailed options and assertions are at the bottom (Chapter 6).

Look for a statement within the cluster that represents the overall subject or theme of the cluster. This statement will be the cluster's label and should be at the "top" of the cluster; that is, at the end of the chains of arrows that link ideas in the cluster. If no existing statement adequately captures the theme, develop this statement with the group and identify it as the cluster heading (Chapters 7, 10).

Cluster labels provide a useful way of summarizing what is in a group of conceptually linked statements (Chapter 9).

Once you have finished identifying the first category or cluster, move on to succeeding groups until the participants are familiar with the entire map (Chapter 7).

Identifying goals, strategies, actions and assertions

To find out what the real goals are, ask "Why would we want to do that?" or "What would be the consequences, or results, of doing that?" Those consequences that are good in their own right are likely to be goals (Chapter 2).

Ask the question "What are the goals?" (Chapter 4).

Ovals representing consequences of addressing the issues can be placed in groupings on the mapping surface above the dashed red line that is meant to divide issues and actions from goals and purposes (Chapter 7).

In order to identify goals, participants are asked "What is achieved if an effective way is found of addressing the issue?" or "What might happen that is undesirable if the issue is not addressed?" (Chapter 9).

Often laddering towards goals continues upwards not to goals, but to a series of negative outcomes, and some of these are "bad outcomes in their own right – we need to make sure they don't happen". If so, these items may need to remain written as negative goals rather than turned into positive outcomes (Chapter 9).

A statement of strategic aims is powerful when it represents the interaction between all of the goals (Chapter 9).

The power of the emerging goals should be tested by the extent to which they are different from those of competitors (Chapter 9).

Ensure that core distinctive competencies are those that are "at the core" of the business model for delivering a successful and realistic strategic future (Chapter 9).

Linking Statements

A useful step in creating an action-oriented map is to ask "How would we do that? What would it take to do that?" (Chapter 2).

Context sometimes gives helpful additional meaning to the problem, so elaborating the context will make for a more "meaning-full" exploration of the problem and very often turns up new solutions (Chapter 3).

Begin the process of laddering up and down the chains of argument (Chapter 8) and draw in causal links (Chapter 4).

When a particular thought occurs, try to explore it further by "laddering up" to consequences, or by "laddering down" to causes or explanations (Chapter 4).

Capturing detailed options and linking them to generic options helps flesh out the idea (Chapter 4).

Typically, an interviewer should start by prompting the interviewee to ladder down into the "hows" of the first option (Chapter 5).

The interviewer should then encourage laddering up to outcomes and ultimately to the purposes of the option – the "whys" (Chapter 5).

Sometimes it is best to ladder up to consequences first before laddering down to what it would take to pursue an option (Chapter 5).

Make the connections between goals and issues (Chapter 8).

Linking focuses attention not so much on what is in a statement but on action: why things are done and what needs to be done to make other things happen (Chapter 9).

Finishing the Map

Link in the "orphans" (Chapter 4).

Review a cognitive map with a friend (Chapter 4).

Revisit each of the workshop tasks to reflect on what has been achieved and to give participants a sense of achievement (Chapter 6).

Preserve the map by using digital photographs, by taking the physical map away, by using *Decision Explorer* software, or some combination of the three (Chapter 7).

Analysing the Map

Look especially for "busy" concepts – those that have many arrows coming in and going out – and "potent" concepts – those that lead to many concepts further up the map (Chapter 2).

By pushing on the consequences of what might be done, you can find out what the real purpose is of doing that thing (Chapter 2).

Once goals are clarified, it is important to re-examine the possible strategies for achieving them to see if there are additional ways to pursue the goals (Chapter 2).

Examine the map frequently to understand what it is saying (Chapter 2).

Think carefully about the contrasting pole of a problem statement – the circumstance that would mean it was not a problem (Chapter 3).

Understand things from others' points of view, particularly those with whom you are in conflict (Chapter 3).

Sit back and look at the properties of the map (Chapter 3).

By capturing the negative links as well as the positive links, you begin to identify some of the dilemmas and trade-offs (Chapter 4).

Examine the clusters to see if there are new aspects to add or missing links between the statements (Chapter 4).

For each linked pair of statements, test which is the option (or action) and which is the outcome (Chapter 4).

Look for busy points (Chapter 8). Look for constructs that connect to many crucial items. They are likely to be especially important constructs and time should be spent exploring them in detail (Chapter 5).

Ladder down from a goal to determine whether the statement(s) immediately supporting it are also goals, albeit subordinate ones (Chapter 8).

Highlight any inconsistencies with the mapping guidelines (Chapter 8).

Check that the goal system map contains at least one contribution from each participant (Chapter 8).

Statements that seem to be at the centre of many others, with many links in or out of them, are often good starting candidates for identifying and prioritizing issues (Chapter 9).

When considering issue priorities it is important to pay attention to "busy" statements as possible high-priority items, except when they are vague "catch-alls" that are not easily actionable; allow the group to suggest other candidate statements; and pay attention to the candidate statements that appear to be supported by all participants (Chapter 9).

Positive feedback loops are very important. Because they are self-sustaining, they may be very important resources for the future of the business. Feedback loops made up of competencies may be especially important (Chapter 9).

Using a Map to Inform Decision Making

Decide which concepts among the various possibilities represent the actual goals, strategies and actions to implement the strategies (Chapter 2).

Getting participants to reveal their preferences concerning which issues they feel have the greatest priority provides useful feedback for the group (Chapter 6).

Carrying out a prioritization exercise gives participants a sense of closure (Chapter 6).

Make sure that the explanation about how to indicate priorities is very clear so as to avoid mistakes and misunderstandings (Chapter 6).

Participants should be allowed to place all of the preference indicators on one of the clusters, if they feel the issue is so important that it demands the entire allocation; or they can scatter their votes on the different clusters close to the cluster labels (Chapter 6).

Group members can be given several red dots and asked to use them to identify the statements they think best articulate desirable goals for the organization (Chapter 7).

Following Up on a Mapping Exercise

Provide a report consisting of the maps and other details within the next two weeks (Chapter 6).

Provide a brief explanation of what the next steps are (Chapter 6).

Have the workshop take place within a psychological week – from the beginning of one week to the end of the next - to keep memory and enthusiasm fresh (Chapter 8).

Facilitating Mapping Exercises

If it is important, make sure that people have enough time to start building a relationship with one another and to establish the beginnings of a sense of common understanding, concern, connection and trust (Chapter 7).

If a group is new and will be working together for a long time, spending time early on developing an effective group will pay off later (Chapter 7).

Give participants a small wad of self-adhesive putty and ask them to attach a small piece no larger than the size of a split pea on the back of each oval in the middle towards the top. The ovals can then be attached to the mapping surface and easily moved around (Chapter 7).

The facilitator can collect two ovals (of the participant's choice) from each of the participants. He or she can then ask the group to help him or her place the ovals one at a time on the mapping surface in clusters held together by a common theme or subject matter. If the clusters will be identifying issues, begin each cluster below the dashed red line (Chapter 7).

Familiarize interviewees with the mapping technique (Chapter 8).

Mapping in an Interview Format

The interviewer and interviewee will have to check with each other throughout the mapping process to make sure that the map really represents what the interviewee thinks (Chapter 5).

The interviewer will need to work with the interviewee to get the right level of disaggregation of ideas, so that the resulting map is as useful as possible (Chapter 5).

The interviewer should push on the importance of the interviewee exploring his or her emotions, and give the interviewee time and space to do so (Chapter 5).

Sometimes it helps simply to stop and talk without doing mapping. Sometimes things – especially when deep emotions are involved – are just too murky to map. You need to talk for a while in order to create enough structure to be able to map. And sometimes it is just better to talk with a friend (Chapter 5).

Remember that if the interviewee wants someone to do something, he or she will have to figure out what that person cares about and therefore what will be motivating (Chapter 5).

If the interviewee is rattling off a long list of concepts, it is often best simply to get the concepts down without worrying about the connections among them. But at some point it will be important to stop and go back to have the interviewee explain the connections among them – that is, the structure of the argument (Chapter 5).

At natural stopping points it is important for the interviewer to summarize what he or she has heard in order to make sure the map is accurate, or perhaps to prepare for the next stage of the mapping exercise (Chapter 5).

Towards the end of the exercise, the interviewer should have the interviewee reflect on what the map or maps are saying. This will help ensure that any important learning points are drawn out and remembered (Chapter 5).

Index